MW01628708

ARQUITECTONICA

ARQUITECTONICA

ALASTAIR GORDON

New York · Paris · London · Milan

WITH ADDITIONAL ESSAYS BY IAN VOLNER

ARQUITECTONICA IN THE WORLD

IAN VOLNER

An architect in Miami today can scarcely stretch his arms without jostling one or the other of his global confreres. With the inaugural edition of the local Art Basel affiliate in 2002, the international art market established a beachhead on Biscayne Bay, and the design scene has since followed. Where once stood unbroken files of stout Deco hotels — those un-Floridian "interiorized" structures, as one European designer has called them, resembling nothing so much as seagoing refrigerators — now the visitor finds a thousand glass-and-steel flowers blooming from Coconut Grove clear to Bal Harbor. Out of Denmark and Italy and Brazil they have come, washing up on the sun-bleached shores of Miami and remaking the city in their own image, an improbable parallel to the waves of eager immigrants who have long flocked (and are flocking even now) to the de facto capital of the Caribbean.

This much the world has brought to Miami. But that is only one half of a crucial urban equation. "What a really great city does," said critic Reyner Banham, "is to furnish an instrument for [a person] to impose their vision upon the world." Mozart's Vienna, Shakespeare's London, Manet's Paris — if Miami is to join that select fraternity, the great sub-tropical metropolis must synthesize and export a recognizable cultural commodity. So what has Miami brought the world? A surprising answer, provisionally at least, might well be: Arquitectonica.

One rushes to qualify the claim. By its own admission, indeed as a matter of high principle, the office launched in 1977 by Laurinda Spear and Bernardo Fort-Brescia has not been confined to any preferred "in-house style," still less one readily identifiable with its hometown. No peninsular motifs — no philodendron green; no bougainvillea pink — mark the firm's projects in such far-flung locales as London and Manila. Neither do the principals put their own individual identities front and center: the firm's very title was devised by the founders as a deliberate act of anonymization, and collaborative teamwork remains their primary modus operandi. Even as their practice has gained momentum over the last three decades, Fort-Brescia and Spear have never sported the trappings of personal fame that have accrued to the many bold-face names with whom they regularly compete. They are, in that sense, the least likely of ombudsmen — he jetting the world over; she the polar opposite, staying in Miami, poring over the nuances of projects; each a little bohemian in their way, children of the 60's that they are. For all their success, they've remained somewhat below the radar, too soft-spoken for proper spokespeople.

Such self-effacement seems especially inapposite to a city purported to be rather brash, and which has already spawned a number of rather brash cultural phenomena that have helped define its image abroad: e.g., the music of thrumming bass and rhythm, the film-and-TV franchise of cops and robbers splashing around in cigarette boats. (The latter famously spotlighted an early Arquitectonica project.) But then consider: in a global age, surely a true cultural ombudsman must traffic in something more than high-end exotica and artistic tourist tchotchkes.

Arquitectonica's deeply-bred cosmopolitanism — and more to come on that subject shortly — has helped, in just the last decade, to yield an architecture of such extraordinary depth and diversity that it can no longer be subject to any reductive, regionalist interpretation. Their architecture today doesn't even look much like their *own* past, much less that of Miami's; it is meant, rather, to look like the architecture of a future city, one staking its claim to global status. Which, presumably, is just the kind of architecture you would expect a truly vibrant twenty-first-century city to produce.

Fort-Brescia has said that if he had not been an architect he would have been an explorer. As it happens, he may have succeeded in being both: French by extraction; Peruvian by upbringing; educated in the US, Switzerland and Germany, his globetrotting bona fides are counterweighted by his wife's background as a native Miamian who has lived in the city for most of her life. This unique cultural blend has become only more varied as their firm, now with offices in ten cities on four continents, has attracted personnel (not to mention clients) from an ever-wider array of backgrounds. And as the couple's children, Marisa and Ray, have lately risen to design positions in the office, they've added their own generational perspectives to the mix, allowing Arquitectonica's diversity to extend along both the geographical and temporal axes. Partly by design, partly by luck, the firm's reach has been able to expand in exact proportion to its grasp.

The impulse behind that grasp does pose a bit of a mystery. With most practitioners, an animating design philosophy — critical, social, aesthetic, what have you — usually compels a designer to want to realize his or her vision, to launch their Big Idea in to the real world. But as noted, Arquitectonica tends to abjure those kinds of master narratives: ask the architects what overarching strategy unifies their current portfolio, and the response is likely to vary from partner to partner, from day to day, or simply to elicit a bemused shrug. One hesitates to gainsay them; silence, after all, can be its own strategy, and a powerful one at that. There may, however, be evidence in the office's work that speaks to impulses which the partners, moving as far and as fast as they do, hardly have time to notice.

The motion itself is a major clue. If anything can be said to bind together the almost 60 projects in the present monograph, it's a restlessness of the architectural imagination, a mercurial intellectual kinesis tempered by a no-nonsense apprehension of the trade, as well as the art of building. As Alistair Gordon observes in his accompanying essay mapping out the firm's cultural origins and formal growth, Aquitectonica's debut project, the Pink House of 1978 (p. 42), began life as an academic provocation, an exercise in surrealist urbanism on Modernist themes. The turn towards a reinvigorated, accelerated Modernism in American architecture would not truly take hold for a decade and more, after the passing of the Postmodernist storm; Arquitectonica was therefore a very early adopter indeed, and some of the chief ingredients of the practice — their hyperactivity, their global outlook, their resistance to theoretical dogma — anticipated the 21st-century "starchitect" phenomenon. But even in that first project, Arquitectonica began to manifest a sensibility at once more freewheeling and much earthier than that of their peers: as Gordon details at length, they made key changes to the Pink House design in order to make it more suitable for its inhabitants, demonstrating a tough-minded functionalism that would serve them well in later years. At the same time, the spirit of the house, its unreserved celebration of Miami's goofball glamour, is both more earnest and more accessible than the coolly impressive monuments of today's "iconic" architecture.

The designers' innate pragmatism and surprising ingenuousness would work in tandem to help mobilize the firm in its turn to the world. In their first significant overseas commission, Arquitectonica was tasked

with designing a new headquarters for the national bank of Fort-Brescia's native country, the Banco de Credito del Peru (p. 62). While it may seem incredible a large foreign financial concern would reach out to an American firm that had never before designed on this scale, as it happens, corporate clients outside the US tend to be far more receptive to untried practices, and Arquitectonica would only break into the institutional realm on these shores by building on their success abroad. In Lima, they proved their chops with a scheme whose complexity both in section and elevation shows none of the tentativeness one might expect in a first outing: a big square donut pierced with projecting geometric volumes surrounds a central courtyard whose distinguishing feature — a naturally occurring hill, originally slated for leveling but preserved at the insistence of the architects — gives the occupants not only a much needed bit of *rus in urbe*, but a fitting emblem for their famously mountainous nation. Together with its highly animated facade and varied, no-two-alike elevations, the bravura project seems almost to enact its creators' gameness in taking it on in the first place, a building-sized billboard bearing the message "Have Architecture, Will Travel."

Capitalizing (so to speak) on their cred in the banking world, Arquitectonica swiftly confirmed their intentions with their subsequent major commission for a non-American client, the Banque de Luxembourg (p. 86). What seems at first a conservative, masonry-clad block with gridded apertures is forcibly disrupted by a semi-conical glass wedge that serves to the announce the building's presence while negotiating its tricky angular site. The paired geometries of cube and rotunda perform a witty kind of role reversal: the former appears to hover over a lofted rez de chaussée, whereas the latter, column-like, descends clear to ground level, imparting a confounding lightness to the heavier volume and an unexpected heft to its curtain-walled counterpart. The visual joke, riffing on the old Modernist preoccupation with dematerilization and floating masses, manages to be land without coming at the expense of contextual sensitivity, as the twinned elements correspond perfectly to their respective urban adjacencies — street wall on the one hand, street corner on the other. Once again, Arquitectonica's playful practicality carriesthe day.

In short order, the firm would add additional notches to their belt, high-profile and logistically daunting blockbuster projects like their 1993 Festival Walk (p. 106) commercial complex in Hong Kong's Kowloon Tong district. Step by step, following a sequence of recognizable formal cues (again, aptly plotted herein by Alastair Gordon), the film built up and out. At last, after the dust had settled from the fall of the Soviet Union, the American design scene would take up the call for an unapologetically urban, globally expansionist model for contemporary architecture. When that happened, and offices big and small looked to Europe, Asia, and to the developing world, they would find that Arquitectonica was already there. Not only that, design watchers would discover that the team from Miami had come to into these disparate locales with a generosity of spirit that seems, in retrospect, almost unaccountable, given how angst-ridden the position of the international creative class has become in our time. Perhaps only a firm that was born in the sun, cooled by the breeze and washed by the tides, could bring to the idea of an opportunistic, interventionist mode of practice so much easygoing confidence. Certainly that would seem a reasonable explanation for how Aquitectonica has been able to sustain that founding spirit into the present day — and not merely to sustain it, but to put it into overdrive.

A cursory survey of the last pages of this volume suffices to show a practice working at fairly astonishing scale and speed. In the current decade alone, the team has undertaken projects spanning almost the entire typological spectrum, from the institutional to the residential, from the commercial to (crucially, given their swelling landscape practice) the urban. Whether working in contexts like dense historic neighborhoods, or in the teeming new metropoles of the developing world, Arquitectonica seems to wolf down commissions with extraordinary gusto — an appetite that would not be at all surprising if, say, they were one of those acronymous corporate offices generally well known for being able to build anything. Only they aren't; they are known, as indeed they are, for being a boutique design firm, and the founders' bristle at the mere suggestion of corporatization. The available facts resolve to a simple, if admittedly tautological conclusion: the motion is the motive. Arquitectonica builds as much as it does, in as many places as it does, because that is what Arquitectonica likes to do.

Taken individually, each of the firm's recent projects can be seen to testify to that same informal disposition. In Vietnam, the firm is presently at work on the Ben Than complex, a twin-spired high-rise to house a Ritz-Carlton Hotel (p. 355) along with a full complement of retail space, offices, and condominium apartments. Perched on the perimeter of Ho Chi Minh City's landmark Liberation Square, the building is of a fairly familiar type, a base-and-tower combo like many similar commercial structures that have appeared in East Asia since the turn of the millennium. Certainly the tastes of the region's emerging middle class have been taken into account here, along with their particular functional expectations (e.g., natural ventilation in the kitchens, windows in the bathrooms). But there is also, folded into the building's striking silhouette, a singular formal maneuver, the two crowns of the towers cantilevering over their respective shafts and each bracing a cubic glass volume. The intent is expressly symbolic: it gives the buildings something of the appearance of the twin dragons that have been part of the city's iconography for centuries, a form sufficiently ubiquitous that local the media picked up on it without having to be told. Yet even such an explicit instance of signification seems to betoken something else — not just a figure, but an attitude, one of daring *jouissance*, like trying out a greeting in an unfamiliar language just to see how its sounds in one's mouth. Ben Than's unique graphic gesture is Arquitectonica at their jump-right-in best.

Graphics are also the vehicle for the architects' ludic instincts in another project, their first in the United Kingdom. On a narrow backstreet in Central London, sandwiched between Trafalgar and Leicester Squares, the firm is working with real estate giant Hobhouse (p. 359) to create a mixed-use infill development that's also a whip-smart visual sendup of the city's signature urbanism. Slated for completion in 2019, the design features an ensemble of grouped facades, each distinguished by a slightly different tone of distinctly London-ish, dun-colored brick. Sensitively scaled, with the flanking members just above the historical datum and the central ones stepping up slightly, the composition could almost be taken for an orthodox exercise in contextualism, but for its signal act of *détournement*: the typical flat-fronted London row house is transformed through a series of deflections that occur irrespective of, and actually involve, the windows, which duly bend around each crimp and fold with gob-smacking ductility. Complemented by rotations in the brick that pick up the light at varying angles, the effect is almost Cubist — a bit of high-minded cheek, given the heaps of chiefly Neoclassical and Romantic paintings just a few steps away at the National Portrait Gallery. Once again, Arquitectonica appears to have blown in from out of town, instantly gone native, and then just as quickly begun to draw fabulous caricatures of its new surrounds with an arch but sympathetic eye.

Closer to home, yet still a world away from South Florida, Arquitectonica is presently engaged in still another commission that seems like a modest attempt to spike the urban punch. Just down the Potomac from the nation's capital, Alexandria, Virginia, is a modest government town of old red-brick buildings in a sea of suburban ramblers. With recent growth in the region, and the expansion of public transit networks, that's begun to change, and Arquitectonica is poised to help pick up the pace. Sitting nearly atop a station of the D.C. Metro, the 34-story, 382-unit residential tower at Carlyle Plaza 2 (p. 365) will be Alexandria's tallest building, punctuating the local skyline with a gleaming exclamation mark. Or, more accurately, a question mark — the rectilinear simplicity of the envelope is shattered by the displacement of the central ten-story block, indenting it by two bays to give the building a kinked outline. The move serves a dual purpose, lending the building (in by-now-familiar fashion) an easily apprehensible visual identity, while simultaneously producing a pair of outdoor terraces that promise stunning views. Yet in truth both objectives, graphic as well as functional, are moved by the same spirit, one that seems almost literally embodied in the building's form: a desire, to recall critic Harold Bloom, to effect a "swerve," taking the familiar Miesian gridiron and then nudging it forcibly into something rich and new.

Subversive formalism aside, it should of course be noted that Arquitectonica never undermines a project's fundamental programmatic prerequisites for the sake of an architectural acte grauit. Be they ever so impish, the partners are hard-headed pragmatists, and they have in any case a huge battery of on-staff specialists and outside collaborators who insure that the i's in every brief are dotted, the t's in every technical document crossed. A firm does not grow to such size without the institutional know-how to get the jobs done; but at many other comparable offices, the relationship between cart and horse is a little different, specifically as relates to getting the jobs in the first place. A typical corporate firm enters a new market and seeks a new commission because that is the nature of their business-model beast. Aquitectonica gives every impression of seeking out work simply for the pleasure of doing so. The exploration-loving hippie-hedonists still love to play, and they seem content with no smaller sandbox than the world itself, a reasonable enough ambition given that they come from a sort of paradise.

If the defining trait of Arquitectonica in its current phase of development is a species of highly refined chutzpah, their whole mission in architecture takes on a peculiar meaning at the moment. For clouds have gathered over Coconut Grove, as in the world at large, and these children of the 60's must perforce be (as one of their own anthems would have it) riders of the storm.

The freewheeling multiculturalism that underwrites Arquitectonica's present sphere of action — the same that has been intrinsic to Miami's ascent as an international mecca for art and commerce — is indeed under unprecedented threat today. The political winds (to say nothing of actual, natural winds) have made the business of building a more fraught enterprise than ever before. Against this background,

Arquitectonica's determination to persevere, to continue to believe in the future of their city and others around the globe, has taken on a moral aspect otherwise alien to their good-natured protean creativity. To simply be protean and creative today, in the face of such vast social and ecological upheaval, seems remarkably like a form of dissent; and for all its growth around the world, Arquitectonica (which continues, on top of everything else, to build constantly in Miami, as in their massive new Brickell City Centre) is as true to those qualities today as in their antic, effervescent first projects for their antic, effervescent hometown. Who would have thought that Miami — neon, hair-gelled, third-button-undone Miami — would suddenly seem like an idea worth for fighting for?

Yet that's what it's become, and in that sense Arquitectonica is the champion of its values. They seem to relish the challenge; or if it causes them any anxiety, it hardly shows in the work. An hour spent in their office is enough to leave the visitor exhausted. Associates bustle, papers fly. Every phone call portends some new opportunity, and will the weather be favorable for flying tomorrow? If it isn't, they'll fly someplace else. Something of a force of nature itself, Arquitectonica thrives in the tempest, and it believes that this is only the beginning.

LESSONS FROM THE SUN

ALASTAIR GORDON

"MIAMI SEEMED NOT A CITY AT ALL BUT A TALE, A ROMANCE OF THE TROPICS, A KIND OF WAKING DREAM IN WHICH ANY POSSIBILITY COULD AND WOULD BE ACCOMMODATED"[1] **JOAN DIDION**

It started as a series of rudimentary sketches and collages: the suburban American house deconstructed, re-imagined as a sequence of subverted facades, splayed out like one of De Chirico's early cityscapes — "The Melancholy of Departure," say — in which barrier upon barrier, wall upon wall, has been stretched out and delaminated over time. This was how the first iteration of the Pink House, appeared on the cover of *Progressive Architecture* and made a lasting impression.

Early studies done while Laurinda Spear was still an architecture student at Columbia — reduced the program to essentials: palm tree, lush foliage, and an egg-yolk sun glued to a tissue-paper sky in full-blooded, Endless Summer orange and yellow. The house is dropped casually between jungle and sea, but the most incongruous features are two highways that extend orthogonally through either end of the facade. This was not just about sun, water and tropical fecundity. It was about expanding horizons and the mythology of drive-through mobility.

A lap pool penetrates the right flank of the house and stretches to infinity. In theory, one could swim, like John Cheever's heroic swimmer, beneath the house and out to the edge of the bay and beyond. "He seemed to see, with a cartographer's eye, that string of swimming pools, that quasi-subterranean stream that curved across the county," wrote Cheever in his short story "The Swimmer" (1964).

The Pink House project was submitted to *Progressive Architecture*'s annual awards program, awarded a first-place citation, and featured in the January 1975 issue of the magazine. Meanwhile, back in Miami, the clients rejected the proposal, seeing it more as a philosophical proposition than a place to live, and encouraged their daughter to try again. After completing her studies, Spear reworked the plans with newfound partner and husband, Bernardo Fort-Brescia.

Spear's renderings for the revised version combine the moody romanticism of Chagall with the hippy innocence of Alicia Bay Laurel's *Living on the Earth*. In one drawing, there's a shooting star and a sliver of moon glowing in the night sky. The house rises out of a cornflower-blue bay like a ghostly scaffolding with square, punched openings. A sleepwalking woman stands by the railing and gazes out to sea, as in Giacometti's "Palace at 4 a.m." sculpture of 1932, but this dream house is inundated by water with a sailboat moored to the banister and steps descending into the bay. A faintly penciled caption reads: "I will wait for you...".

As built, the Pink House, 1978, (p. 42) is a progression from water to water, a color-coded conversation between lap pool and Biscayne Bay, setting up a sequence of rhythms, reflections and alternating syncopations, beginning at the 115-foot wide facade and proceeding through other layers and colored foils — from blushing rose on the first wall, to wild flamingo on the second, to a paler conch-shell pink on the two-story wall of the main house. "The alignment of colored planes seems to evoke the idea of screens to protect the nucleus of some secret spatial heart," wrote Fulvio Irace, an Italian critic who wrote the first analysis of the project ("The Dream of a House," *Domus*, January 1981). But where, exactly, does this secret spatial heart hide itself?

There are subtle hints of numerological symmetry throughout. Six square windows in the house correspond to the six palm trees in the front courtyard. Three panels of translucent glass block are rippled like water and suffused with sea-flecked light. The foundation plinth was not so much a neo-classical affectation as it was a practical response to flood-control laws that required the first floor to be eleven feet above grade.

The entry staircase leads to an open-air terrace that, in turn, surrounds a narrow, sixty-foot-long pool and confirms the project's conceptual bias towards wetness. A first-time visitor can preview the underwater "chamber" through a luminous eye that gazes out from the front facade in cool, chlorinated blue. Round like a porthole or camera lens, it is the true metaphysical entry, and conjures forth other ironic subversions of the American Dream — from Cheever's "quasi-subterranean stream" to David Hockney's homoerotic pool culture and Joan Didion's "subaqueous suspension." (Both Jay Gatsby and Joe Willis, narrator of Wilder's *Sunset Boulevard*, are found dead, floating in their respective swimming pools). The aquamarine lens is also a peephole for watching unsuspecting swimmers — what Irace refers to cryptically as the "voyeur's ambiguous game" — a ritual device that recalls Miami's early days of Aquacade ballets, glass-bottomed boats, and the underwater bar that Morris Lapidus designed for the Eden Roc Hotel that featured a much larger porthole for watching scantily clad mermaids dance in dreamy syncopation.

When the house was completed in 1978, some of the responses were negative. "NEIGHBORS SEE RED OVER PINK HOUSE," ran a headline in the *Miami Herald*, while Councilman Ralph Bowen grumbled about the color being "inappropriate." Most reviews, however, were ecstatic. Soon the house became a pop icon and was featured not only in design journals like *Progressive Architecture* and *Domus*, but in mainstream publications like *Vogue*, *Time*, *The New York Times* and *House Beautiful*.

It also became a favored location for fashion shoots and TV commercials. Bruce Weber shot a 10-page spread for the February 1980 issue of *Gentleman's Quarterly* (*GQ*) with male models lounging around the pool and terrace. A feature in *Life* magazine included the double spread of a bikini-clad woman, faceless and floating on the surface of the pool, in an unabashedly erotic pose — "a study in integrity" — with her long legs dangling off a rubber raft.

The Pink House embodied a certain moment and mood: European rationalism cross-fertilized with the tropical surrealism of Miami. Everything about the place — colors, pool, translucency — seemed to exude a simmering, barely sublimated sexuality. Suddenly, Miami appeared to have a culture that went beyond retirement plans and palm trees, a culture that was edgy and slightly dangerous, with fast cars, cocaine cowboys, cigarette boats and outrageous architecture.

"WE ARE NOT TRYING TO CREATE A NEW STYLE. WE ARE JUST TRYING TO MAKE MODERN ARCHITECTURE MORE LIVELY AND UP-TO-DATE."[2] **LAURINDA SPEAR**

Pink would be the color associated with Miami. Maybe it had always been that way, what with flamingoes, sunsets and bougainvillea, but now it was ingrained into the DNA of the place, connoting an environment that was both exotic and irreverent in its *pinkness*, an impression reinforced by Christo's "Surrounded Island" installation in which eleven small islands in Biscayne Bay were collared with bright pink polypropylene fabric, and a few of those islands could be seen — *pink to pink* — from the terrace of the Pink House.

URBAN FOLLIES

By 1978 the fledgling firm had moved into a 600-square-foot studio in Coconut Grove that sat on the corner of Oak Avenue and Rice Street (just across from Arquitectonica's present headquarters). They paid $600 a month for a second-floor studio above a mini mall and began work on a series of modest infill projects in which they were able to expand the ideas they'd experimented with in the Pink House, continuing to explore the poetics of sun and shadow. These urban follies used stucco walls, bold blocks of color, and elemental geometries to attract the maximum attention while keeping budgets within reach. For a property in El Portal, Fort-Brescia and Spear converted two low-lying buildings on NE 2nd Avenue into a plastic surgeon's clinic (Kitsos, 1979) with a courtyard surrounded by four elementary forms: a red gateway, a yellow tower with blue-tiled roof, a blue staircase that leads up to a secret chamber, and an undulating studio wall.

Spear's renderings show the tower and colonnade inhabited by tragic Greek figures: a naked Adonis, a goddess in long diaphanous dress and flowing hair, similar to the dreamy figures in her Pink House renderings. On the upper margins of a night sky, there's a sliver moon and angelic emanations, while below, a palm tree droops, as if swooning against the side of the solitary tower.

In the built version, the stucco walls are featureless foils for the subtropical sun and a play of changing shadows — "a disturbing linear succession of colored architectural ghosts"[3] — while slender palm trees replace the colonnade of Spear's renderings. Openings are more like punctures than conventional doors or windows, and the entry cube appears to be a solid block of matter, penetrated through its core by a mysteriously arched passageway.

A similar play of form and color was used at the Decorative Arts Center (1982) in Miami's Design District. An L-shaped warehouse was divided in half by an undulating passageway, and a pedestrian plaza was furnished with a turquoise archway and an orange pavilion with a peaked roof. Two 40-foot-high pylons, painted red, were placed on axis with NE 40th Street to signal the main entry and catch the eye of motorists passing on I-195.

These toy-like constructions were mere finger exercises leading up to a series of much more ambitious projects.

BREAKTHROUGH ON BRICKELL

The Babylon (p. 48) sits prettily on SE 14th Street just where the street begins to turn into Brickell Bay Drive and curve around to the south, along the bay, in a bulging crescent. Lying low among so many stodgy beige condos, the 1982 building seems both quaint and radical at the same time. It is conspicuously small, six stories high with only 13 units. In form, it is a mongrel construct, a "building in the process of metropolitan mitosis," as one critic noted, a two-sided ziggurat with stepped Dutch gables at either end.[4] The red gables may have been self-conscious pastiche and/or self-mocking, but there is also beauty in the pure geometries and daring choice of color that helped to wake up the entire neighborhood. Although the jury had mixed feelings, the project won a citation from *Progressive Architecture* (January 1978). Charles Moore admired the wit and "Chagallian, Star Wars quality of the graphics... drawn in a pseudo-archaic manner" and thought it would be a fun place to live." That same feeling of joy might occur each time you return to the building," he noted.

While there are obvious historic allusions, they are never as literal as the historical appropriations that avowed postmodernists like Robert Venturi, Robert Stern, and other architects of the period were committing. Michael Graves' Portland Building, with its strident classicism and pseudo-fascist detailing, was completed the same year as the Babylon. With all of its incongruities, the Babylon represented a significant shift in the architectural thinking of the day, showing the way from late corporate modernism and the indulgent pastiche of post-modernism to a new kind of urban landmark.

If the Babylon represented the last of Arquitectonica's early period, then the shift from early to mature was hardly perceptible. Within months of its completion, the firm took on a series of large-scale commissions that would have been impressive for even the most established firm.

The Palace, Atlantis and Imperial were all built in rapid succession between 1981 and 1983, and all were slab-like residential towers built within a seven-block stretch of Brickell Avenue.

Norman Mailer described the ubiquitous condominium towers of Miami as "ice cube trays on end," but Arquitectonica's new structures were anything but predictable, taunting the old order, verging on subversive.[5] All three could be recognized from a distance because of their height and unusual profiles. The Palace was 41 stories, making it for a short interval the tallest building in Miami, and it rose incongruously behind the humble Romanesque facade of a Greek Catholic Church.

The Atlantis was 20 stories and the Imperial 31 stories. A slender slab presents a two-dimensional quality, as if the building were a flattened foldout, pressed and rendered in shallow perspective, like a Cubist collage. At such a width, rooflines become exaggerated and loaded with meaning, cutting against the sky.

In each case there was a singular move: a stepped mass crashing through another mass at the Palace, a four-story void through the center of the Atlantis, a perforated red wall at the Imperial. All three shared the dynamism of early Constructivism: powerful geometries, tesselations, playful displacements, honest structural expression; offset by overlapping grids, skewed planes and cantilevered balconies; while exterior walls were polychromed with the bold Euro-primaries of Rietveld, Memphis and Lego.

The Atlantis (p. 56) was wafer-thin, 37 feet wide, with only a single apartment in depth. The 37-foot high void that penetrated its middle was a stylized x-ray of the building's inner anatomy, a cross-section. Early drawings show the so called Sky Court as a giant window, a refined urban lens, through which the city is reframed and reconfigured from an idealized point of view, that of a man dressed only in a bathing suit, standing on the diving board, gazing out at the horizon. In fact, it's an allegorical vignette for all of Miami, a new kind of tropical utopia, miniaturized and framed on the eighth floor. (In early iterations, the spiral staircase looks more like an umbilical cord than a staircase). To further emphasize the metaphor of a lost and sunken city, Spear designed a tapestry of dolphins and fish swimming against a sea-blue background that hung on the back wall of the lobby. (The tapestry was based on the ancient Minoan "Fresco of the Dolphins" found on the island of Knossos.)

The red masonry wall of the Imperial was an enormous flat shield sliding down the north side of the building, punctured at regular intervals by a thousand square openings, an ecstatic grid that echoes through the rest of the design.[8] As with the Atlantis, there was a major erosion, in this case, an eight-story void that makes for a dramatic "drive-through lobby." The Palace, first to be finished and most northern of the Brickell triad, was built for Harry Helmsley, legendary New York developer, on a skewed waterfront lot near the corner of SE 15th Road.

"I DON'T CARE IF YOU ARE YOUNG OR OLD, AS LONG AS YOU ARE GOOD."[6] **HARRY HELMSLEY**

Fort-Brescia, then in his late 20s, was on his way to Rome to visit Spear who had a fellowship at the American Academy. Along the way he stopped in New York and managed to get an appointment with the 72-year-old developer who was planning to build a condo tower on Brickell Avenue, but hadn't yet settled on an architect. Fort-Brescia told Helmsley how they had just finished building the nearby Babylon and were familiar with the neighborhood. He reassured the developer, "I know Miami."

Helmsley agreed to come see the firm's work and a few weeks later he and his wife Leona showed up at their studio, an inauspicious, 600-square-foot walk-up in Coconut Grove. It was a major opportunity for such a young, inexperienced firm. Helmsley had one of the most successful real estate companies in the country, and among other iconic properties, owned the Empire State Building. "I don't care if you are young or old, as long as you are good,"[6] said Helmsley.

They had just enough time to prepare a pin-up presentation of their plans, and Fort-Brescia explained how the main building would be perched on an elevated plinth with a grid of square pavers. From out of this Euclidean base rose two primary slab-like structures. The site plan was similar to Le Corburbier's Unité d'Habitation (Marseille, 1952), both featuring bar-like forms skewed in relationship to the main entry access. The higher of the Palace's (p. 52) two slabs was encased in a cast-concrete grid, white and uniform, and was penetrated by a shorter stepped section clad in bright red stucco, which appeared to be crashing through the bigger slab while descending towards the bay in steps with extra-wide balconies on every level. The connotation of one building penetrating the other was fairly blatant and Arquitectonica referred to the smaller of the two buildings as the "aggressor." A three-story glass cube contained a penthouse apartment, while a teardrop-shaped blob projected from the southeast corner of the building, creating a free-form oriel and sky terrace.

At first there was silence. Helmsley cleared his throat and asked his wife what she thought of such a radical proposal.

"I think that the kids have done their homework," said Leona.

After another extended pause, Helmsley looked across at them and said: "I like it!" And that was it — the firm's first big break — winning a $30-million project over five more experienced firms for one of the top developers in the country. (Up to that point, Arquitectonica had made a total of $25,000, mainly for their work on the Babylon.)

"We were still in our twenties!" recalled Fort-Brescia. "It was quite amazing."

"THE DRAWING IS THE DREAM OF WHAT THE BUILDING COULD BE."[7]

LAURINDA SPEAR

PROCESS

For Spear and Fort-Brescia, the creative process was largely intuitive but it was also about understanding context, budget, and the politics of securing a job and managing it through completion. "When we first present a concept I give all the numbers, square footage, scale, construction costs, how much material will be needed," said Fort-Brescia. "It's important that the client is reassured."[8]

Even their biggest, most complex ideas started with a small, elementary sketch, drawn on a paper napkin or scrap of paper during brainstorming sessions in coffee shops and restaurants. While Spear often did the initial drawing, it was a collaborative process. "We sit down, and one sketches something and the other one suggests something else, or a modification of that sketch until we agree that this is a solution," said Fort-Brescia. "We reinforce one another."

The rough sketch would evolve into a more developed concept but there was usually a single prime image that remained as a conceptual touchstone and captured the essence of the design, the "dream of what the building could be."

Working from their sketches, the architects would then improvise with an additive, cut-and-paste process derived in part from Cubism, Futurism, and Russian Constructivism, but seen through their own uniquely sub-tropical lens. "Our buildings are collages," explained Fort-Brescia. "As in a collage, things don't match; scales aren't corresponding. When you look out over a city, not all buildings are coordinated. That's what makes a city lively."[9]

For projects like the Pink House, Spear's drawings were rendered in a kind of dreamy Chagall style, "all moons and starry skies and airborne maidens," as Joan Didion described them.[10] There was also a slightly later transitional style during the early 1980s, executed in the shadowy spirit of Hugh Ferriss's moody urban renderings. Charcoal drawings for projects like Kitsos, Atlantis, and the Helmsley Center, were brooding and dystopian, with much finger smudging of charcoal into textured paper.

By 1983, the Ferriss-type chiaroscuro, as well as the airborne maidens, gave way to a brighter, less romantic style: axonometric projections drawn in outline with a Rapidograph pen and then colored in by hand with Prismacolor pencils on translucent vellum, which lent the images a luminous quality, as if they were lit from within. (Prismacolor pencils featured a soft, waxy core of pigment and came in a range of 150 different colors.)[11] The axonometric projection, by its very nature, transforms a building into an abstract object, like a sculpture, skewed off-axis, self-contained, while revealing multiple facades in rotation. These richly colored projections became the firm's signature style, delighting critics, charming clients, and helping to make sure that Arquitectonica's work was published in journals throughout the world.

A similar sensibility was translated directly from drawing to built project — the dream of what the building will become — as singular, free-standing objects, often perched on a plinth (for parking), leaving extra-wide perimeters, not maxing out the lot, with room for plazas, gardens and swimming pools. While this was partially in response to setback laws, it was also a way to achieve sculptural integrity.

Arquitectonica learned to work with the subtropical light of Miami as an essential design medium. The Miami sun can flatten perspective and diminish mass, but it can also bring out previously hidden dimensions. Shadows shift and fold, while true edges lose definition, as if in a watercolor wash. At certain times of day and season — depending on the angle of light, cloud cover and humidity — a building might appear vague and edgeless to the point where it dissolves in a haze of milky midday torpor. "Buildings swim free against the sky," noted Joan Didion during a visit she made to Miami in the summer of 1985. "Surfaces were reflective, opalescent... Angles were oblique, intersecting to disorienting effect."[12] In mid-winter light, the same buildings might stand out with razor-sharp corners and cantilevered balconies.

They understood the poetics of sun and shadow, how a simple stucco wall became animated when struck by tropical sunlight, turning it into a foil, a blank screen, for the play of interlacing shadows. Stucco, a material that seems dull and unlovable in northern light, comes to life in the tropics. A simple overhang with undulating fascia breaks up the monotony of the wall and the sun does the rest. Filigrees of crisscrossing shadows could further animate a brightly colored surface. Six tall palms, planted in front of the Pink House, cast shadows across the pink facade, like Corinthian columns, suggesting, however subliminally, a modern temple. Cantilevered balconies at the Imperial were stacked vertically to create a rippling shadow dance.

Where possible, nature was encouraged to intervene and play compositional counterpoint to the geometric volumes and rigid gridwork of the architecture. Venerable old banyans with dangling aerial-roots, were preserved and allowed to grow around the eastern end of the Atlantis property. Clusters of mangrove were cultivated along the water's edge at the Imperial to create a green buffer between land and bay.

Ralph Waldo Emerson wrote that "water understands civilization," and Arquitectonica understood how to integrate water in much of their work, for its surface textures, its sense of mystery and for the ways that it reflected light, dissolved edges, and enhanced color. Water became one of their trademarks. The Pink House bracketed itself around a 60-foot lap pool, as if it were the foyer of the house. A kidney-shaped pool was used at the Palace to offset the rigidity of the relentless grid. A narrow lap pool was placed on a perpendicular axis with the Atlantis, while the eastern end of the Imperial stepped cautiously into a circular pool.

"WHAT WE'RE TRYING TO SAY IS THAT THERE IS A MIAMI, AND IF THERE ISN'T ONE, WE'RE GOING TO INVENT IT."[13] **BERNARDO FORT-BRESCIA**

In the final months of 1979, Arquitectonica moved from their tiny office in Coconut Grove into a 2,500-square-foot space, a former car repair shop, on Ponce de Leon Boulevard, in the industrial area of Coral Gables. Expectations were high, even soaring. As *Progressive Architecture* reported: "Accounts of the young firm's meteoric rise over the last five years have chronicled the process by which its principles have changed the face of Miami."[14]

The work was radiant and poetic, qualities that hadn't been seen in mainstream architecture for some time, and the buildings on Brickell became instant landmarks. "They might shock the public," wrote one critic, "but the shock is always a pleasant tickling sensation."[15] Others called the Arquitectonica look everything from "Romantic Modernism" to "Ecstatic Modernism."[16] Esquire described a certain "child-like naiveté."[17] Time thought the work was "visually noisy," while Wolf Von Eckardt compared the buildings to abstract paintings by Mondrian and Miró. One critic described the firm's "Prismacolor habit" as being mere packaging, while dismissing it as "wet T-shirt architecture,"[18] and Beth Dunlop, architecture critic for the Miami Herald, called it "child's play."[19] Such critical responses often come with overnight success and Arquitectonica's exuberant buildings made easy targets.

On the evening of September 16, 1984, the American viewing public sat in their living rooms and watched NBC's pilot episode of *Miami Vice*. A hard-driving theme song by Jan Hammer continued through the credit roll to a fast-cut montage of Miami plumage. After the palm trees and pink flamingos, after the fractured waters of Biscayne Bay and a speeding cigarette boat, came a helicopter shot of Miami's skyline and then, finally, the most startling image of all: the west facade of the Atlantis on Brickell Avenue.

Here was the prime image for the cool-hot Miami, more than speedboats or sexy women: a square hole in the middle of a blue building, tricked out with a red spiral staircase and a solitary palm tree. Here was the essence of American leisure magnified, even weaponized — a palm tree in the sky! It instantly became the symbol for a city in transition, a city that was outrageous, wildly colored, and slightly dangerous.

REVERSE RUINS

The scope of Arquitectonica's work would expand in the mid-1980s to embrace larger, more exploratory projects, while moving further away from their Miami-centric visions, taking on commissions in sprawling cities like Houston and Dallas, attempting to create "place" in placeless edge conditions, while offering radical alternatives to the conventional suburban typologies of shopping center, office park, and residential subdivision. They were still experimenting with many of the same themes as the early Miami work — color, clustering and colliding of forms with punched-out windows and cantilevered roof planes — but elevating scale and complexity that was more on par with megastructures of the 1960s and the works of the Metabolists, Archigram, and Superstudio.

The Horizon Hill Center (San Antonio, Texas, 1982), a towering, 1.4-million-square-foot structure with four vertical members, 45 stories high, and connected along the top by a massive crossbar of reflective glass. (One thinks of Fuller's dome over Manhattan and Superstudio's mega grids.) This monumental gesture would be seen from miles away, signaling the entry to a new suburban development being built around the intersection of two major expressways. The base took the form of a six-story plinth — a kind of modern earth mound — that pushed the project even further towards the fringes of science fiction, as did the red pyramid, oblong swimming pools, palm trees and crystalline arcade of shops, all of it evoking the imagery of a lost civilization. After several starts and stops, the project was ultimately abandoned.

Arquitectonica's master plan for the G Street Mole in San Diego (1982), integrated restaurants, shops, offices, a park and residential units, into a riotous, candy-flavored urban landscape of whimsical shapes and comic-book colors while playing off the odd trapezoidal shape of the waterfront site. The Planets development (1984) was a utopian shopping center that Arquitectonica designed for a 25-acre lot outside of Dallas. Each of the twelve "planets" possessed its own distinctive character: a tower clad in pink glass with a green globe rising from its roof, a bright red restaurant that projected out over a boomerang-shaped reflecting pool. Other planets featured zigzagging roofs and swooping, catenary curves.

Capital Park West (1983) was a 3.3 million-square-foot office complex near downtown Houston that featured seven towers with a radical assortment of roof treatments: fin, wedge, wave, zigzag. The highest tower, at 42 stories, was a vertically extruded triangle resting on slender columns with curvilinear glass blobs for the lobby and roof. The 34-story tower was a stack of displaced cubes, while the 22-story tower took the form of a truncated cone. All were connected to peripheral parking structures via elevated pedestrian bridges.

Even though New York is only 1,280 miles north of Miami, it's a thousand light years away in terms of cultural hegemony, and New Yorkers' inbred sense of superiority does not always take kindly to outsiders. While the city's newspapers and magazines heralded Arquitectonica's early rise to stardom, the praise usually came with a caveat: their brand of sun-drenched flamboyance was fine for the tropics, but it lacked the intellectual gravitas that New Yorkers expected from their architecture. It was too "Latin," too colorful, too playful.

"We wanted to go beyond Miami, but New York was tough," confessed Fort-Brescia. How would the firm's ebullient designs play in a city that never slept, a city known to be obdurate, unforgiving and gray? Early proposals for the Big Apple in the 1980s included an edgy fashion center that was to be built in a former Con-Ed Station in Soho. The plan was to gut the old brick structure and insert a multi-level cocoon, amorphously shaped and fully transparent, that would float on a pool of water and support a series of showrooms for hip young fashion designers.

Arquitectonica's 1983 proposal for the South Ferry Plaza in lower Manhattan assumed the form of a 68-story tower with wildly cantilevered platforms, observation decks and a strident television mast that rose several stories above the roof, a playfully Constructivist monument in the spirit of Ivan Leonidov's Tower for Red Square (1934), an ode to verticality and modern technology. But it was deemed too radical for the retro, post-modernist tastes of the moment, and it would be another twenty years before Arquitectonica got to build their first project in New York City.

Other parts of the country proved less resistant and Arquitectonica found success with a new kind of residential hybrid that was aimed at young urban professionals who wanted to live closer to downtown areas. Partially derived in response to setback laws and height limitations, the new typology also responded to climate, changing demographics and an expanding work force in car-centric cities like Houston and Dallas where suburban fringes were rapidly being absorbed and transformed.[20] Attached living units introduced low-rise urbanization and higher densities to previously single-family neighborhoods. They were conceived from the inside out, doing the most with a minimum of material, contrasting forms and colors, often layered with false fronts, brise-soleil panels, balconies, recesses, gaps, and other kinds of interstitial spaces that created more depth and sculptural complexity, while the interiors featured loft-like spaces, high ceilings, nautical railings and multiple skylights. Boxy sections were clustered together with overlapping planes and square or triangular openings punched through the tautly pulled envelopes that were further delineated by multi-hued partitions. Vertical cleavages delineated different sections of the Milford and Taggart townhouses, allowing for natural light to penetrate the deeper recesses of the buildings, while providing access points for staircases and doorways.

The Haddon Street Townhouses (1983) brought density to an otherwise bland suburban neighborhood of single-family houses in west Houston. Instead of filling a single lot, the complex stretched across two corner properties with white walls and jaunty, multi-colored features: saw-toothed roofline, portholes, bright red indentations, yellow fins and extruded blue cubes, "something put together by a gifted child with an oversize Lego toy set," as *Time* magazine described it.[21] Instead of the proverbial front yard, the ten units addressed the street with an unbroken wall of vertical frontage that expressed interior configurations. Vertical red slots contained entryways. The blue cubes were bedrooms, while the yellow fins were a kind of organizing armature, not only concealing structural supports but defining the two-story living spaces while screening off the staircase and loft-like dining area. Arquitectonica would go on to design more than eight similarly attached residential projects over the next few years.

By 1986 the firm's staff had increased to more than sixty employees, and Arquitectonica needed room to grow. Fort-Brescia and Spear purchased a corner lot on Miami Beach, at 420 Jefferson Avenue, in an area that was just beginning to gentrify. They designed a 25,000-square-foot building with 10,000 square feet for their own studio. What was essentially otherwise a stucco box was brought to life with a variety of decorative interventions. (The general feeling was subaqueous.) Colors were softer — aquamarine blue, teal green, sky blue — more pastel in tone than the bold primaries of their earlier work. Multi-hued tiles were based on traditional Miccosukee Indian patterns. Perforated cutouts evoked an underwater world of stylized jellyfish, seaweed and starfish.

The same type of eccentric imagery was repeated inside and outside and carried up to the roof terrace and Arquitectonica's design studio with undulating walls and a palette-shaped roof with deep overhangs supported by slender, chopstick columns that leaned at different angles.

Their next big projects — a courthouse, a private banking complex, an embassy — had more to do with authorship and long-term legacy than impulse and overnight success. Where they had experimented with verticality and three-dimensional collage, the next generation of buildings were less conspicuous, lower and more horizontal in profile. "Our current work is more expressionist," said Laurinda Spear. "The forms are freer, less rigid, therefore, less limited in the vocabulary."[22] Whether splaying along a roadway, negotiating a natural landscape, or presenting a dignified but defensive posture, they were now dealing with a hierarchy of programmatic issues that they hadn't had to deal with in their residential projects — complex circulation and security issues — while delivering a more civically responsive brand of iconography. In place of bright blocks of color and visual puns, surfaces were treated like tapestries with overlapping patterns, while more sophisticated materials — stone, marble, ceramic tile — were used in place of painted stucco.

The North Dade Justice Center (1983) was built on a 12-acre site shaped by both natural and man-made forces. There's a mangrove swamp out back, and a busy four-lane roadway in front, that curves through the cluttered suburban landscape of North Miami Beach. (A curving wall of glass looks out over the mangrove preserve, as does a stained-glass window that features a crisscrossing pattern of red-and-gray glass panels based on a Seminole Indian pattern.) In plan, the 39,000-square-foot building is a pale pink boomerang resting on an ovoid-and-rectangular base of perforated green walls with four steeply pitched skylights that stick up from the roof like wedges of yellow cheese. The convex facade of the upper level follows the bend of highway and bulges towards the west as a kind of anamorphic distortion, hovering on slender pilotis, shifting and spinning as one moves past, either by car or on foot through the central breezeway. All together, it made for a highly animated civic space, a vivid drive-by experience designed for consumption at 50 miles per hour. A cross-axial promenade skewers the site, creating a link between Route 1 all the way east into the wetlands preserve — between noisy highway and quiet sanctuary.

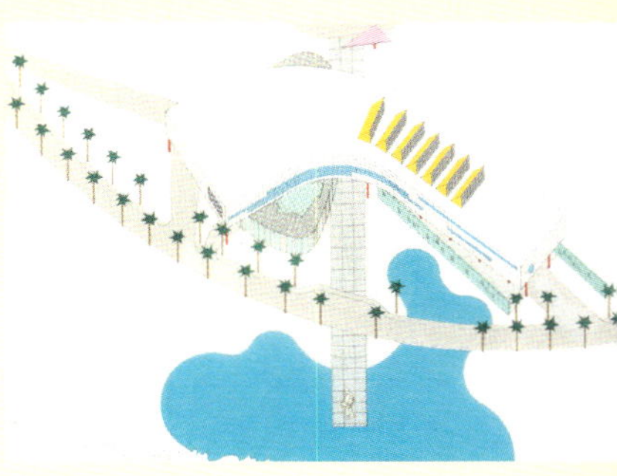

While some architects shunned the retail genre, Arquitectonica embraced it as yet another American typology to be disrupted and reconstructed, pushing their aesthetic to the limits of good taste, while turning shopping into performance art. "Rio will hit town like a wired rock band," boasted developer Charles Ackerman, who envisioned a kind of McLuhanesque tribal village in which customers became willing participants in an interactive environment, stimulated by electronic media. Arquitectonica designed the $10 million center for a six-acre site in midtown Atlanta and it would be one of the firm's most experimental interventions.

"If Rio is a Shock, Blame it on Arquitectonica" ran a 1987 headline in the *Atlanta Journal*.[23] Original plans called for a gas station with transparent pumps and attendants wearing luminous uniforms. While these features were cut, there was a five-story laser light tower and an interactive video wall, heralded as the "electronic bulletin board for Rio's post-modern town square," that consisted of 25 television screens stacked on top of one another. "You are going to experience things the minute you walk in," said developer Ackerman. "It's going to be a new gathering place for Midtown, a big turn-on." A gridded

plane was subverted by ramps and prisms rising or sinking below a central plaza. The prisms contained shops and restaurants that surrounded a reflecting pool with a 15-foot-high waterfall, a 40-foot geodesic sphere, a peach grove, and an army of 350 cast-concrete frogs.

The Sawgrass Mills mega mall lays less than 2,000 feet from the edge of the Everglades National Park, making for a swampy netherland between wilderness and civilization, alligator habitat and discount retailing. Described by the architects as a "series of boxcars set at angles," the four main sections were joined in a zigzagging configuration. Seven anchor stores branched off the central core, and long allées of palm trees led to the primary entrances, each of which featured a roofless, skeletal structure, as if the building process had been deconstructed and left to stand as a series of partially finished monuments, "reverse ruins" — one being a jungle-gym scaffolding painted bright yellow; another being a super grid curving out towards the parking lot, skewered by giant chopsticks. Another took the form of a shadow box with white masonry walls punctured by irregularly shaped openings. The entry follies served as spatial markers, reference points to help guide disoriented shoppers from their cars to the desired destination within the 120-acre sea of discount mania.

Architecture deferred to history and the natural order of topography as the Banco de Credito, Lima, 1988, (p.62) became a peripheral framework — more background than foreground — a conceptual corral for a rugged, Peruvian landscape that featured jagged rock outcroppings, native plants, waterfalls, and an ancient Incan burial site uncovered during excavation. Arquitectonica's overarching idea was to give the country's biggest private bank an identity, a physical presence it never really had before: an idealized meditation between wilderness and city, history and modernity, open to mountain gods on one side, while processing international capital on the other.

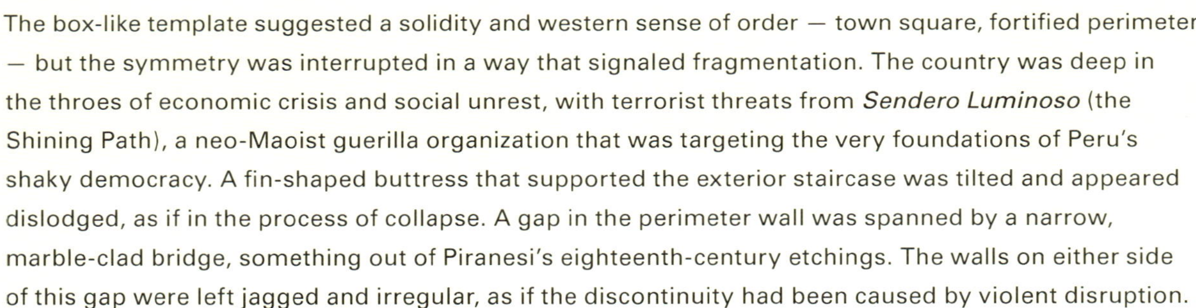

The box-like template suggested a solidity and western sense of order — town square, fortified perimeter — but the symmetry was interrupted in a way that signaled fragmentation. The country was deep in the throes of economic crisis and social unrest, with terrorist threats from *Sendero Luminoso* (the Shining Path), a neo-Maoist guerilla organization that was targeting the very foundations of Peru's shaky democracy. A fin-shaped buttress that supported the exterior staircase was tilted and appeared dislodged, as if in the process of collapse. A gap in the perimeter wall was spanned by a narrow, marble-clad bridge, something out of Piranesi's eighteenth-century etchings. The walls on either side of this gap were left jagged and irregular, as if the discontinuity had been caused by violent disruption.

"Arquitectonica's building has become the ironic new symbol of a country presently under political siege," wrote Karen Stein in *Architectural Record*.[24] The construction of a $54-million banking complex under such circumstances was a decided act of faith in the country's future.

A 119-foot-high atrium rose through the roof to announce itself as both entry and guiding metaphor. Natural light filtered through 8,000 glass blocks that enclosed this elliptical glass eye — evoking visions of Étienne-Louis Boullée — not only a filter for light and circulation, but a crystalline connector between exterior and interior spaces, and a transcendent architectural moment that symbolized the highest of civic aspirations.

The same might be said of the United States Embassy (1994), also built in a suburban area of Lima, and set well back from La Encalada, a busy, four-lane avenue that runs through the residential neighborhood of Monterrico. It is a simple rectilinear mass, perched on a precast concrete plinth that acts as a blast wall. There are no extraneous projections, cantilevered ledges, or balconies. Windows are small, tinted with dark glass and there is only a single, centrally controlled point of entry. It is, essentially, a bunker and most of Arquitectonica's design choices came out of the need for heightened security. But what is the role of the architect in such a constrained situation? How does one work with blast-proof facades and create something artistic? Arquitectonica wrapped the building with a monumental mosaic, inspired by traditional Incan textile patterns, camouflaging the bulk of the building in a series of horizontal bands, as if revealing a cross-section of geological strata in alternating bands of color.

Most of the materials used in construction were from local Peruvian sources including a type of white volcanic stone known as sillar that was quarried in Arequipa, in the southern part of Peru. The blast-wall base resembles rugged stone blocks set in tiers like the ancient walls at Machu Picchu. The next section features squares of tinted glass set against a background of white native stone. The upper facade was made from two-toned slate tiles of a golden hue, set in triangular patterns. This kind of layering not only helped to diminish the mass of the 200,000-square-foot structure, it also drew the eye back to the ochre-colored reaches of the San Cristobal foothills and beyond to the upper reaches of *El Pino* and *Muleria*. This is how the building connects to the indigenous spirit of the place; not only to Incan culture, but to Lima's rugged terrain and the astringent light of its 5,080-foot altitude.

TRANSGRESSION

The single-family house is often considered to be the sonnet form of American architecture, a form that allows the architect to return to core artistic values while testing out new ideas without the pressures of a larger-scale project. Following the spectacular success of the Pink House, Arquitectonica was eager to take on a similarly experimental commission. They designed the Magaziner house for a narrow, bay-front lot in Coral Gables, with a bright yellow facade, three pronounced gables, and steeply pitched roofs, pushing conventional iconographies of the American home toward pure abstraction, while also addressing a 12-foot-high flood regulation and a design-review ordinance that stipulated a historic "blending in."

The tri-gabled facade extended itself away from the street and broke into elongated wings: short, medium and long. This was where domestic certainties began to erode. The middle wing was sliced midway, on the diagonal, to reveal a transverse cross-section of angular incongruities. A narrow lap pool stretched to the back of the property and ended abruptly above a man-made crater. Outer volumes were further breached by a suspended balcony and a bright red prism that crashed through the longest wing of the house. The furtive exterior was expressed in reverse on the interior with an assemblage of converging forms: a cylindrical fireplace, a spiraling staircase, and an elevated pedestrian bridge.

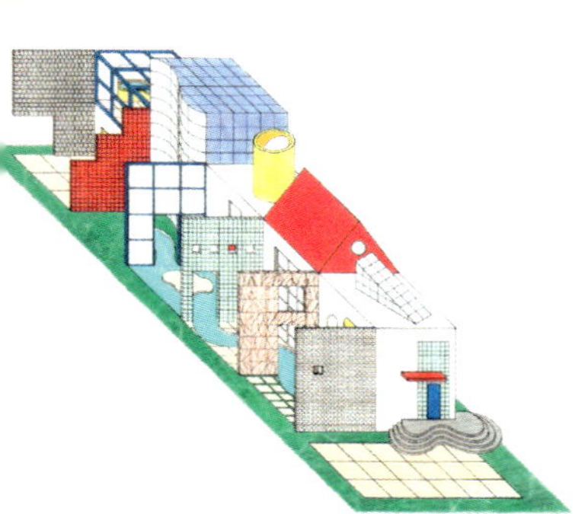

In an ingenious house that Arquitectonica conceived for developer Jerry Maba, rooms took the form of separate volumes, miniature buildings. Like the Pink House, it was low and linear with a pool as central metaphor, but it was fractured with autonomous elements divided by terraces and connected by a river-like pool that snaked between the open-air rooms. The preferred mode of circulation was, therefore, *swimming*. Each section, each wing wall was expressed by a different material: brick, aqua-blue tiles, pink marble, translucent glass, concrete block. (The living room had a red, pitched roof. The guestroom featured a wedge-like skylight.) It was a brilliant subversion of the suburban American home, all about liquidity, opening up, and peeling back the underlying mythologies of domestic architecture.

Another house, also for Jerry Maba, was a speculative beach house "for a bachelor," to be built on an oceanfront lot in Malibu. The flesh-pink walls echoed the wavering line of the sand dunes and concealed a central courtyard with vulva-shaped swimming pool and single palm tree. With its "V"-shaped openings, glass-block apertures and suggestive protrusions, the house was a study in voyeurism, concealing and revealing — beach house as a kind of architectural foreplay. As the architects wrote: "a getaway house for aspiring movie stars whose programmatic needs included the heroic master bedroom and exercise terrace with Jacuzzi."[25]

In place of a linear layout, like the Pink house or first Maba house, Mulder (p. 70) featured a cross-axial armature around which different rooms and terraces extended out as independent sculptural entities in pinwheel fashion. None of it was apparent from the street as most of the house was blocked from view by a 12-foot-high peripheral wall, the only point of entry being a small, unassuming doorway framed in red. The house was published extensively, with cover stories in *Architectural Record* and several other journals. "A small work from the open-minded American office sums up its design preferences for collage, collision and calculated sophisticated transgression," wrote the approving editors of *Domus*.[26] With skewed site lines, incongruous fenestration, and seemingly random patterns of pink and black granite cladding, the Walner House (1987) was an expressionist assembly of mismatched components spliced together in a Z-shaped layout that zigged and zagged across a 2.9-acre property, just to the north of Chicago. "We wanted it to appear to be moving," said Fort-Brescia, who designed the house with alternating facades, prismatic forms, and sudden juxtapositions, as if the extended linearity of the Pink House had been bent to fit the high ground of a heavily wooded knoll overlooking Lake Michigan. Interior spaces are suffused with natural light and furnished with the owners' collection of contemporary art (Sol LeWitt, Larry Rivers, Ed Ruscha) and one-off pieces of modernist furniture. A black granite fireplace was cranked at an angle in the middle of the living room like a monolithic sculpture. A space-age doorway was surrounded by several randomly placed portholes that percolate up the side of a wall like soap bubbles.

Water begets water in the liquid, drifting composition that Arquitectonica conceived for a newspaper magnate who wanted to build his dream house on an oceanfront site in Florida. The proposed 15,000-square-foot plan was a delirious concoction that compressed Arquitectonica's larger-scale urban visions into a single-family house, a city in miniature. Conventional house anatomy is broken apart into eight semi-autonomous components that rotate outward in a centrifugal pattern. A discretely integrated system of ramps, terraces, elevated catwalks, and open-sided galleries provide circulation throughout, but the real connective tissue is water. A series of architectural follies that make up the rooms of the house, rise above the salt-water reflecting pool that is, in turn, bisected by a narrow, chlorinated lap pool and the owner's trapezoidal study is perched precariously above this liquid intersection.

The Beverly Hills house, 1989 (p. 78), is a complex arrangement of elements that project out from a incline with shifting planes and angular extensions of space. It borrows some of the organizing principles of the Mudler house but consolidates them in a more uniform template of color and surface tension. The deep, overhanging roof provides shade for the owner's collection of twentieth century art and creates an additional canopy for privacy. The mood is urbane and sophisticated but grounded to the site with various landscape features that appear to spin off from the main house like so many shards of pottery.

ARCHITECTURE AS INFRASTRUCTURE

Although Arquitectonica rarely entered design competitions, there were two important exceptions in 1989, one for the United States Pavilion at the World's Fair in Seville, Spain, and the other for the new Bibliothèque Nationale. Their Paris submission was a sequence of overlapping forms that echoed the curve of the Seine with a split ellipse, a hybridized form that would reappear in some of the firm's future work. It was divided into lecture halls, reading rooms, and rare-book repositories. The building was anchored to the shore, like a ship at its mooring, by a long armature that held administrative offices and led to a grand public plaza.

"WE WANTED TO TURN THE PATRON INTO AN ACTIVE PERFORMER."

LAURINDA SPEAR.

Arquitectonica's proposal for the Seville Expo was an invocation of new technology that bristled with multimedia events, laser lights and giant projection screens within a sculptural assemblage of dislocated parts, an "anti-building," as the architects called it, with a conical tower, spiraling ramps, and cantilevered performance decks. While the firm failed to win either the Seville or Paris competitions, their proposals were published, which helped spread their reputation in Europe and led to several major projects including the commission to design the headquarters for a banking headquarters in Luxembourg.

Boulevard Royal is a one-way arterial road that skirts the northwestern part of Luxembourg's historic *Ville Haute*. The road sweeps in from the east and makes a sharp left as it crosses Avenue Amélie, and it was this intersection that provided Arquitectonica with the generative form for the venerable Banque de Luxembourg, (p. 860) their first major building in Europe. It is a restrained and dignified composition, an idealized balance between past and future, honoring the bank's 70-year history while making a modern statement of aspiration and global connectivity. The palette throughout is muted, each section employing a different color, texture and height to differentiate it from the others — the lowest being a beige limestone block, the next a glass ellipse, while the highest is a black granite slab that serves as backdrop to the other two sections.

Interior finishes were designed to match the exterior, and the shapes expressed on the exterior were carried inside, as an ongoing dialogue between tradition and modern efficiency.

While it may have shared some of the intersecting collage features of Arquitectonica's earlier projects — the rotations and alignments of North Dade, the overlapping envelopes of Banco de Credito — the Luxembourg bank was more resolved in execution, integrated in plan, and suggested a more enlightened reading of both the urban context and the client's program. It was also, by far, the most convincing argument to date that the still-youthful firm from Miami was ready for international prime time. (They never once resorted to bright colors or flashy gimmicks.) Arquitectonica proved itself capable of a subtle and sophisticated level of design while gaining a whole new level of respect.

The brief for the City of Dijon called for a master plan (1999) to revive and bring clarity to a 30-acre site in the Clémenceau quarter and included a 1,650-seat performing arts center, a conference center, hotel, retail center, and several new office buildings. Medieval Dijon was surrounded by stone ramparts that were demolished in the twentieth-century and replaced by a series of peripheral boulevards and parks that followed the circular trace of the old wall. Working from this historical and concentric imprint, Arquitectonica rethought the traditional gateway and instead made a sweeping urban gesture that would not only redefine the perimeter, but create a modern point of arrival and a catalyst for economic growth in an unmemorable hinterland of light industry and Brutalist apartment blocks from the 1970s. The arts complex has a broadly curving facade that echoes the man-made geometries of the immediate neighborhood: the circularity of the transit lines, the roads that radiate from the center, the busy traffic circle where five boulevards converge. Here was a case of architecture expanding into infrastructure, with a variety of extensions, connections and complexities. Approaching from the east, from the direction of Vesoul, the pale limestone facade appears, at first, to be an encompassing wall, but it unfolds and opens up as the motorist speeds beneath the curving wing of the arts center and merges with the traffic on Place Jean Bouhey.

Urban patterns in and around the periphery of Paris were going through dramatic changes during the late 1990s and early 2000s, swelling outward from the historic center and beyond the Périphérique highway, northwards towards Charles De Gaulle Airport, westwards to Nanterre and La Défense, the sprawling business district. For all of the attempts at order and alignment, it remains a discordant jumble of confusing intersections, wind-swept plazas, and flashy corporate towers, each one vying for architectural supremacy. When Arquitectonica designed the new headquarters for Mazars (p. 132), an international consulting company, they did not want to add to the cacophony of the place.

Early sketches show a curving parallelogram, "as if sailing towards the esplanade propelled by an imaginary force,"[27] that evolved into a semi-transparent slab that was concave on one side and convex on the other, a gracefully neutral form, a quiet architectural solution for a frenetic urban condition. Even though the 15-story structure was dwarfed by some of the tallest buildings in France, the architecture managed to hold its own within the cluster of looming skycrapers. The bottle-green glass and fins of black steel appear supple, lending a sense of movement to what would otherwise be a static office tower. Vertical slots, as if carved with a chisel, are indented above the portals on either end and emphasize the tautness of the building's outer skin while identifying twin points of entry.

The site chosen for Microsoft Europe's headquarters, 2009 (p. 224), was just as complex and cluttered as La Défense, located at the confluence of the Seine and the multi-lane Périphérique that encircles Paris. A tripartite splitting of space into elliptical wings breaks up the bulk of the 500,000-square-foot complex and brings it down to a more approachable scale. It also allows natural light to penetrate every part of the building.

The elongated ellipsoid extensions create lens-like distortions as one moves past, creating the illusion of tangencies and mirrored repetition as the three wings fold back and reveal courtyards, a swooping ramp, and an underground entry for pedestrians.

For a site adjacent to Microsoft, Arquitectonica created a self-contained campus arrangement for Accor and EQ Water (p. 248) that borrows direction and movement from the surrounding infrastructure with curving tangencies and neatly nesting configurations. Two primary forms play off of one another — one vertical, the other horizontal — while converging lines pick up on the cartilaginous condition of the neighborhood, wedged as it is between the intersection of Rue Barra and Rue Henri Farman to the south and the tracks of a commuter railway that curves along the northern edge of the property. There is movement and an undercurrent of sublimated urgency.

As the firm continued to expand, their priorities and architectural visions evolved beyond the scope of their early practice, but while scale and budgets escalated, the basic principles regarding light, sculptural integrity, density, architectural symbolism, and proportion remained consistent.

URBAN COLLAGE

Herb Caen, columnist for the *San Francisco Chronicle*, used to refer to the city's Mid-Market District as "*le Grand Pissoir*" due to the number of vagrants and the ever-present scent of urine that wafted along Market Street. The long-blighted area was known mainly for its homeless shelters, S.R.O. flophouses, drug dealers and gang warfare, but the Mid-Market District has entered a period of gentrification after the city offered tax incentives and made a concerted effort to revitalize the neighborhood. In 2012, Twitter Inc. moved its headquarters into the old San Francisco Furniture Mart, a million-square-foot showroom at 9th Street and Market, and brought with it more than 2,000 employees. In return, the micro-blogging company received a six-year tax break, which encouraged other companies like Uber, Spotify and Dolby to follow suit along with a spate of trendy restaurants, boutiques and cultural venues like the American Conservatory Theater that opened at 1127 Market Street.[32]

Anticipating further growth, Angelo Sangiacomo, legendary Bay Area developer, commissioned Arquitectonica to design Trinity Place, 2018 (p.188), a multi-phase master plan for a 4.5-acre block that lies between Mission and Market Streets, on the former site of a motel. All of those young, well-educated new workers needed a place to live. Fort-Brescia called Trinity Place a "dormitory for the hi-tech generation" with price points aimed specifically at the new-age work force. More than 230 of the 1,900 units were offered at below-market rates. The affordable units were mixed in with the market-rate apartments and featured the same amenities.

John King, architecture critic for the *Chronicle*, called Trinity Place a "super-size urban collage."[28] It might also be seen as a Chinese puzzle of interlocking fragments that appear to shift and slide into one another, even though they remain completely static, but together create a sense of movement in what might otherwise have made for a monolithic urban fortress. A white section embraces a gray section that is, in turn, penetrated by a sand-colored section, and all of it rests on what appears to be a transparent substructure, a one-story band of glass that surrounds the base of each building and makes them appear to float ten feet above the ground.

Similar kinds of geometries and color treatments were used in other projects that Arquitectonica designed in response to San Francisco's housing shortage. As with Trinity Place, the tendency was to break down mass into smaller parts to meet local zoning requirements, but also to address the scale of smaller, pre-existing buildings of the immediate neighborhood. A restless shifting of parts and surface treatments create movement as well as a subliminal reminder of the tectonic slippage that occurs in this earthquake-prone city.

At Avalon Mission Bay, 2009 (p. 230), also in the Mission District, alternating blocks of red and gray masonry surround a garden courtyard and are perforated, here and there, by voids. At Linea (pg. 316), 2014, built on a corner lot in the Hayes Valley area, cubic forms are even more pronounced and appear to tumble and push against one another for position as they reach out from the building's two street facades. 33 Tehama, 2017 (p. 360), assumes a showcase position in the South of Market (SoMa) neighborhood, near the Financial District. The 35-story residential tower faces out from a narrow lot on Tehama Street toward the southwest like a giant billboard, greeting motorists streaming off the Bay Bridge with a sculpted ribbon-like facade that alternates transparent and tinted panels of glass in the architectural version of a Möbius strip, creating a sense of suspension and visual continuity while dematerializing the mass of the 280,000-square-foot structure.

Meanwhile, back in New York, Arquitectonica was finally ready for prime time and won the chance to design the Westin Times Square, 2002 (p. 114), a 680-room convention hotel in the very belly of the beast, on Times Square, at the corner of Eighth Avenue and 42nd Street, a location that would be seen and judged by everyone. For such an honor they beat out the likes of Zaha Hadid and Michael Graves, so it was a propitious opportunity. Early sketches show a cavalcade of outrageous pop imagery and cartoonish silhouettes, gargantuan figures, robots, Godzilla-like monsters, as well as more abstract configurations that feature crenellated, serpentine and Z-shaped profiles. The drawings are fast and nervous, one idea overlapping the next. The final plan was a brightly colored, three-part composition with street a level, 14-story podium and a soaring 45-story tower that was split in half by a curving incision. "We could have held back and made it more tasteful, but we decided to go all the way," said Fort-Brescia. It was a building that shook up New York's architectural establishment and caused something of a sensation — receiving both negative and positive responses, and opening the door for a more diverse, open-ended conversation. One critic compared the finished project to an Almodóvar movie: a "building on the edge of a nervous breakdown."[29]

The following year, Arquitectonica completed a master plan for Hudson Yards, a 59-block area in the old Hell's Kitchen neighborhood, one of the last undeveloped sites on Manhattan's west side. "We felt it needed a whole new geography," said Fort-Brescia. "It had to have a reason to exist."

An expanding swath of green would link 42nd Street down to 34th Street with clusters of shade trees, gardens, raised walkways, water features, as well as new roadways and overpasses to ease congestion, finally wrapping around the Jacob K. Javits Convention Center and terminating at the Penn Station rail yards.

The Bronx Museum of the Arts, 2006 (p. 168), made for a calmly restrained presence on the Grand Concourse that runs through the heart of the South Bronx. The pleated metal facade engaged with the street and allowed passersby to peer into the all-white gallery spaces. In comparison to Arquitectonica's other New York projects, it was modest, low-scale and relatively low budget. "It's going to put the 'grand' back in Grand Concourse," pronounced Mayor Bloomberg at the ribbon-cutting ceremony held on October 3, 2006, while the *New York Times* praised the museum as being a "reminder of how architecture can have a profound public impact when its values are in the right place."[30]

"THE FLOATING LIFE IS BUT AS A DREAM..." LI BAI (TANG DYNASTY POET, 701-762)

While most of Arquitectonica's designs derive from the twentieth-century legacy of European and American modernism, projects for the Pacific Rim are subtly reconfigured for the "Economic Tigers" of the twenty-first-century with familiar metaphors and symbolic undertones. Fort-Brescia compared the shifting forms of a building he designed in Hong Kong to stalks of bamboo swaying in the wind, while the hyper-elongated form of a high-tech campus made for a "dragon-like chain of prismatic volumes." Monolithic slabs for a bank in Shanghai formed a "moon gate," while a tower in Jakarta was inspired by the traditional two-handed *sembah* greeting of Indonesia, and a residential complex in Singapore made allusions to Chinese landscape painting with subtle brush-stroke gradations of color.

Arquitectonica's first Asian project was Festival Walk, 1998 (p. 106), a major retail complex in Hong Kong that celebrates a sense of perpetual movement throughout a 1.5-million-square-foot space flooded with natural light. The otherwise static art of architecture was stretched even further at the Cyperport Technology Campus, also in Hong Kong, 1999 (p. 154), a long, serpentine extrusion that wriggles across the 59-acre site of reclaimed land on Telegraph Bay. Like a thing in gestation, breaking away from conventional typologies, it provided a highly flexible environment, not only housing multinational giants like Microsoft and IBM, but offering nurturing spaces for start-ups and small tech incubators.

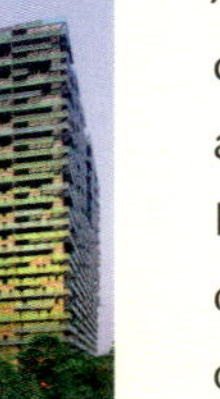

At Mangrove West Coast (2006), in Shenzen, China, three V-shaped towers rotate around the perimeter of a man-made lagoon in a windmill configuration. Each block has an arch-like opening that takes advantage of prevailing breezes and provides views out over mangrove wetlands, and across Shenzen Bay to the faraway hills of Hong Kong. Foreground replaces background as the towers and an all-glass clubhouse straddle the edge of the water. Glass parapets and balconies are positioned in semi-random order to create a shimmering effect on the glass facades in shades of sky blue, turquoise and verdigris.

The architecture and landscape of the Asian projects were sympathetically linked, suggestive of a floating world in which water, earth, buildings and sky merge into a single, integrated composition.

CONTINUITY

By the mid-2000s, Miami was growing from a seasonal resort to a major cultural destination with new museums, concert halls and theaters, as well as a series of annual art fairs. The change was fueled, in part, by an infusion of investments from South America and other parts of the world. Arquitectonica played a decisive role in this transformation, helping to shape a new urban identity by encouraging density and verticality over horizontal diffusion. "This movement towards densification responded to a determination not to continue the expansion of urban sprawl farther into the Everglades," said Fort-Brescia.

By this point, the firm had spread its reputation to more than thirty countries and had close to 500 employees spread among ten offices in different parts o the world. They were no longer the young outsiders, but had matured to become the city's most prominent firm. In 2010, they would move into a new, much larger headquarters on the corner of Oak Avenue and Rice Street in Coconut Grove. It was

directly across from the site of the original studio they had occupied thirty-two years earlier, when they were just starting out. In a sense they'd come full circle, and even though they never really left, this move represented a return to the firm's roots.

Roughly laid brick pavers led through a breezeway, past a ten-foot-high metal gateway, into the central courtyard, a tranquil sanctuary planted with shade trees, native grasses and casual seating where employees can gather during breaks. The gates are perforated with large, cut-out words in ancient Latin that read: *Utilitas, Firmitas, Venustas*, after Vitruvius's principal virtues of architecture: "function, structure, and beauty." The courtyard and other landscape features were designed by ArquitectonicaGEO, led by Laurinda Spear and Margarita Blanco, who planted a mini eco-system within the six-foot setback that wrapped around the periphery of the building, with edible fruits and vegetables that were free to be picked by passersby. All irrigation, for both courtyard and street-side plantings, came from rainwater that was captured on the roof, filtered and channeled into holding tanks at the back of the property. ArquitectonicaGEO, launched by Laurinda Spear in 2005, brought to the firm a heightened awareness of natural environments and native species.

The building itself was a basic 18,000-square-foot box with concrete block walls that wrapped around an open-air courtyard. The steel mullions of the 10-foot-by-10-foot windows were painted in shades of bronze and brown and set in an alternating pattern that was based on traditional Seminole textiles. Interior spaces were equally spartan, with polished concrete floors, high ceilings, industrial steel staircases, exposed ductwork and open, loft-like workstations. "We left it as raw as possible," said Fort-Brescia, "no sheetrock or carpeting, all concrete and exposed ductwork."

As revealed in the new headquarters, the firm had already begun to redefine its priorities with a deeper commitment to community, urban planning, civic space, climate change, sustainable design, and the natural environment. During the first 15 years of the new century, the firm went on to complete a series of significant civic and cultural projects that would effectively reshape Miami into a vibrant, twenty-first-century metropolis — including a federal courthouse, the Aventura Government Center, the American Airlines Arena, the Miami Children's Museum, the School of International Studies at FIU, a student center for the University of Miami, and the South Miami Dade Cultural Center, the design of which Fort-Brescia described as two hands clapping in an "homage to the act and art of performance."

For the Wilkie D. Ferguson Federal Courthouse in downtown Miami (p. 140), 2006, Arquitectonica set out to redefine the standard courthouse template, creating a commanding, vertical presence, but one that felt modern and transparent, and conveyed a "message of democracy and being open to everybody," while meeting the most stringent security requirements. From an urban-planning point of view, the building serves as a gateway, giving a ceremonial sense of procession to a nondescript part of downtown Miami, reintroducing the scale and order of the original city grid.

ArquitectonicaGEO's design for the PortMiami Tunnel, 2014, (p. 330) for Bouygues Civil Works, tells a story about its functional purposes as well as the site's significance. Unfolding from the center lanes of the MacArthur Causeway, two concrete ribbons join to mark the entrance to the tunnel. Protecting the

tunnel floodgates from the corrosive effects of maritime Miami weather, the enclosure also acts as a monument to the port and to the tunnel's construction.

The folding exposed-concrete structure is embossed with text relating to the ideas of travel and navigation. Gaps in the concrete planes are covered with a transparent metal mesh which glows from within, acting as a shining lantern visible on both sides of the underpass. Inside the mile-long tunnel, an undulating graphic pattern softens wall surfaces and smooths the transition from sunny exterior to the passage deep under earth and water. To provide a complementary setting for the contemporary architecture, the landscape is planted to restore the unique character of coastal Florida — open plains of native grasses contrast with dense clusters or "hammocks" of native coastal trees and shrubs.

EFFERVESCENCE

While the beachfront condo represents a fairly exhausted typology — restricted as it is by the developer's bottom line, setbacks and strict zoning — Arquitectonica has managed to breathe new life into the genre by picking up where Morris Lapidus left off, updating it for the twenty-first-century with a series of exuberant beachfront projects that acknowledge Miami Beach traditions while playing off the loaded line between sea, land and sky. Arquitectonica understood sun. They understood shadow. They understood the principles of cross-ventilation and what could be done with a relatively minimal set of design options. The angle of orientation and shaping of the balcony were just two of the architect's most effective tools. "You have to express the balcony," said Fort-Brescia. "It's a part of life."

Arquitectonica used wave-like railings at the Rimini in Surfside (1996) to create a dynamic surface treatment and set something of a precedent for later beachfront experiments. A woven, crisscrossing facade at Icon Bay (pg. 320), 2011, serves as a reflective foil for the watery, bay-front light of Edgewater. Undulating balconies and softly contoured overhangs give the 43-story Regalia, 2006, (p. 274) a cloud-like presence while echoing the rippling, sandy surfaces of the beach itself. Sloping, terraced corners at Fendi Chateau, Surfside, 2012 (p. 342), catch the evening light in the dancing, overlapping balconies and glass railings, bringing the entire building to life. The broad glass slab of Oceana is relieved by a large breezy opening that serves as a kind of theatrical passageway between street and beach.

As part of the presentation for Paraiso Bay, 2013, (p. 362) Arquitectonica showed the image of a girl swimming underwater with bubbles drifting up from her mouth. These bubbles became a metaphoric device around which the entire complex was developed, a kind of underwater tableau. Two towers face Biscayne Bay like oversized soda bottles with effervescent facades. Bubble-shaped balconies appear to percolate up toward the sky, lightening the bulk of the otherwise static buildings, making them appear to float and pop up from their waterfront site in Edgewater.

"WE ARE NOT SEEKING A SHAPE. WE ARE SEEKING AN EXPERIENCE THAT IS AN EXTENSION OF THE CITY." **BERNARDO FORT-BRESCIA**

CITIES WITHIN CITIES

While closely connected to Miami's booming downtown, the Brickell neighborhood is surprisingly self-contained, bounded as it is to the north by the Miami River, to the west by Interstate I-95, and to the east by Biscayne Bay. The 70-block neighborhood is, in many ways, a city within a city, and has, for the past decade, established its own identity with new residential and commercial buildings that offer a tighter, more vertical kind of urban experience. Between 2008 and 2018, Arquitectonica developed a series of large-scale projects that, in many ways, redefined the character of the area. It was also a return to the scene of the firm's early successes, a short distance from the Palace, Atlantis and Imperial, all built in the 1980s, and all still functioning.

500 Brickell (p. 220), 2003, was the first large-scale residential project to be built there in fifty years. Twin towers and a sky court rest on top of a ten-level parking structure. Instead of trying to hide it, the architects turned the functional podium into a giant work of art, an optical abstraction of multi-colored perforations. A similar strategy was used at the 4.6-million-square-foot Icon Brickell (pg. 244), this time with three towers placed around a sun plaza, and all of it raised on top of a 12-story parking podium. A white metallic grid encases the towers, providing shading from the sun as well as a grille-like surface effect that helps to break down the sense of mass. "The idea transforms three large towers into eleven smaller prisms, creating a village of cubes," explained Fort-Brescia.

By respecting the existing grid and opening itself to the street on every side, the five-million-square-foot Brickell City Centre (BCC) (p. 286) weaves itself into the very grain of the city without massive disruptions. The open-air complex spans more than nine acres and includes three levels of retail shopping, two office towers, residential blocks, as well as a 352-suite hotel, clustered together on a site that borders the Miami River on one side and 8th Street on the other. All of it has been tied together by the undulating blades of the patented Climate Ribbon that snakes between the buildings, providing shade, cool breezes — a "corridor of the wind" — and spatial continuity while also collecting rainwater for irrigation purposes.

The idea was to create an urban nexus in a place that lacked any sort of center and in that it succeeds. Brickell City Centre reconfigures the idea of the town square for the twenty-first-century. It is a place to gather and wander in real, non-digital space. There are moments of unexpected intersection, sudden drop-offs and vistas that reach into the surrounding streetscape. There is also a certain meandering randomness in the pathways of movement that are neither linear, nor fully prescribed.

Further south, around SW 13th Street, the regulated grid of downtown Miami breaks apart in response to the bend of the shoreline and the westward broadening of Biscayne Bay. The disruption of the orthogonal street grid creates a series of irregular, wedge-shaped building lots that Arquitectonica was able to exploit as a kind of starting point for a 51-story tower that they designed for SLS Brickell on South Miami Avenue.

Envisioned as a "luxury urban oasis," the building contains 450 condominium units and a 133-room hotel that occupies the first ten floors. Exterior walls were angled in response to the diagonal intersections of the surrounding streets, and these same divergent lines extend around the slab-shaped tower like glacial striations. "The building is a prismatic glass wedge that resolves the geometry of the city's grids," explained Fort-Brescia. Triangular viewing points project from the cantilevered balconies like the teeth of a band saw and are staggered in such a way as to set up a secondary surface contour of diagonal markings. Lines appear to converge and change angle as one moves past on the street level, while from afar, the multi-faceted treatment makes the building seem like a living, reptilian entity. "The triangular balconies cascade diagonally off the facades like wind-driven rain," said Fort Brescia. "When you stand at their tip, you float out over the street and feel suspended in space."

LINES OF DESIRE

Much like a city unto itself, a college campus is a crisscrossing network of pathways and intersections, an allegorical landscape where each building represents another subject — philosophy, mathematics, art history, economics — and students walk between these abstractions, weaving their own threads of inspiration and discovery. The so-called desire lines become a natural template and structural foundation that Arquitectonica would apply to all of their campus commissions, something like miniaturized versions of their larger urban planning schemes. "You can read the desire lines, the shortest routes that students walk between different points on campus," said Fort-Brescia. "We always try to think about that sort of connectivity throughout the planning process."

Early studies for the East Los Angeles College of Performing Arts, 2011, (p. 202) show two smooth stones, vaguely triangular in form, laid over a site plan of the existing campus. "We wanted to make artistic boulders in the landscape," said Fort-Brescia. "The buildings are like outcroppings from a hillside." The organic forms of the stones evolved into three separate structures sculpted into wedge-like shapes with angular openings and rooflines. Together, the buildings created a protected compound, a cohesive sense of place for walking, quiet reflection, and student gatherings, a recognizable "campus," while softening the impact of the automobile-centric neighborhood that surrounds the college, just north of the Pomona Freeway and east of downtown Los Angeles.

Within two miles of their Coconut Grove headquarters lies the University of Miami where Arquitectonica was commissioned to design several major projects in the past ten years, including a student center (p. 208), a new studio building for the School of Architecture (p. 358), and a student housing complex (p. 364). Less than a hundred years old, the campus has grown with a fairly random assortment of buildings that appear to have no connective tissue.

Due to a lack of on-site housing, only 4,000 of the university's 10,500 undergraduates currently live on campus. Many commute to class by car and the grounds are broken up with parking lots and looping access roads. The university is making a concerted effort to entice more students to live on campus, to foster a stronger sense of community.

Arquitectonica saw their mission as establishing a logical sequence of environments that further enhanced the educational context while creating a more walking-friendly condition, a "pedestrianized car-free zone" with outdoor rooms, greens, and extended walkways. All car-related infrastructure would be pushed away from the center, towards an outer, peripheral ring, and parking lots would be replaced by pedestrian plazas.

The new Design Studio Building is essentially a big open space with floor-to-ceiling glass along the north and south elevations, 18-foot-high ceilings, exposed ductwork, and narrow steel columns that support the center of the roof. It's a raw, functional workspace for architecture students that can be easily reconfigured at a future date. A curving wall of cast concrete disrupts the perimeter and signals the main entry at the western end of the building while, overhead, the roof melts down over the southwest corner and acts like a visor to block the rays of the afternoon sun.

The building defines a new east-to-west axis at one end of the campus in an area that previously felt disconnected and frayed around the edges with parking lots and service entries. The studio also creates a non-vehicular plaza at the intersection of several walkways, and helps to unify the eclectic mix of buildings that make up the School of Architecture.

Still a work in progress, the Student Housing complex was positioned at the very center of campus life, broken down into a village-like scale of separate but connected clusters. Inspired, in part, by the water-bound houses of Stiltsville in Biscayne Bay, the clusters are raised on pylons and circle around in a looping formation to create enclosed courtyards. Beneath the hovering dormitories lie shaded arcades penetrated from every direction by pedestrian walkways. "It's as if the buildings were trees themselves, providing shaded spaces below and a green canopy above," wrote the architects.

As part of the master plan, ArquitectonicaGEO reorganized the surrounding landscape with lush, tropical plantings and new walkways to give order and an organic sense of procession to what had been a fairly haphazard matrix of footpaths and streets. The 525,713-square-foot complex not only provides room for 1,100 beds, it also creates a new hub for the University of Miami, fostering a closer, more interconnected campus community.

FRONTIERS

As Bernardo Fort-Brescia and Laurinda Spear continue to expand their practice, they are laying the groundwork for a new generation of goals and aspirations, in which their children — Raymond and Marisa — play an increasingly integral role in the future direction of the company. If there's a shift of interest, a new direction, it's a growing commitment to community development, resiliency, and sustainable design practices in response to climate change and global population patterns.

"A lot of our work has been on the waterfront and our firm has spent years worrying about and planning for hurricanes and sea-level rise," said Fort-Brescia. "It's in our DNA." Similarly, working in the subtropical city taught the partners the importance of using natural light, sea breezes, open-air courtyards and cross ventilation, to reduce energy consumption and enhance lifestyle.

The roofs of the International Finance Center, Seoul, South Korea, 2013, (p. 238) were equipped with photovoltaic solar panels, and a recently completed project in Rio de Janeiro, BG Group Global Technology Centre, 2017, (p. 336) is largely fueled by solar power, while the Infinity, an environmentally responsive urban project in Luxembourg, features a multi-level series of green roofs and pedestrian byways.

ArquitectonicaGEO has been at the forefront of sustainable design from its inception in 2005. Its design for the green roof on the School of International and Public Affairs, FIU, 2006, (p. 258) was the first of its kind in Florida with over 9,000 square feet. It is planted with a native palette that can restore habitat for local wildlife. The green roof for a five-million-square-foot "urban oasis" in Guangzhou, China, takes the form of a public park that absorbs radiant heat and insulates the shopping center that lies below.

Four corner plazas planted with mature *Terminalia* trees invite visitors into the retail mall and provide shade during the summer months. This multi-level landscape was seamlessly integrated both vertically and horizontally with the use of a cohesive plant and hardscape palette that blurs the line between indoor and outdoors.

Arquitectonica continues to explore new territories, as they are doing with the "Spirit of Saigon" (p. 355), a major mixed-use project built on Ben Thanh Square, in the heart of Ho Chi Minh City, Vietnam. "It's a new geographic frontier," said Fort-Brescia. "It's a cultural frontier."

Hobhouse Court (p. 359), Arquiteconica's first building in London, explores a different kind of scale, material and urbanism in a dense area of Westminster, near Trafalgar Square. Facades of the five-story structure are broken up and tilted back to create a slightly skewed, multifaceted effect. Pre-existing walls have been incorporated into the final design, and surfaces are textured with old and new masonry, making subtle allusions to the historic neighborhood.

Bernardo Fort-Brescia and his life-long partner and wife, Laurinda Spear, are nothing if not prolific — with more than 1,200 built projects around the world. They are also dedicated "urbanizers," as they call themselves, and continue to explore both the poetics and practical possibilities of architectural culture.

1 Joan Didion, *Miami.* New York: Simon & Schuster, 1987, p. 33

2 Laurinda Spear, as quoted in Wolf Von Eckardt, "Design: Jazzing up the Functional", *Time,* July 23, 1984

3 Fulvio Irace, *Domus,* January 1981.

4 Koeper, Frederick. Arquitectonica, Yesterday, Today, and Tomorrow: An exhibition of drawings, models, plans and photographs, 1977-1984. Center for the Fine Arts, Miami, Florida, 1984.

5 Norman Mailer, *Miami and the Siege of Chicago.* New York: World Publishing Co., 1968, p.13

6 Larry Birger, "Coral Gables 'Kids' Make their Mark at Arquitectonica," *Miami Herald,* July 20, 1981

7 "Romantic Modernism: Arquitectonica," *Process Architecture* (Japan), #65, February 1986

8 BFB, interview with author: September 3, 2016, Coconut Grove, Florida.

9 "Architectural Firm Alters Miami's Skyline," L. Erik Calonius, *The Wall Street Journal,* July 7, 1983

10 Joan Didion, *Miami,* New York: Simon and Schuster, 1987, p. 31

11 Prismacolor pencils were first manufactured in 1938 by Berol, a British stationary company, and were later produced by Newell Brands.

12 Joan Didion, *Miami.* New York: Simon & Schuster, 1987, p. 31

13 BFB as quoted in Patricia Leigh Brown, "Having a Wonderful Time in Miami," *New York Times,* October 25, 1990

14 *Progressive Architecture,* February 1983, p.99

15 "Arquitectonica: Casa Los Angeles (Mulder House) Lima," *Domus,* no. 692, March 1988.

16 "Romantic Modernism: Arquitectonica," *Process Architecture* (Japan), #65, February 1986; Patricia Leigh Brown, "Having a Wonderful Time in Miami," *New York Times,* October 25, 1990; Charles K. Gandee, "Those New Kids in Town," *Architectural Record,* June 1985.

17 Patricia Leigh Brown, "Designs on Miami," *Esquire,* December 1984, 194.

18 "Prismacolor habit" and "wet T-shirt architecture": Nory Miller, "Knights of Tropical Splendor," *Metropolis,* April 1984

19 Beth Dunlop, "Out of the Blue: Arquitectonica Turns Design into Child's Play," *Miami Herald,* April 4, 1982.

20 Steve Brown,"Out of this World in Grand Prairie," *The Dallas Morning News,* April 15, 1984

21 Wolf Von Eckardt, "Design: Jazzing up the Functional," *Time,* July 23, 1984, p. 91

22 Interview with Laurinda Spear and Bernardo Fort-Brescia: "Romantic Modernism: Arquitectonica," *Process Architecture,* No. 65, February 1986, p. 5

23 Tom Walker, "If Rio is a Shock, Blame it on Arquitectonica," *Atlanta Journal,* July 27, 1987

24 Karen D. Stein, "Bankers' Trust," *Architectural Record,* February 1989, p. 90

25 As quoted in "Romantic Modernism: Arquitectonica," *Process Architecture* #65 (Tokyo), February, 1986

26 "Arquitectonica: Casa Los Andes (Mulder House), Lima," *Domus,* No. 699, March, 1988

27 From: "Mazars La Defense, Paris, 2006," project description, Arquitectonica Archives.

28 John King, "S.F. Planners back Bold Original Vision for Mid-Market Project," *San Francisco Chronicle,* February 22, 2016

29 Herbert Muschamp, "A Latin Jolt to the Skyline," *New York Times,* October 20, 2002

30 Nicolai Ouroussoff, "Art to the People, and Vice Versa, in the Bronx," *New York Times,* October 6, 2006

PROJECTS

PINK HOUSE

MIAMI 1976 | 1978

As built, the Pink House was a progression from water to water, a color-coded conversation between lap pool and Biscayne Bay, setting up a sequence of rhythms, reflections, and alternating syncopations. The unveiling begins at the 115-foot-wide facade and proceeds through other layers and sequential foils, from reddish rose on the first wall to wild flamingo on the second, to a paler, conch-shell pink on the two-story wall of the main house. There are subtle hints of symmetry and numerology throughout. Six square windows in the main house correspond to the six palm trees in the front courtyard. Three panels of glass blocks, rippled and translucent like water, further dematerialize the mass of the facade while maintaining privacy and reflecting sea-flecked light. The foundation plinth was not a Neoclassical affectation, but arose from necessity; a 1976 flood-control law required the first occupied floor to be at least 11 feet above grade. The entry staircase leads to the piano *nobile* and the first "room": an open-air terrace surrounding a 60-foot-long pool that assumes a central role and emphasizes the project's conceptual bias toward liquidity.

A narrow, streetlike corridor cuts through the center of the house, transversely, north to south. While it is only 4.5 feet wide, it is 18 feet high and more than 100 feet long, opening on the east to a two-story living room, a library, a dining room, a kitchen, and a bayside terrace. While the Pink House may have appeared to some as slightly decadent and garish on first impression, it was, in fact, highly structured and logical in its composition: European rationalism converging with surfer culture and the tropical surrealism of Miami.

Then there is the strange luminous eye gazing out from the center of the pink wall, perfectly round like a porthole or a navel, a cool chlorinated blue. This is where the entry sequence begins, beside the staircase, revealing the subaqueous heart of the house — neither living room nor hearth, but lap pool.

Opposite
Ground and second floor plans

Arquitectonica's first built project, elongated in plan with three tones of pink, the house, a foil for sun and shadow with a 60-foot lap pool at its center.

BABYLON

MIAMI 1978 | 1982

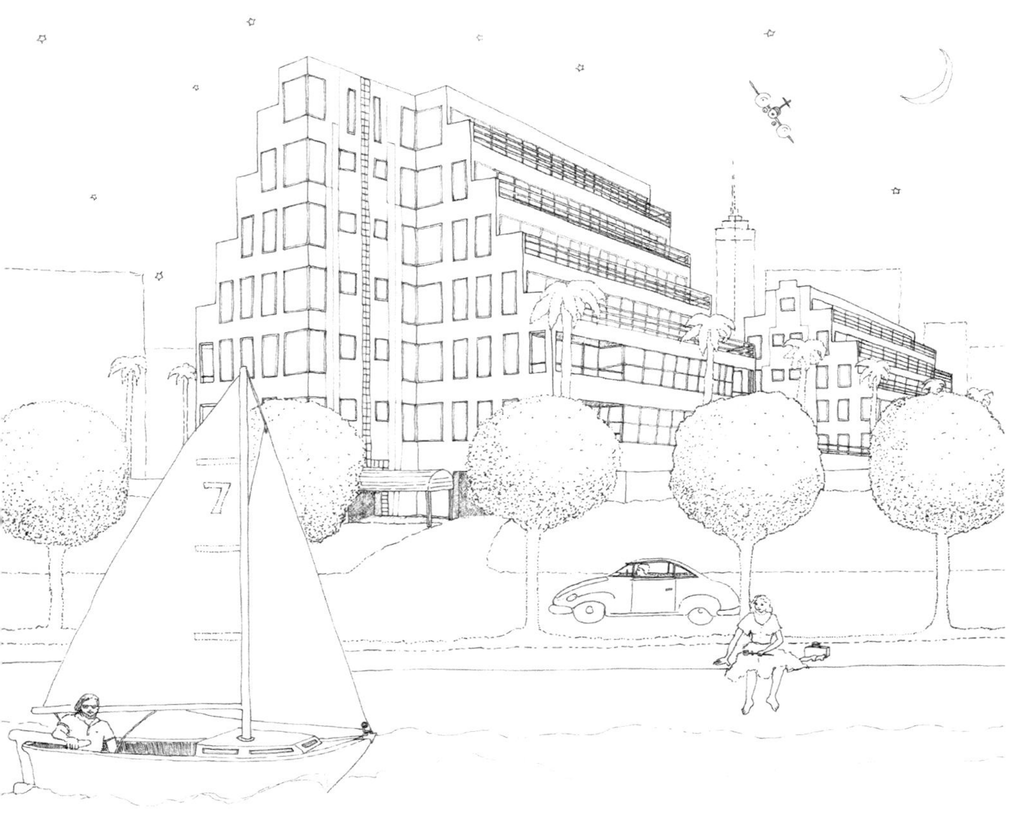

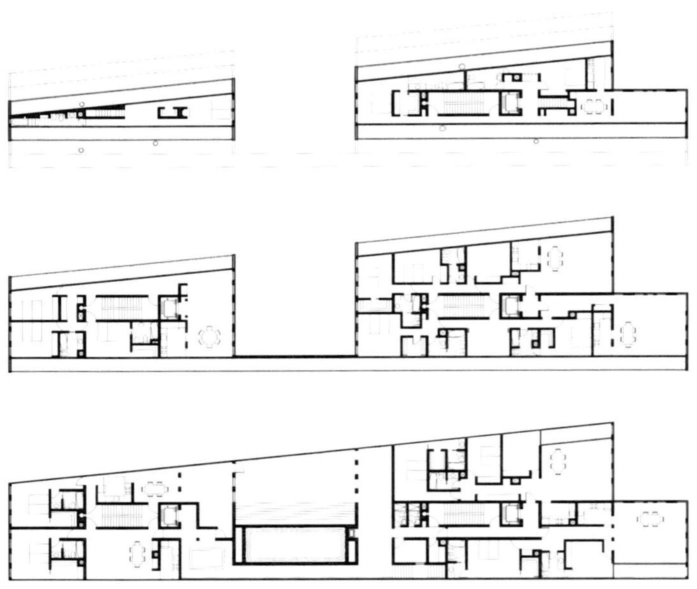

Despite romantic allusions, the Babylon was, in fact, shaped as much by the city's prosaic building code as it was by any poetic allegory. The site was within the high-risk coastal flood zone, so the first level had to be raised 7 feet above grade. The ziggurat-type configuration was the architect's attempt to gain maximum volume within the code's tightly prescribed envelope of setbacks.

The front facade folds back to create a formal entry that is grounded to the site by a concrete foundation wall. Windows are flush, unadorned, and without conventional trim, borders, or mullions, as if punched out from sheet metal, further emphasizing the idea of the exterior being little more than a paper-thin wrapping.

Once you move beyond the street facade, the building opens up and stretches to the southeast — as if the gable had been extruded — with stepped-back terraces, white nautical railings, sliding glass doors, and a rooftop swimming pool. The back facade — another Dutch gable but unfolded and flat — floats freely above the ground on slender pilotis, like a boat in dry dock.

Arquitectonica started planning the Babylon in 1978, about the time they were finishing the Pink House, so it has the freshness and thrill of discovery that often characterizes early work. (It would take almost four years before the building was actually built.) Initial drawings by Laurinda Spear are loosely rendered and romantic, more Chagall than Le Corbusier, a mix of 1930s moderne, Morris Lapidus, and Fritz Lang's *Metropolis*. She presents a dreamy landscape of classical sculptures and antique figures in repose.

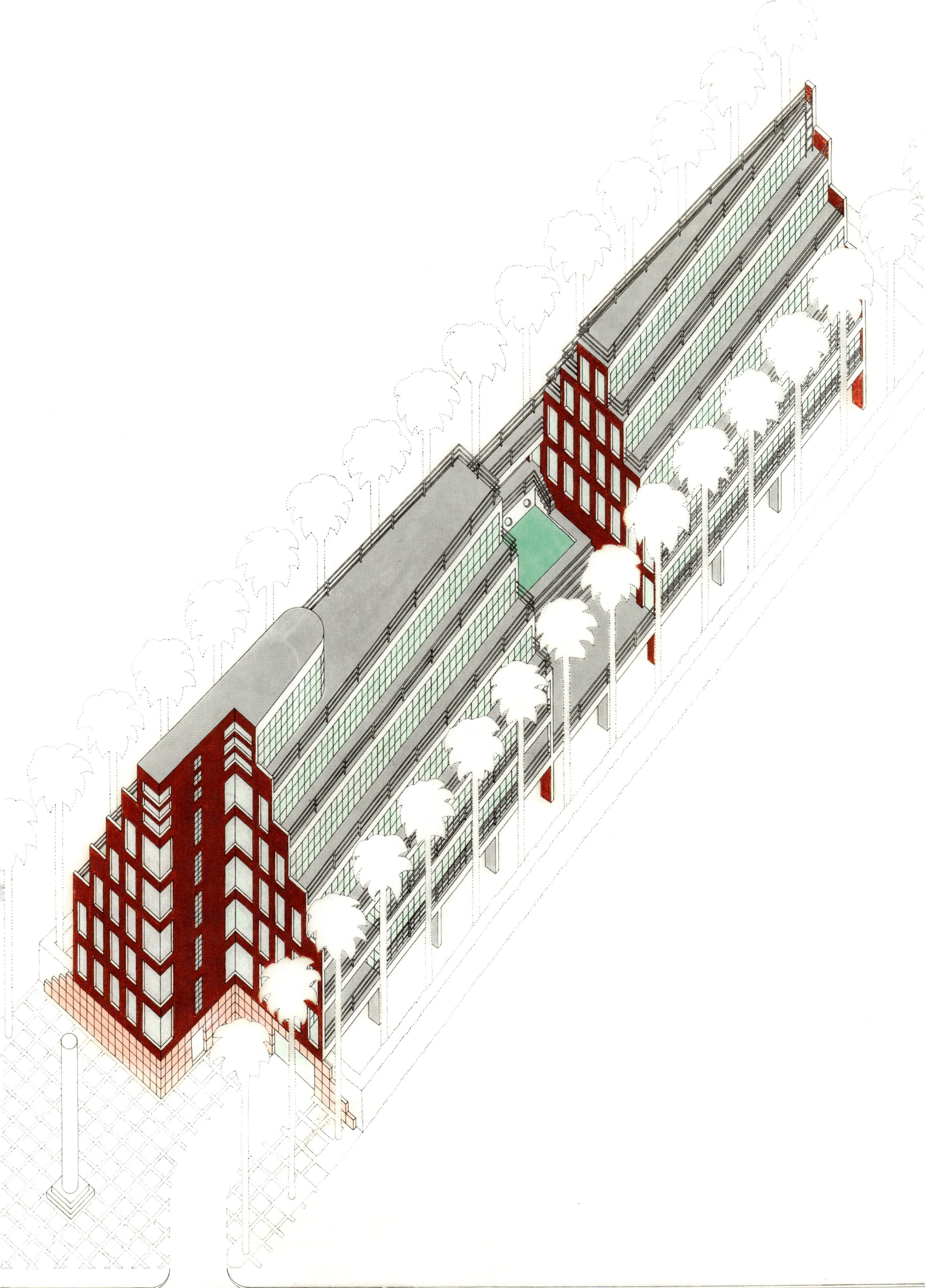

A ziggurat extrudes itself to the back of the property, shaped in part by set back regulations. Once the highest structure in the neighborhood, it is now dwarfed by tall condo towers.

As with the Pink House, the Babylon appears water centric, an ocean liner berthed on dry land, its decks projecting toward Biscayne Bay. In one of Spear's renderings, a woman with long blonde hair stands at the railing and gazes out to the water. We cannot see the woman's face, but her pose conveys a sense of expectation and imminent departure. There are shooting stars and a scimitar moon in the night sky, while the silhouette of an urban skyline looms in the background. It might be a prewar city — Casablanca or Monaco — with lines of stylized palm trees, men fencing on the pool deck, prop planes flying overhead, and a mysterious boat moored out on the bay.

PALACE

MIAMI 1979 | 1982

From out of a pure Euclidean foundation rise two slablike structures. The higher of the two is encased in a cast-concrete grid, white and uniform — like a Sol Lewitt sculpture — and is penetrated by the shorter, stepped section clad in bright red stucco that appears to be crashing through the bigger slab at a right angle while descending toward the bay with extrawide balconies on every level. (The site plan has similarities to Le Corbusier's Unité d'habitation [Marseille, 1952], both featuring barlike forms skewed in relationship to the main entry access). At the top of the main building, a three-story glass cube contains the penthouse apartment, while a teardrop-shaped blob projects from the southeast corner of the building, creating a free-form oriel.

The Palace commission came with one major compromise. The original plan called for a large opening with a sky terrace and pool where the two sections intersected. Client, Harry Helmsley, felt the big opening would be too expensive. So, as built, the stepped red slab only appears to crash in from one side as a separate entity, sticking out the other side to create a monumental portecochere and arrival court, creating only the illusion of separate buildings in full penetration.

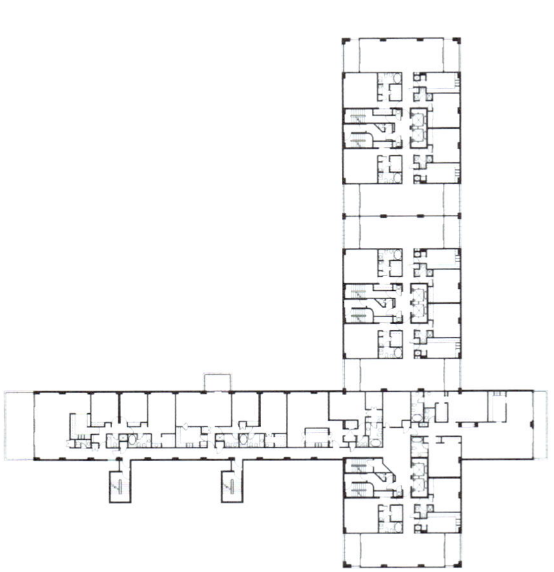

Typical floor plan

A red ziggurat penetrates a white grid as it descends toward the bay.

ATLANTIS

MIAMI 1980 | 1982

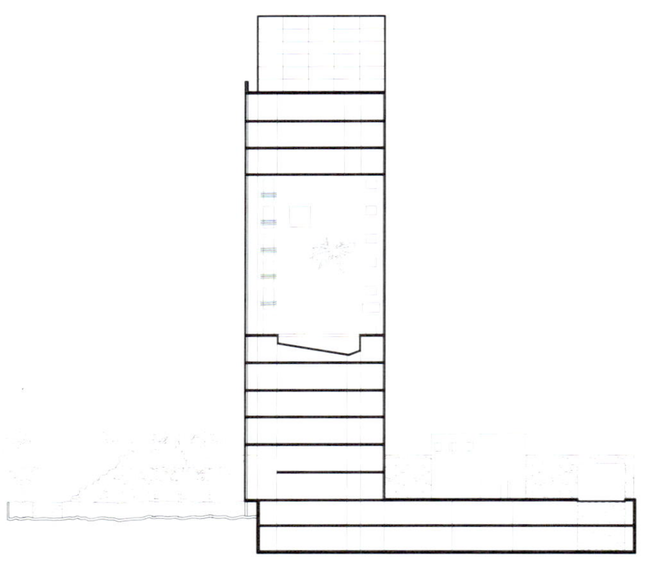

Arquitectonica's partners were still working on the Babylon when Bernardo Fort-Brescia met Chilean developer Hugo Zamorano, who had purchased a waterfront lot at 2025 Brickell Avenue, the site of the old Tiffany estate. Zamorano wanted
to build something spectacular, and while it took several years to develop, the end result became one of Arquitectonica's most celebrated works.

Stretching from the street to the edge of Biscayne Bay, the twenty-story condo tower makes an elegantly slender mark on the Miami skyline. It is 300 feet long but only 37 feet wide, with six apartments on each floor. To further set it apart from neighboring buildings, Arquitectonica added a series of playful embellishments: a red pyramid-like structure on the roof; yellow triangular balconies jutting out from the northern facade; a single peg-leg column that supports the rounded "prow" of the building; and a blue supergrid that hovers like a waffle grill in front of the southern facade, serving as a brise-soleil to block the harsh rays of the tropical sun.

The architects were not allowed to move or demolish the historic Tiffany house that was still standing on the property, so they restored the structure and incorporated it into their overall design. Now the white, Shingle Style cottage appears to be yet another abstract object possessing its own autonomy within the greater master plan. (It is used as an events center.)

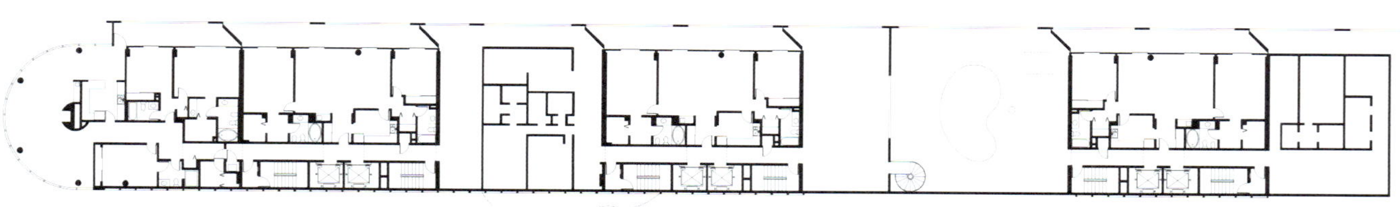

Named after the mythical sunken kingdom, the Atlantis features a sky court with red spiral staircase, Jacuzzi, and a single palm tree. The building, featured in the opening credits for *Miami Vice*, became an "instant cultural icon."

The most memorable move of all is the "sky court" void that cuts through the middle of the building with its sensuously spiraling staircase in lipstick red, a kidney-shaped Jacuzzi, and the undulating yellow wall off of which a small red balcony thrusts itself into open space like a space-age pulpit.

"You look at that building and you see a perfect square opening, a triangular shape above, a perfect semicircle at the end," said Fort-Brescia. "There is a certain concern with the perfection of form." The same playful colors and geometries are borrowed from the exterior and brought inside the main lobby with a grid of white marble tiles on the floor, undulating yellow pilasters, and oversized interior "follies" — enlarged blue frames, gateways, or portals of some sort. Spear designed the deep cubic armchairs covered in yellow and red leather, similar to the LC2 lounge chairs by Le Corbusier and Charlotte Perriand, but without metal framing. There's also a small round table by Memphis with red, yellow, and black feet that brings the primary-color palette down to the smallest scale. A marble fountain snakes through the lobby and butts up against a triangular column. It all reads like a metaphysical landscape: the fountain as a stylized river seeking its source, the blue follies as remnants of a lost civilization, possibly Atlantis itself.

Within a few months of completion, the Atlantis was lauded as an architectural sensation, an icon for the new Miami, and was featured prominently in many publications, including the *New York Times, Esquire, Time,* and *House & Garden,* and reproduced on the cover of *Progressive Architecture* (February 1983).

BANCO DE CREDITO

LIMA 1982 | 1988

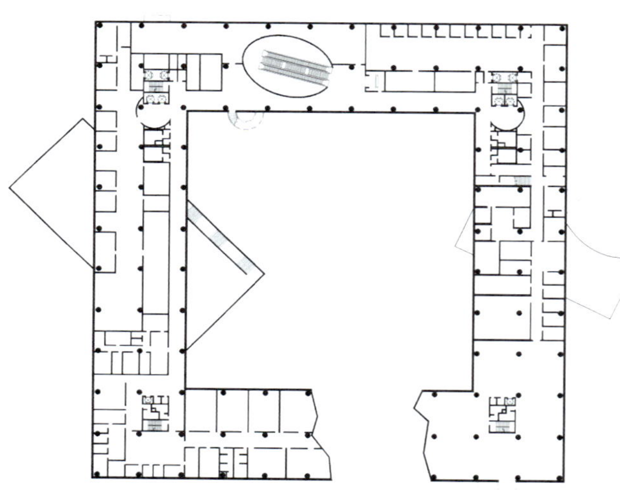

"We wanted to give the bank an image," said Fort-Brescia. Instead of leveling the rugged topography or spanning it, as one of Arquitectonica's early proposals suggested, the architects chose to celebrate the rocky terrain as both the physical and symbolic centerpiece of the plan. The perimeter is broken and open to the southeast so that the talus — an outcropping of the Andean foothills — comes cascading right inside the compound, and the building embraces the land while looking inward. It is a modern variation on the sixteenth-century Spanish courtyard, built at the edge of the Andes, within an active earthquake zone, where city meets sierra and creates its own context.

At the opposite end — the city side — the building is elevated on silver pilotis to mediate the severe drop in grade, while presenting a stolid, corporate facade to the streets of La Molina, one of Lima's more upscale neighborhoods. The architecture of the Banco de Credito speaks of continuity and order, but it also acknowledges an undercurrent of instability, even entropy. As the critic Deyan Sudjic wrote: "With its fractured forms and its counterpoint of solidity and transparency, mass and fragility, Arquitectonica seemed to be deliberately exploring the architecture of the fault line."

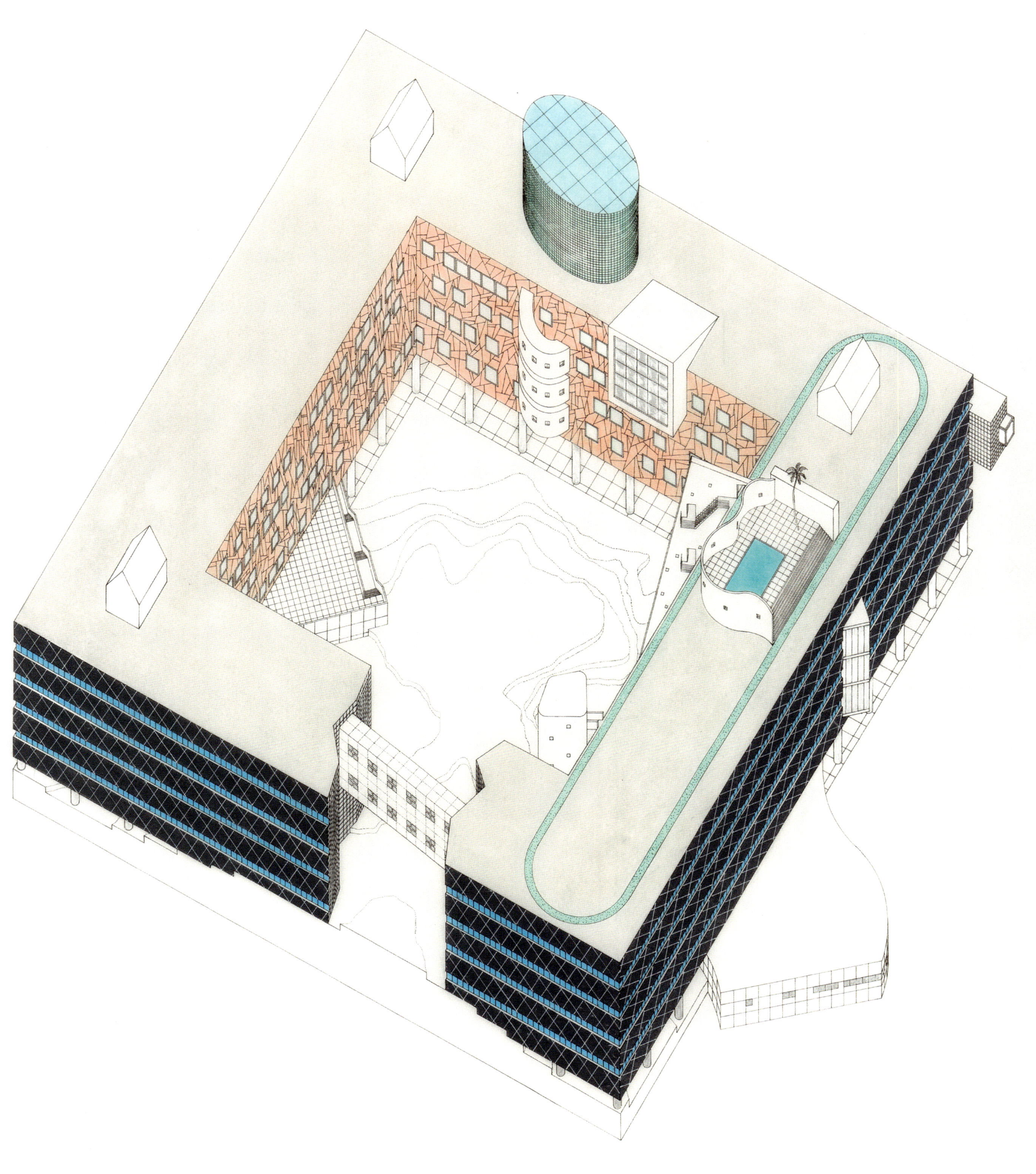

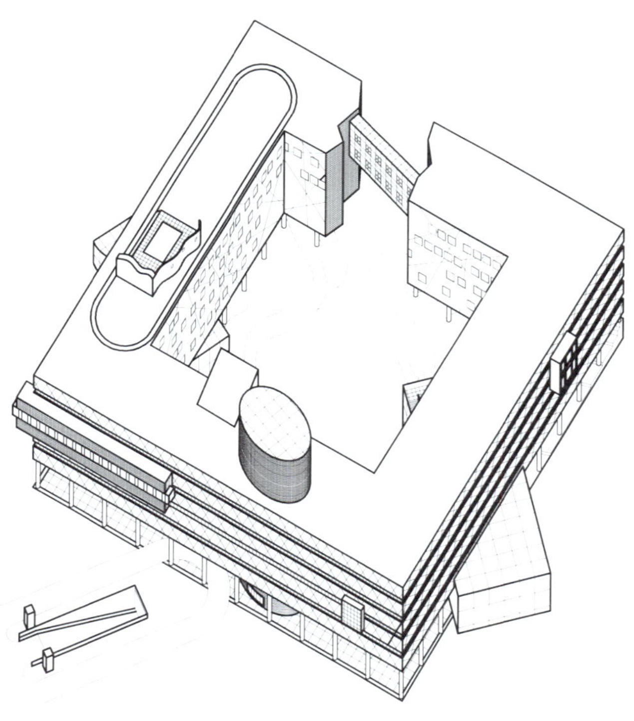

The outer walls of the four-story structure are clad in black Peruvian marble, cut into square tiles set at 30- and 60-degree angles in jazzy contradiction to long, horizontal bands of blue-tinted glass. Eccentrically shaped appendages and window projections break the monotony of the 203-foot-long facades while bringing natural light to interior spaces: a triangular oriel, a three-story wedge of glass, and a white-marble bar of executive suites that juts out from the northeast corner of the building.

In contrast to the dark severity of the exterior walls, the courtyard is clad with a locally quarried pink slate called silla that creates a softer interior surface, something like the lining of a seashell's chambers. A spiraling helix protrudes from one of the courtyard walls, as does a boxlike dormer with a sloping shed roof that houses the spacious boardroom, command central for the entire complex. A large floor-to-ceiling window looks over the rugged inner landscape and beyond to the Andean mountains. "We wanted to remind them of the country they are serving and the original source of its wealth," said Fort-Brescia, who was born and raised in Peru.

The additions and extrusions break the boxy bulk of the building into manageable sections, helping office workers and visitors navigate the 530,000-square-foot complex. Small, folly-type structures domesticate the roofscape along with a swimming pool enclosure, a running track, helicopter pad, and telecommunications equipment.

An elevated square disrupted by divergent forms and set within the rugged landscape of the Andean foothills.

A black marble balcony projects into the 119-foot-high elliptical glass atrium.

The 119-foot-high atrium pokes its head through the roof, announcing itself as the building's main entry and guiding metaphor. Banks of escalators rise through the luminous void and disappear into a darkened opening, as if to the afterworld. (The ledge, in fact, provides space for a security checkpoint.) A cube-shaped balcony of black marble, reminiscent of the red cube at the Atlantis, is the only other feature that breaks the pure geometry of the elliptical shaft, jutting out from the third level, as if to provide scale and a single vantage point from which to view the glass-lined spectacle that lies below.

With its collarlike form, its deference to the natural setting, and its use of native stone and traditional Incan patterns, the Banco de Credito combines international modernism with the archaic roots of a pre-Columbian Peru.

MULDER HOUSE

LIMA 1982 | 1985

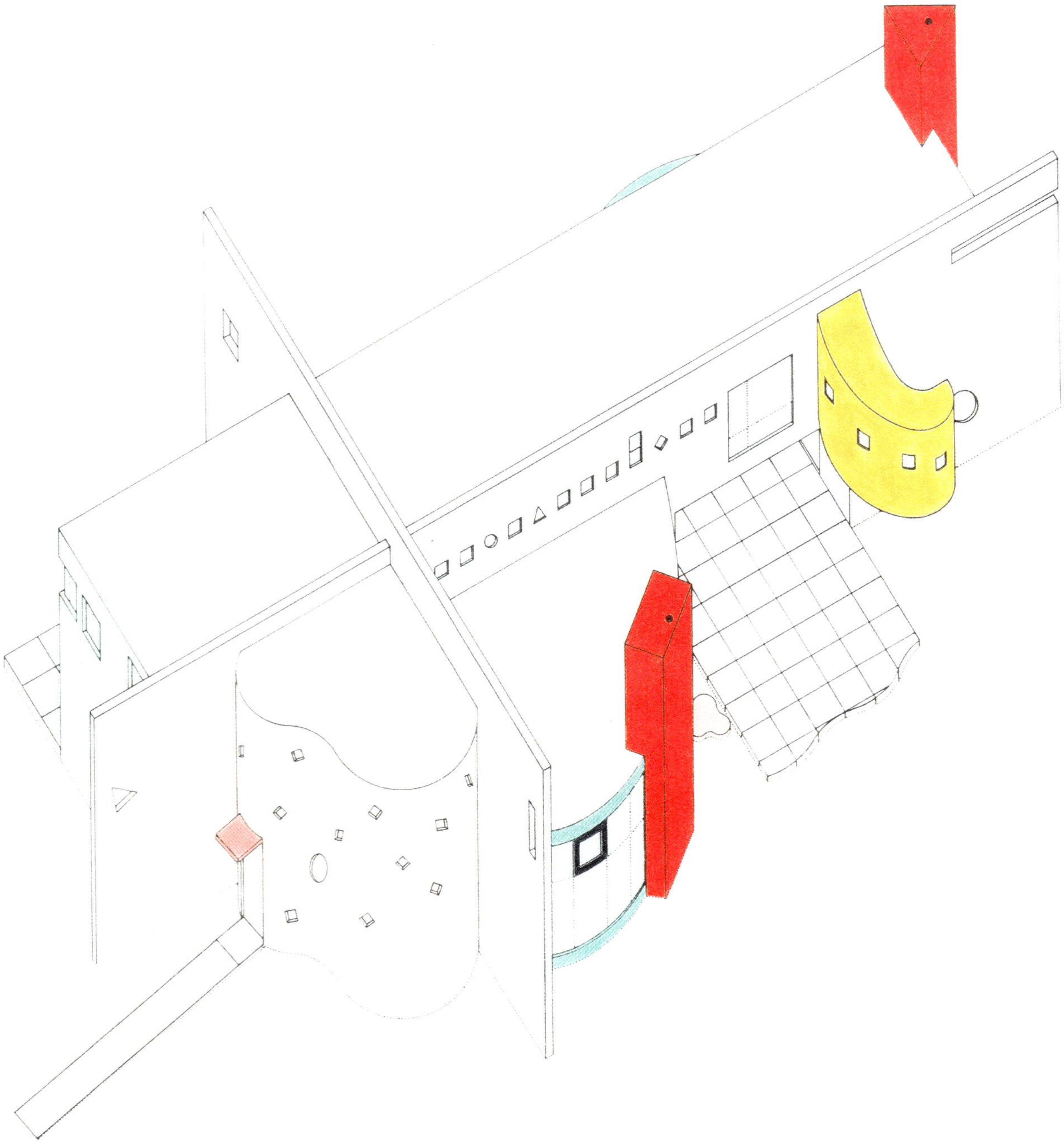

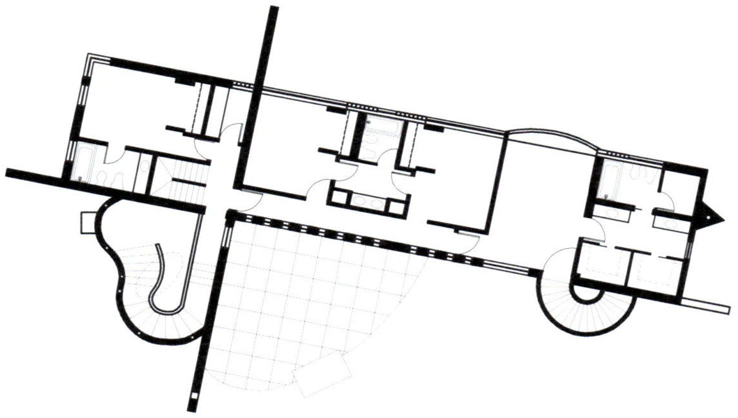

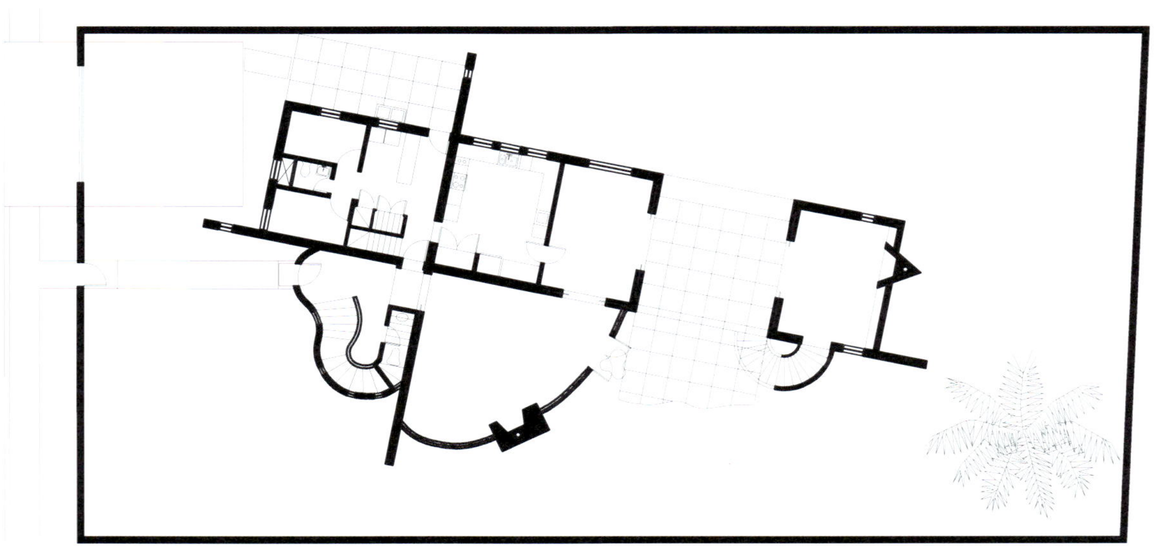

Wildly playful elements project from the bone-white armature of the Mulder House. It resembles a house turned inside out, an internal anatomy revealed in bright colors, breaking through the outer skin: a bulging pink marshmallow with an undulating free-form wall that surrounds the entry foyer; a yellow helix that spirals up from the ground-floor library and encloses a back stairway; and a bright red triangular prism that conceals the chimney. All are powerful volumes accented by primary colors and further articulated by a variety of openings punched through the main body of the house: small square windows and a porthole in the foyer; a large triangular window in the dining room; a narrow glass-block aperture in the library; and a shaded breezeway for outdoor dining. The east facade is penetrated by a series of geometric cutouts — squares, circles, triangles, and rectangles — providing natural light for the second-floor corridor and upstairs bedrooms.

Throughout the design, there is a cut-and-paste aesthetic, both additive and subtractive, like a large-scale constructivist assemblage. The cruciform walls extend past the outer envelope of rooms, further abstracting the composition and destabilizing any notion of domestic hierarchy. The house presents a highly scripted collision of forms, and, as one critic, writing in *Domus*, noted, "it is from this collision that the house derives its disturbing, slightly surrealistic poetic quality," Domus, March 1988.

A diminutive entry leads to the undulating pink foyer.

The fireplace in the living room uses one of the collaged elements as its chimney.

After walking through a relatively diminutive doorway, one enters the foyer to a pure phantasmagoria in pink with deliriously dancing perforations, oval skylights and circular openings, a rippling stairway, and other disorienting effects that set the temperament for interior spaces still to come. After the amoebic expansion of the foyer, which acts as an "aesthetic air lock" between public and private zones, space deflates as one passes into the cavelike living room — a place for family intimacy on cold Peruvian nights, with a freestanding fireplace and a floor of randomly laid planks of caoba, a native type of mahogany from the Amazon jungle.

The living room flows effortlessly outward into the gardens surrounding the Mulder House, with terraces made from dark laga, a local, slatelike stone laid out in biomorphically shaped "carpets," with roses blooming in the southeast quadrant, fruit trees in the northwest courtyard, and a lush perimeter of bougainvillea, palms, avocado, and apple trees. A 12-foot-high perimeter wall blocks out most of the neighboring villas, but one can still see tiled roofs and church steeples all the way beyond to the ruins of Incan pyramids, and farther still to the ocher foothills and higher peaks of the Andean range.

A three-dimensional collage of lively colors and shapes

BEVERLY HILLS HOUSE

BEVERLY HILLS 1989 | 1992

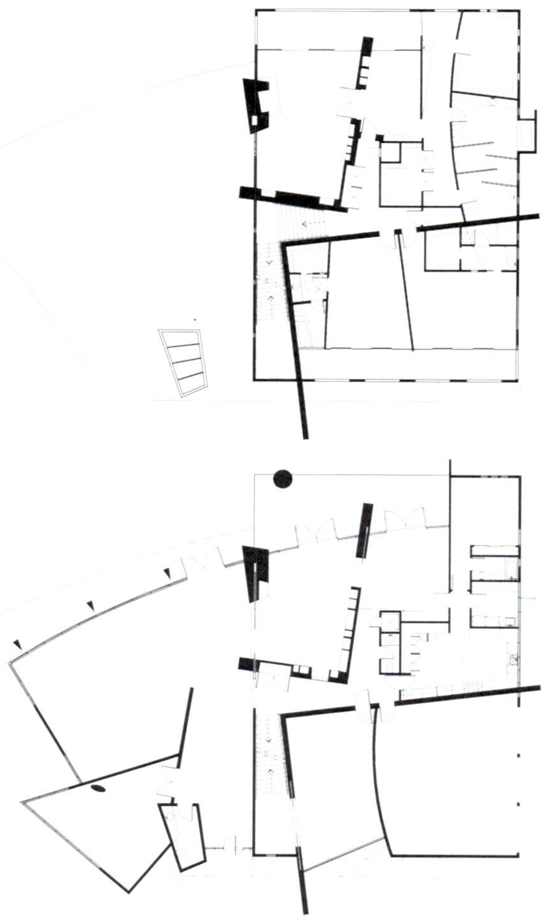

The house is a complex convergence of elements that project from a beveled incline in Beverly Hills, with shifting planes and angular extensions of space. The main house holds five bedrooms, a library, a private study, and a dining/kitchen area within a floor plan of restless interior spaces conjoined by zigzagging skylights and clerestory windows that gradually open up — in the expansive living room — to a curving wall of glass and sweeping views toward the Pacific Ocean, across a grassy ha-ha and a sunken tennis court. (The deeply overhanging roof provides shade and protection for the owner's art.) The mood is Neo-Cubist, frenetically urban but also whimsical and grounded to its site by a number of subsidiary landscape features — flaring terrace, narrow lap pool, and small guesthouse pavilion — that appear to spin off from the main house like so many shards of broken pottery.

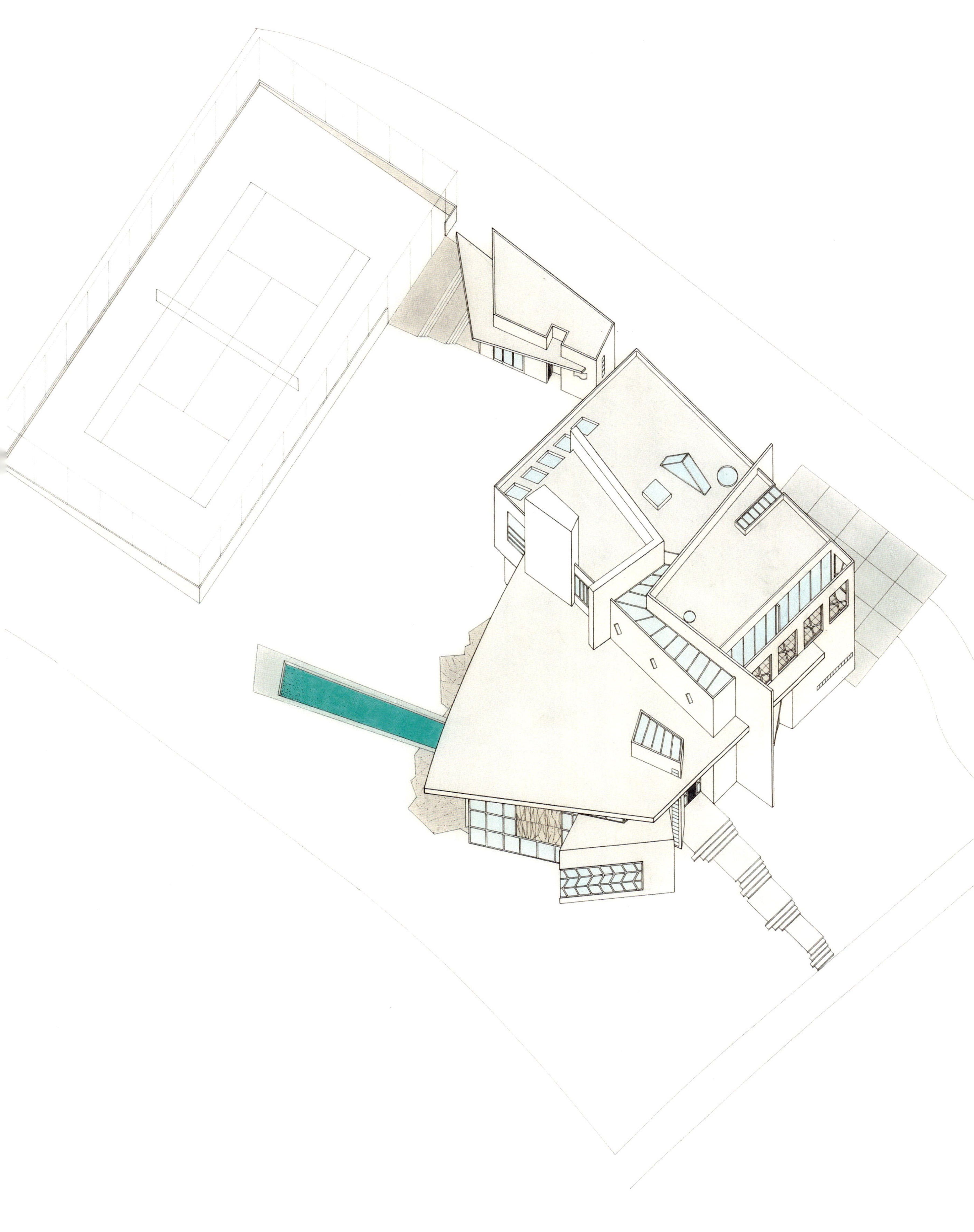

A convergence of shifting planes and angular extensions follow the contours of a beveled-off hill in Beverly Hills.

Next spread
The subtext of decorative elements plays counterpoint to the orthogonal

BANQUE DE LUXEMBOURG

LUXEMBOURG **I** 1989 | 1994 **II** 2009 | 2012

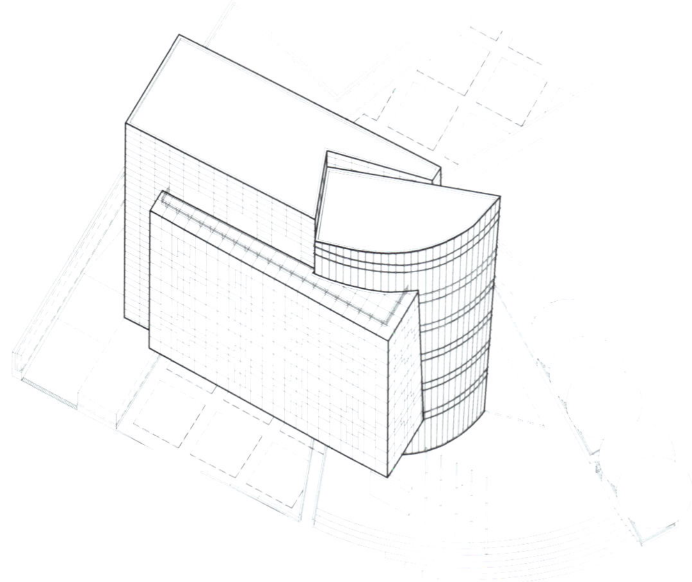

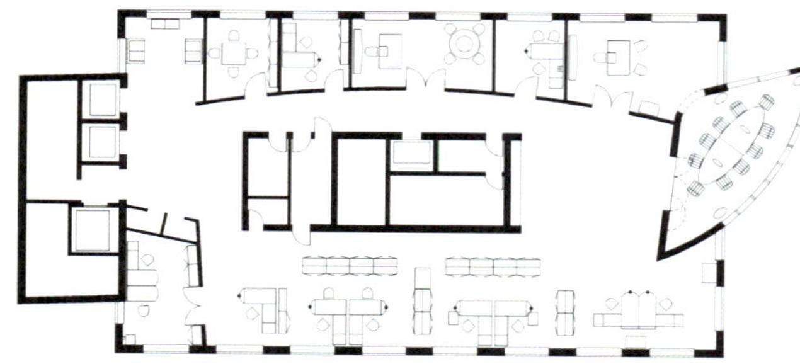

View of facade across Boulevard Royal

The plan grew inevitably from the site, playing off of scale, tone, direction, and rotation. In place of a single monolithic structure, Arquitectonica chose to break down the mass into discretely separate parts that were stepped in height, and set back from the street, as a way to resolve the shifts in scale and to bridge the old and new parts of the neighborhood. Three primary platonic volumes are combined into what Fort-Brescia called a "collage of building typologies."

The five-story block is clad in local Chassagne limestone, punctured by a grid of square windows. Openings of amber-tinted glass are set back in such a way as to make the entire block appear as a hollow shell, while referring to the other buildings along Boulevard Royal, many of which use the same kind of limestone. A seven-story block — a "shadowlike parallelogram" made from black granite with black-tinted windows — houses a cellular arrangement of offices and meeting rooms. A limestone grid projects 10 feet above the street level and appears to hover, while the southeast corner cantilevers out over the main entry court and rests on a massive chunk of rough-hewn granite. It is as if the weight of the entire building were bearing down on this single piece of rock, a detail that signifies financial solidity and longevity.

The third, and most important, of the primary volumes is a six-story glass tower — a partial ellipse in plan — that appears to penetrate the other two volumes, completing the tightly knit assemblage. The curving facade turns the corner from Boulevard Royal to Avenue Amélie and gives the building its most distinctive character, reflecting surrounding buildings while deflecting lines of energy streaming up Boulevard Royal. The director's boardroom is situated here, on the top level, commanding views over the city in several different directions. The conference table, also designed by Arquitectonica, is an ellipse of polished black granite that matches the shape of the room.

Arquitectonica was able to keep the 290,000-square-foot building relatively intimate in scale by submerging many functions in eight underground levels that house private banking facilities, meeting rooms, vaults, a corporate dining room. and an art gallery to showcase the bank's impressive art collection. An elliptical-shaped elevator transports clients to the subgrade banking hall that is illuminated by a large, sloping skylight. Alternately, one can take the dramatically poised spiral staircase — also a partial ellipse — made from stainless steel.

An expansion was completed in 2011, sixteen years after the first building opened. Using a similar vocabulary of Chassagne limestone and curtain-wall glass, the 130,000-square-foot extension continues the bank's facade up Boulevard Royal with seven floors above grade and four below. "The new building responds to the growing needs of the bank, while recognizing the permanence of the corporate identity," said Fort-Brescia.

A semielliptical glass tower intersects with a cubic mass of limestone.

Conspicuous forms of internal circulation: a spiral staircase and open-platform elevator descend to the banking hall.

Bridges connect phase one to phase two

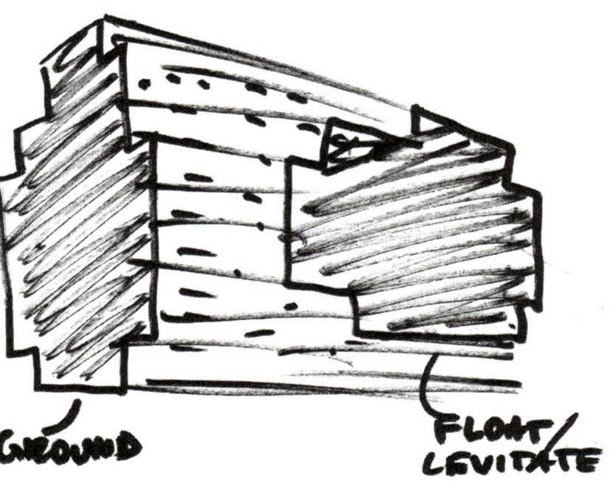
GROUND
FLOAT/
LEVITATE

A recent extension of the bank continues the lines and limestone facade of the original building down Boulevard Royal.

BANQUE
DE LUXEMBOURG

PERFORMING ARTS AND CONVENTION CENTER

DIJON, FRANCE 1991 | 1998

OPÉRA
DE
DIJON

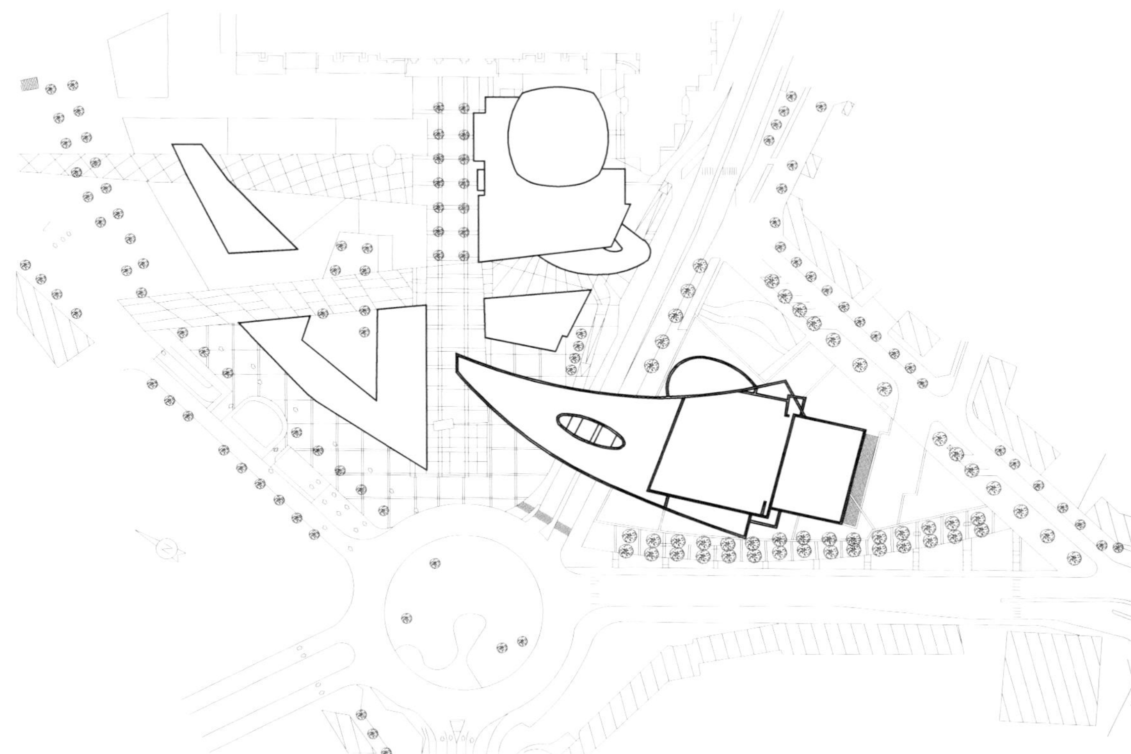

The main body of the performing arts center in Dijon is finshaped, curving away from Boulevard de la Marne and Place Jean Bouhey. Similar to the scissoring effect of the North Dade Justice Center, the upper level shifts off axis and pivots to the east as it narrows to a point. Both the upper and the lower parts of the center are clad in Chassagne, a local, beige-colored limestone, applied horizontally on the upper level and vertically on the lower. Instead of stopping at the border of the triangular lot, the building extends farther to the west as a bridge that crosses the four-lane Boulevard de Champagne — a multilevel intersection where cars, city trams, cyclists, and pedestrians converge for a moment beneath the overarching foyer of the concert hall.

Art patrons, milling around the lobby or entering the main hall, can look down through an elliptical oculus that penetrates both the roof and the floor, and watch the traffic streaming below. This is the centerpiece of the elongated lobby. It is a magic eye, a transparent well with curving panes of tempered glass that reflect the changing colors of the sky above while shedding natural light onto the street below. At night, the oculus projects a column of electric light into the sky, a celebratory beacon that can be seen from miles away. The extended passageway not only serves as a lobby with art gallery and bar, but turns into an elevated skyway that connects the arts center to other parts of the civic center, including a hotel, a restaurant, and a convention center (Parc des Expositions et Congrés de Dijon), as well as access to an underground parking structure.

The eastern end contains the 1,650-seat hall that was designed as a multipurpose performing arts space for symphony, ballet, and opera. Dark and pale wood veneers are set on the walls in angled stripes to create an abstract, dazzle-camouflage effect. Large acoustic baffles hang from the ceiling on either side of the great hall like oversized quotation marks.

An elliptical oculus becomes the all-seeing "eye" for a master plan that reflects the energy of a modern city while acknowledging historic underpinnings.

A raised terrace looks out across Boulevard de la Marne, toward the old city, and is screened off by a wroughtiron grille that the architects based on the layout of the Parc de la Colombière in the south part of Dijon. On sunny afternoons the diagonal lines, sweeping arcs, and intersections of Antoine de Maerle's eighteenth-century plan are cast as shadows across the terrace, further grounding the project in Dijon's historical context, and confirming that the underlying forms of the architecture derive — at least in part — from the ancient ligaments of the city itself.

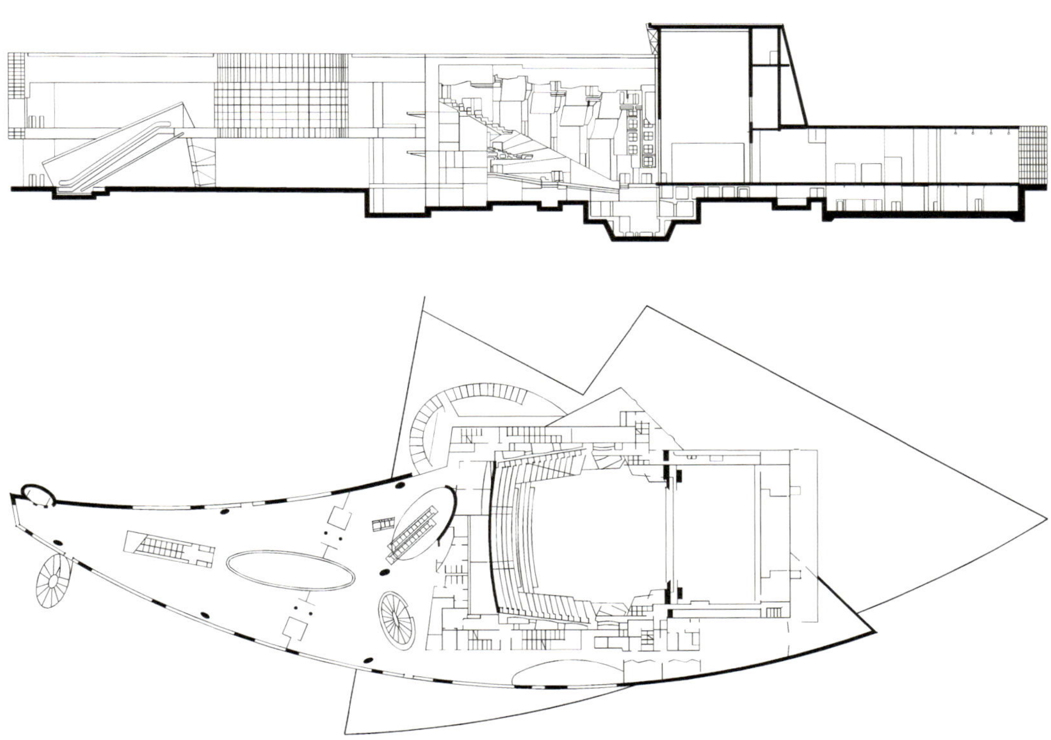

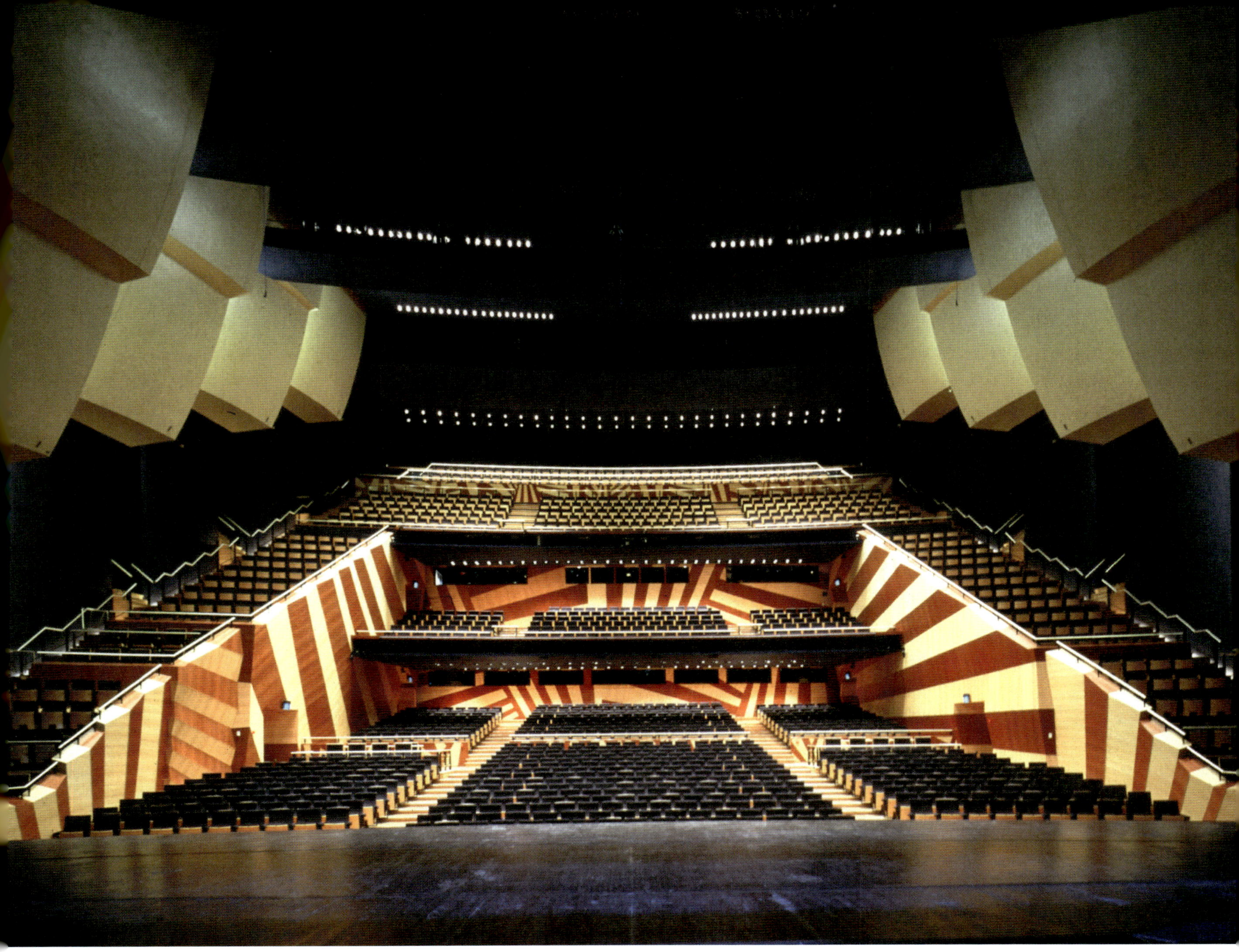

Brings the energy of city and circulation into the interior of the building

A performing arts space for symphony, ballet, and opera, with dazzling patterns of dark and pale wood veneers

FESTIVAL WALK

HONG KONG 1993 | 1998

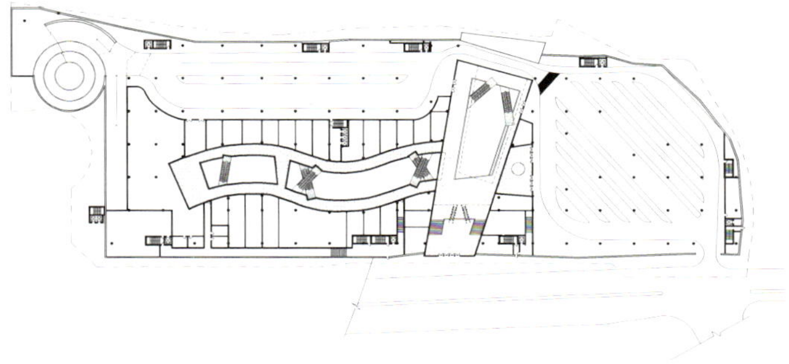

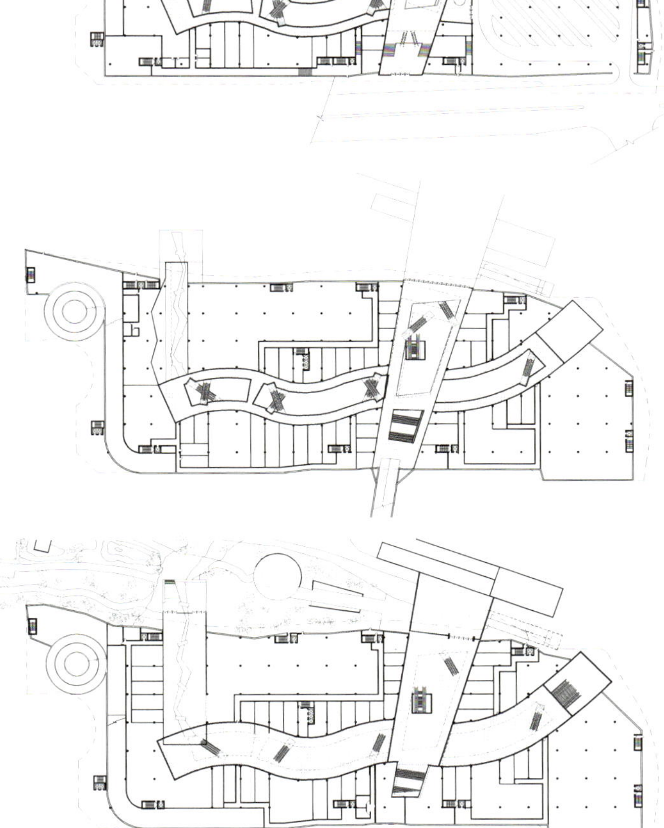

Festival Walk was Arquitectonica's first project in Asia. The client had an office in Miami and became aware of the firm's early commercial/retail work — in particular, the Sawgrass Mills Shopping Mall in Sunrise, Florida (1990). The 1.5 million-square-foot complex is perched on the edge of a hill in Kowloon Tong that separates Hong Kong from Mainland China. It was from the natural contours of this setting that Arquitectonica developed initial plans to create a place of mobility and high-speed transition, an undulating void that flows from west to east across the site like a river canyon, defining an intuitive way-finding path for the busy consumer who has access to seven levels of stores, cinemas, restaurants, and a skating rink. The man-made canyon is connected vertically by eighty-five escalators that cross the central void at different angles and appear to hover, however briefly, before cascading down like so many chromium waterfalls. (Initial plans called for an eight-story-high aquarium, but this was deleted along the way).

Throughout the design process, the metaphor remained that of a natural landscape — canyon, river, lakes, waterfalls — and while Arquitectonica's master plan evokes elements of traditional Chinese landscape painting, it is a thoroughly modern — almost futuristic — environment, a nexus of movement and interconnectivity. "It's like the abstraction of a mountain ridge with these crystals breaking through," said Fort-Brescia. The largest "crystal" is a long wedge of glass and metal that penetrates the facade along Tat Chee Avenue, providing entry and connection to retail areas as well as access to the major transportation hub that lies below. The Kowloon Canton Railway intersects with the Hong Kong Metropolitan Transit line here and then continues through Lion's Rock Tunnel into China. One ascends into a 232,000-square-foot office block or descends into a pedestrian tunnel that connects to the Hong Kong Polytechnic Campus across the way. When it opened in 1998, Festival Walk was hailed as the largest and most popular shopping complex in Hong Kong.

A nexus of movement and interconnectivity, with escalators that cascade down like chromium waterfalls

ORCHARD SCOTTS

SINGAPORE/ 1994 | 2005

A triad of sculptural entities gather around a man-made lagoon at Orchard Scotts, a 736,000-square-foot condominium project near the junction of Orchard and Scotts Roads in central Singapore. The buildings are casually laid off-axis within a triangular plot of land formed by Peck Hay Road, Clemenceau Avenue, and Anthony Road. Each of the towers has a unique configuration: One is punctured through the middle with a square void, reminiscent of the sky court at the Atlantis. Another has a wedgelike profile and a vertical cutout. The third features a curving roof.

"Each volume originates as a functional rectangular plan," explained Fort-Brescia. "It is then 'carved' in section to create form and profile." Two of the towers are twenty stories high; the third is eighteen stories. The voids help to diminish the mass of the glass volumes while creating urban-scale "windows" that allow light and air to flow into the compound. The towers are also differentiated by color: one blue, another green, and the third red. Facades are animated by alternating stripes in different shades to create something of a moiré effect. "This simulates giant brushstrokes reminiscent of Chinese calligraphy," said Fort-Brescia. There is an almost childlike innocence to the composition — partly pop art, partly functional — and a painterly quality in the use of colored glass and painterly, detailing. Eccentrically shaped landscape elements — pools and terraces — can be read as giant splatters in juxtaposition to the prismlike geometries of the buildings.

A triad of sculptural entities gather around a man-made lagoon.

M
HOTEL

WESTIN TIMES SQUARE

NEW YORK CITY 1994 | 2002

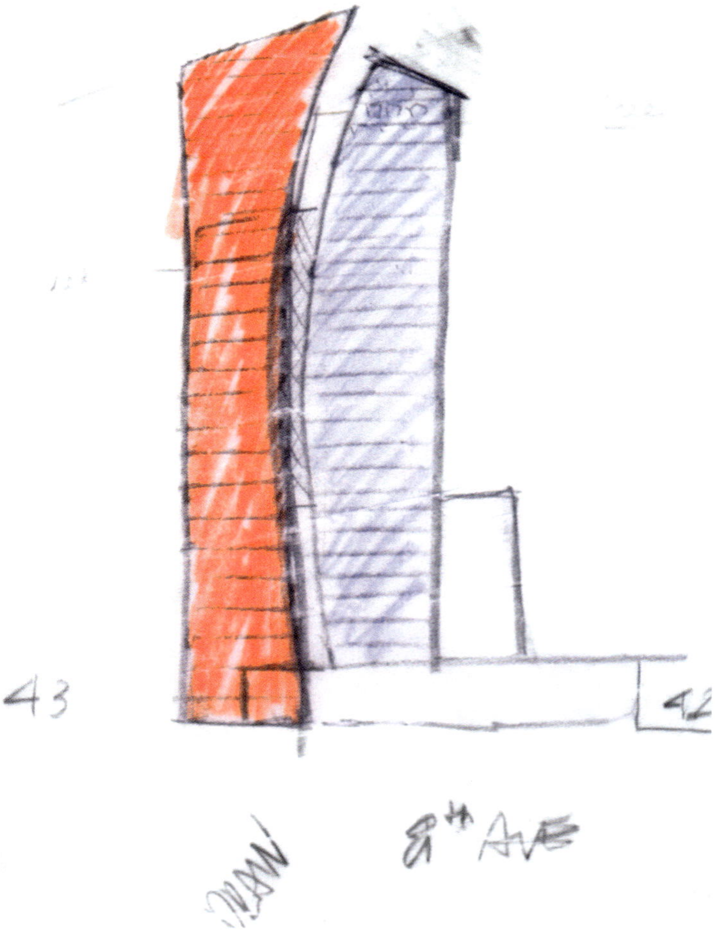

An early study for the Westin Times Square showed a zigzagging column with glassed-in voids. Another resembled Claes Oldenburg Torch of Liberty. After many improvisations, the architects returned to the essence of the problem: how to design a high-rise that would be original and immediately recognizable. Arquitectonica wanted to celebrate the flashing colors, lights, and jumbled disorder of the city that never sleeps. "Times Square was super funky and we asked ourselves: Do we really want to take away that funkiness?" asked Fort-Brescia. "We certainly didn't want to do some kind of corporate intervention."

Preliminary impulses gradually merged into a relatively minimal solution — think Ellsworth Kelly — first embodied in a napkin sketch by Spear. It couldn't have been simpler. Two slender forms — one reddish-orange, the other blue — are separated by an arcing elliptical gap, a "curving streak of light," as if a single tower had been cleaved in two. The red part is slightly higher than the blue part, which suggests a kind of tectonic displacement — one sliding past the other, ascending or descending — giving it a unique profile that could hold its own against so many other iconic buildings on the Manhattan skyline.

"We wanted to create a new typology of the skyscraper, a modern statement, an expression of movement," said Fort-Brescia, who felt compelled to take a risk. "Times Square is the entertainment district of New York," he said. "The building had to be theatrical, like a stage set."

As realized, the bipartite tower rises from a fourteen-story podium made up of two sections. A four-story "retail base" addresses the gritty reality of 42nd Street and contains the E-Walk entertainment complex with an IMAX theater, tourist shops, and restaurants. It's a pastiche bristling with billboards and signage intended to "reinstate the cadence of the original block," and evoke the chaotic patchwork of the old Times Square, albeit a sanitized, family-friendly version.

Out of the retail base rises an irregularly shaped block, fractured and jagged in profile, colored with an abstract pattern in brown, ocher, and orange. This transitional section — originally designed to resemble an exploding meteor — contains eight floors of executive suites and serves as the base for the tower that rises another forty-five stories above it.

CARTER
HOTEL
Back in therapy
December 6
Robert De Niro
Billy Crystal
analyze
that
On DVD And Video
Oct. 8
NY
MORE FIGHTS THAN ANY OTHER PREMIUM NETWORK!
SHOWTIME
Chevys
Chevys
Tommy Tune
ONLY

Rising from the street clutter of Times Square, a multihued glass tower is cut in half by a curving incision.

"We cut the tower in half to verticalize it," said Fort-Brescia. "In a Broadway play there is often a man and a woman, and we thought of the building as two actors wearing different costumes." The taller tower, at fifty-two stories, is skybound, sheathed in vertically striped, blue glass, with "brushstrokes" of silver and violet. The opposing tower, at forty-five stories, is more earthbound and anchored to the ground. It features bronze, horizontally striped glass accented with streaks of brown and gold.

A similar palette was brought inside the Westin with asymmetrical folding walls and floor patterns, tinted glass panels, and other elements that refer to the exterior, including a curving shaft of light that shoots through one end of the seven-story lobby.

AMERICAN AIRLINES ARENA

MIAMI 1996 | 1999

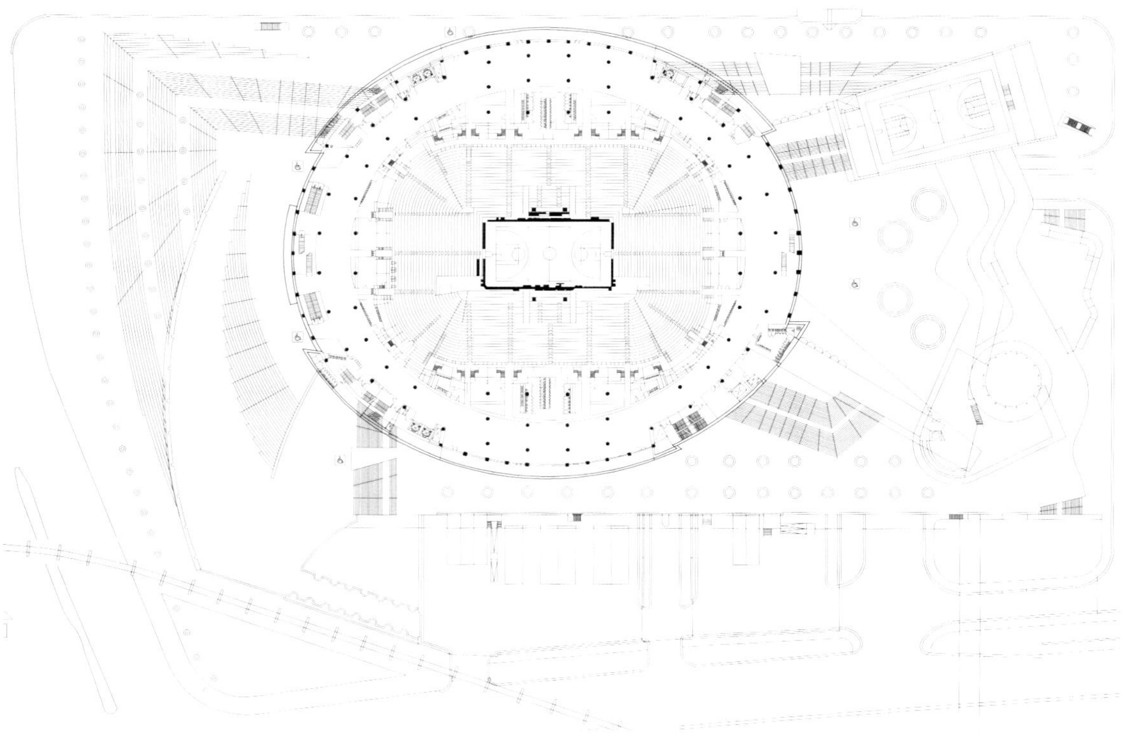

The American Airlines Arena was designed to serve as the new home of the Miami Heat basketball team, and to replace the out-of-date Miami Arena. "We wanted to remove the preconception that sports buildings are ungainly," said Fort-Brescia. "We wanted this arena to prove that they could be artistic." Beyond the task of designing a state-of-the-art sports arena, Arquitectonica saw its mission as creating a landmark for a part of downtown Miami that was largely bereft of character. It would be an anchor for urban development and stimulate the economy by luring in new businesses and tourism.

"We didn't want the building to look like a can of tuna," said Spear. "We wanted it to be open." Unlike most arenas, which are usually windowless and detached from their surroundings, the American Airlines Arena connects with both the bay and the city through six-story-high glass walls at both the eastern and western ends, as well as open-air porches and private sky suites that look out toward the Port of Miami. The arena sits atop a plinth that rises 20 feet above Biscayne Boulevard and the flood plain. A long, sweeping ramp and a monumental stairway with more than thirty-two steps ascend from the sidewalk to the main entrance. Most sports arenas are surrounded by a sea of parking, but this was avoided here, and parking was hidden beneath the man made podium.

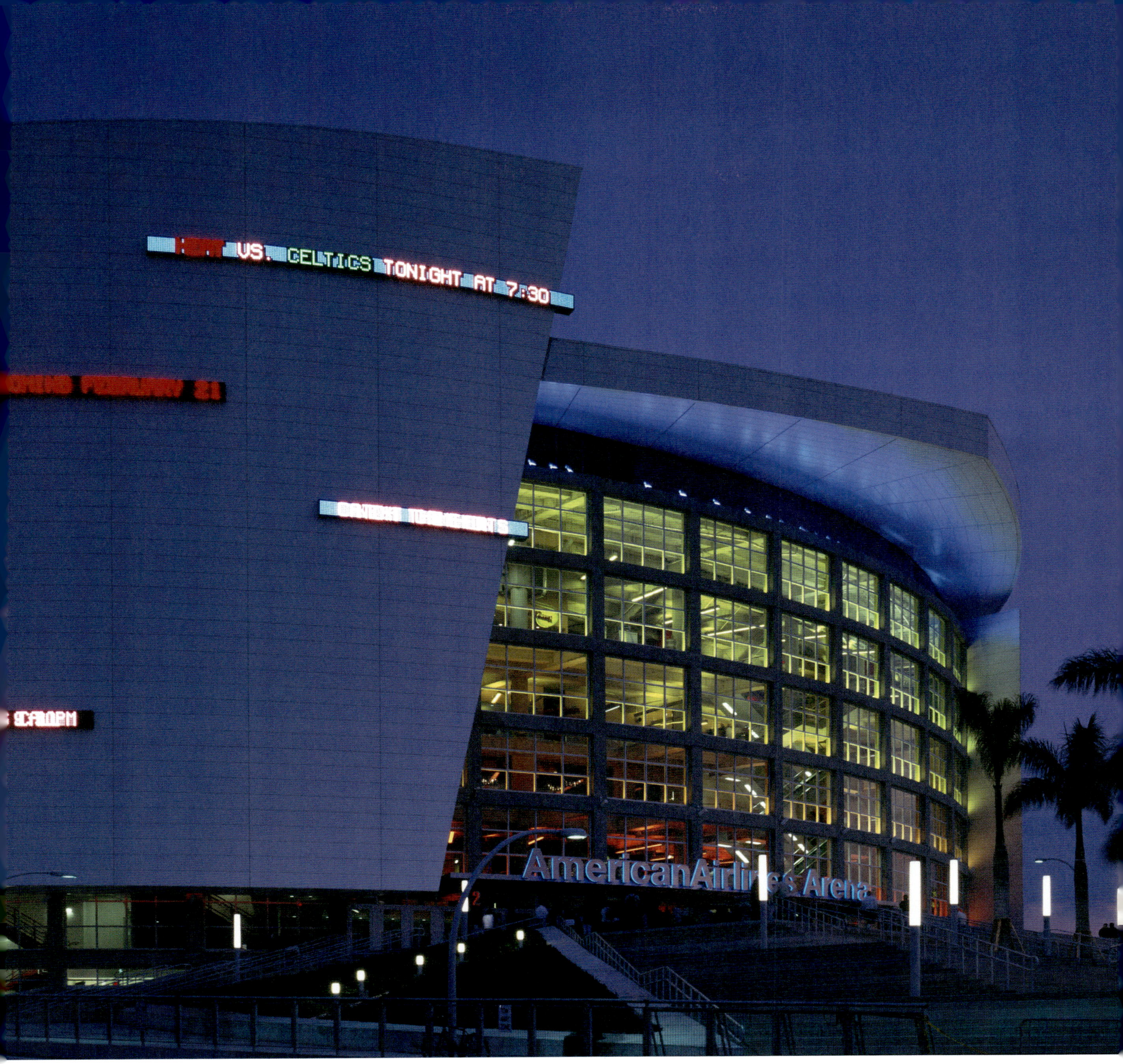
VS. CELTICS TONIGHT AT 7:30
AmericanAirlines Arena

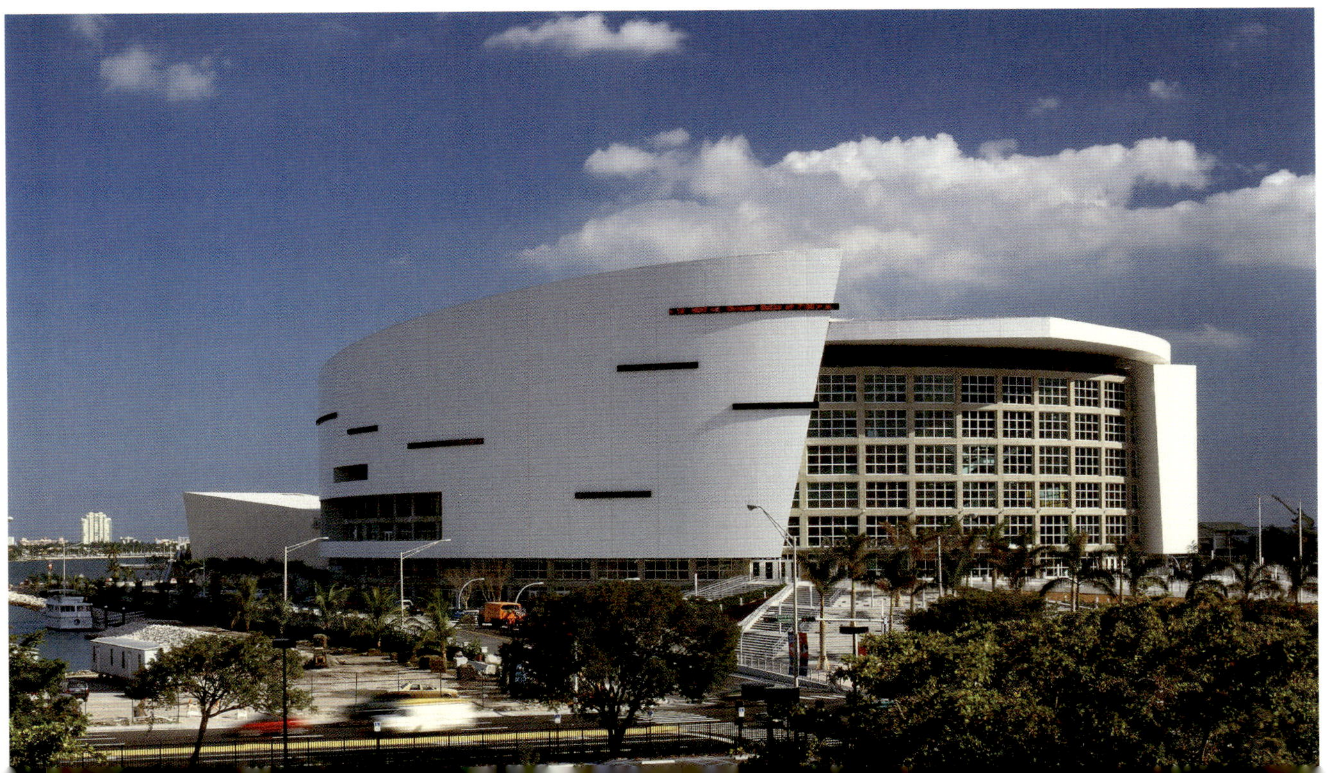

AmericanAirlines Arena

The arena curves around on itself with billowing forms, open-air terraces, and a six-story wall of glass that looks out over the city.

The elliptical building curves around on itself with finlike waves that flare out on either side, one rising into the sky, another descending toward the ground. The white aluminum panels create a taut surface tension like billowing sails. The bay side of the building features a cluster of multifaceted extensions, undulating terraces, and overhangs reminiscent of the midcentury beach hotels of Morris Lapidus. A wedge-shaped structure houses the Heat's practice court and locker rooms, with water views through a high window. Off-season, the practice court can be used as a ballroom or a multipurpose event space. The curving lines of the exterior are echoed on the inside with similarly curving lines of submerged lighting in the ceilings and matching patterns in the terrazzo flooring. "Once inside, it's raw and honest with colored tiles and concrete block," said Fort-Brescia. The multi-tiered concourse, with escalators and concession stands, looks toward Biscayne Boulevard through a six-story wall of glass. "We thought all of the glass would help to dematerialize the building," said Spear.

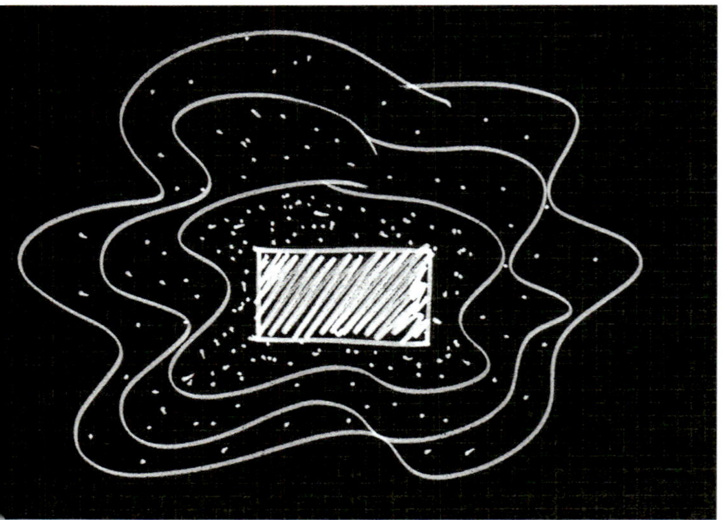

The central bowl provides as many as 20,000 seats for basketball, as well as a standing-room-only balcony. It can be adapted for concerts and other sporting events, such as ice hockey and boxing, or be broken down to a more intimate 5,000-seat theater layout. Acoustically absorptive materials were used on ceilings and walls to reduce the clamor of the crowds. Spear designed the upholstery for the general seating in a radiating "Heat Wave" palette of yellow, orange, and red, while a flamboyantly sculpted "Turn up the Heat" scoreboard was designed by artist Christopher Janney in the shape of a giant sea anemone.

PHILIPS ARENA

ATLANTA 1995 | 1999

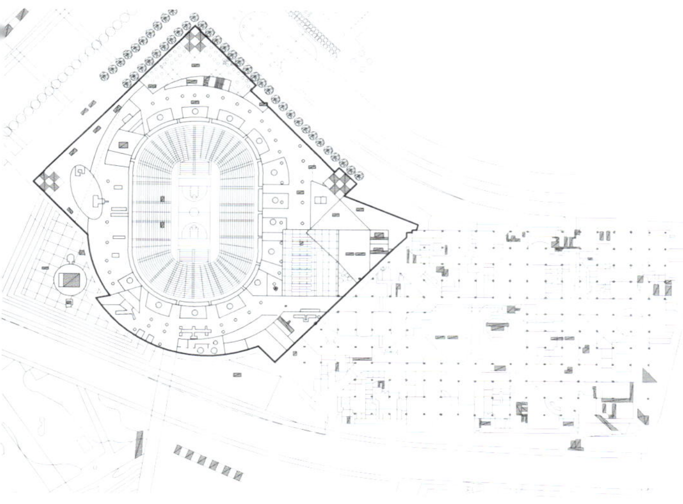

The 750,000-square-foot arena was situated in a dense downtown site, a 4.4-acre lot wedged between busy surface streets and bordered by overpasses, multilevel parking structures, and public plazas, as well as a railway station and the sunken switching yards of Atlanta's mass transit system. Picking up on the energy of the surrounding infrastructure, Arquitectonica designed the building as if it were a viaduct hanging over the train yards, with elevated bridges, sunken pedestrian passageways, parking structures, and numerous shifts in level. Forms and materials fit seamlessly into the city's gritty hardscape. A series of curving trusses hold up the barrel vaults of the main roof in a fanlike sequence of overlapping parallelograms that are splayed, rotating and cupping one another like shallow domes.

The building communicates the civic pride of the city of Atlanta.

Structural integrity takes the form of municipal identity with a trestlelike arcade and overlapping vaulted roofs.

"The curving rooflines are important as you see the building from the upper levels of the CNN Center and from the skyscrapers of downtown Atlanta," said Fort-Brescia. The vaulted roofs descend in height as they turn toward the south. The lowest of the three extends over Centennial Olympic Park Drive and creates a long, curving entry canopy that is supported by a trestlelike arcade of structural girders that spell out the word "ATLANTA" in 60-foot-high steel-clad letters. Structural integrity takes the form of municipal identity. Crowds walk beneath the looming letters on their way to sports events, and this then becomes the overarching allegory of the complex, signaling the new Atlanta — a modern, self-starting city of innovation and new technologies — while also celebrating its wunderkind and chief entrepreneur Ted Turner, a philanthropist and founder of the Cable News Network (CNN). The 21,000-seat arena connects to the CNN Center via a streetlike concourse that features food courts and the Hawk Walk retail corridor.

PHILIPS ARENA
TICKETS
MARTA ENTRY

EXALTIS TOWER

PARIS 1996 | 2006

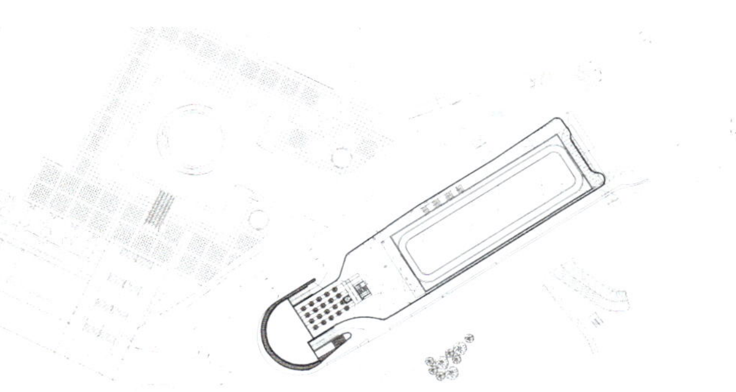

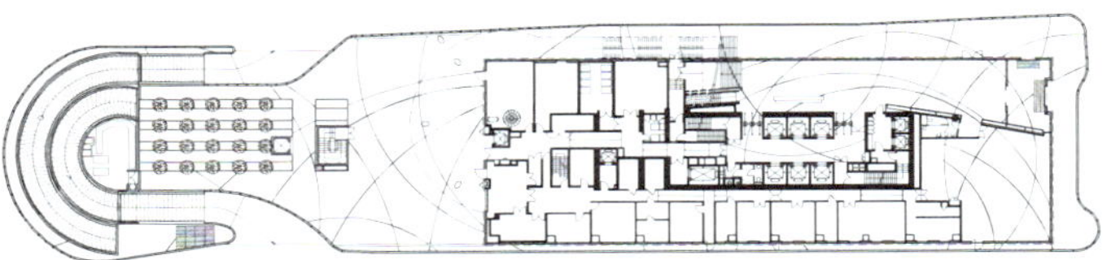

Shaped like a windblown leaf, the fifteen story tower stands among some of the tallest skyscrapers in France. Curving lines of the exterior are reflected throughout the interior.

"The prism began its design life as a pure rectangle," explained Fort-Brescia, and early sketches for Exaltis Tower show a curving parallelogram, something like a leaf blown in the wind, "as if sailing towards the esplanade, propelled by an imaginary force." As the idea evolved, it turned into a semitransparent slab with curving sides — concave on one end and convex on the other, bulging out on the northeast, while bending inward on the southwest — a simple, harmonious solution for a frenetic urban condition. The narrow ends of the "speeding building" are not, however, symmetrical mirrors of one another. They are off-kilter, fooling the eye, radiating from different points below the ground, spreading outward as they rise toward the sky, amplifying the biomorphic irregularity of the building's outer shell, while suggesting an invisible geometry of even greater trajectories.

The building site was a narrow lot wedged between one-way avenues and parking complexes. Even though the fifteen story mass is dwarfed by some of the tallest buildings in France — including the nearby Coeur Défense (forty stories high) and the Tour Areva (forty-four stories high) — the architecture manages to hold its own within such a cluster of skyscrapers. Vertical slots have been indented above the portals on either end — as if carved with a chisel — emphasizing the tautness of the envelope and identifying the twin points of entry to the grand lobby that runs the length of the building with soaring, two-story ceilings and a restaurant that overlooks an adjacent park.

(exaltis (

The curving lines on the exterior of the building suggest greater circumferences and radii (some seen, others unseen) and these phantom lines have been inscribed in the walls, floors, and ceilings of the lobby space with curved lighting elements and semicircular lines of white stone inlaid to the black marble floors. "The lobby is an expressionist synthesis of the forces that shaped the exterior," said Fort-Brescia. "The curves multiply like a wild scribble on a sketchpad. They describe the emotion of architecture, the emotion of the architect, the emotion of the urban moment."

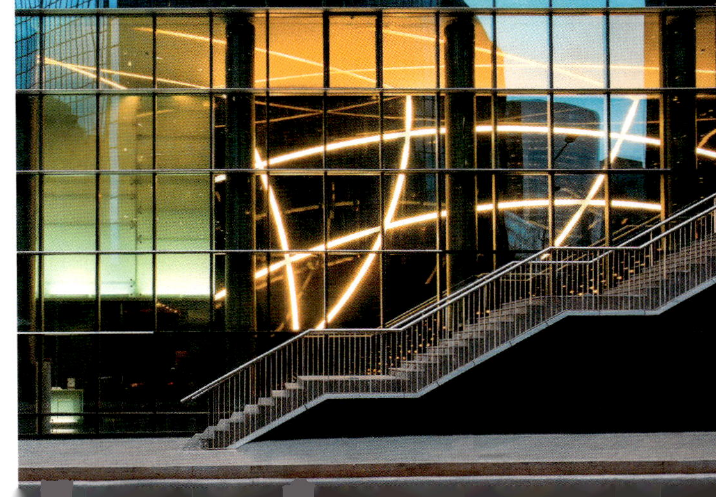

MIAMI CHILDREN'S MUSEUM

MIAMI 1997 | 2003

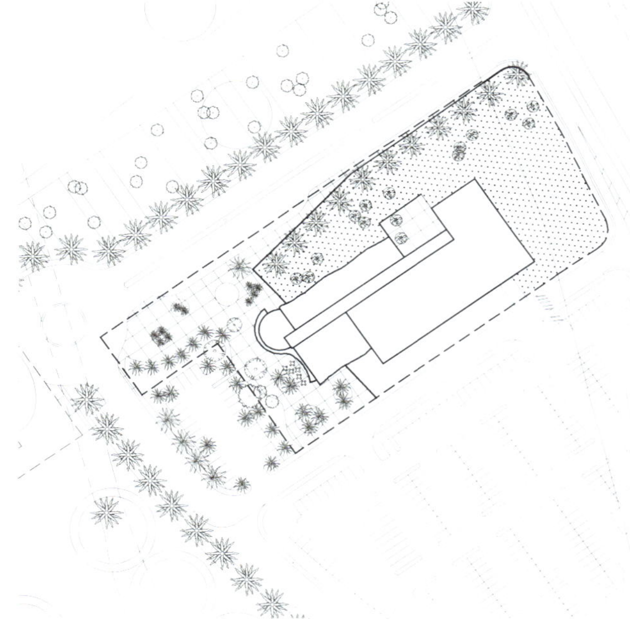

The Miami Children's Museum was designed for a site along the MacArthur Causeway, which links downtown Miami to South Beach, on Watson Island, across from the Parrot Jungle amusement park and looking out over the Port of Miami. It is playful architecture designed to enchant the children who visit every day. The 60,000-square-foot museum is composed of bold multicolored elements, with intersecting planes and contrasting forms that make an eye-catching impression on motorists passing on the nearby highway.

The architecture tells a story. Each section represents one of four elements: earth, wind, water, or fire. The entry pavilion (wind) is a 30-foot-high cone with an internal ramp that spirals up three stories to the exhibition areas. It might be a giant teepee, a nautilus shell, or a witch's hat. Walls fold back and light filters through translucent panels to give the interior spaces an underwater luminosity. Terrazzo floors are embedded with swirling patterns. Another section (water) is painted blue and cuts through the center of the museum with an undulating, wavelike roofline, skylights, and bubblelike perforations. Horizontal bands of orange, ocher, and brown represent earth, while a jagged, saw-toothed section represents the element of fire. In addition to 20,000 square feet of exhibition space, the museum has a cafeteria, classrooms, a gift shop, a birthday party room, and an outdoor play area.

A 3-D collage of brightly colored geometries, the architecture tells a story about earth, wind, fire, and water.

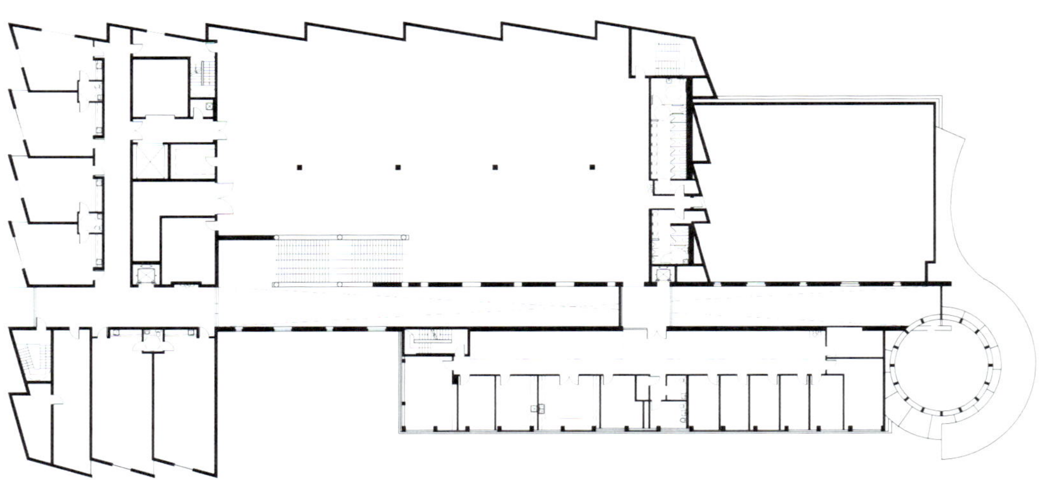

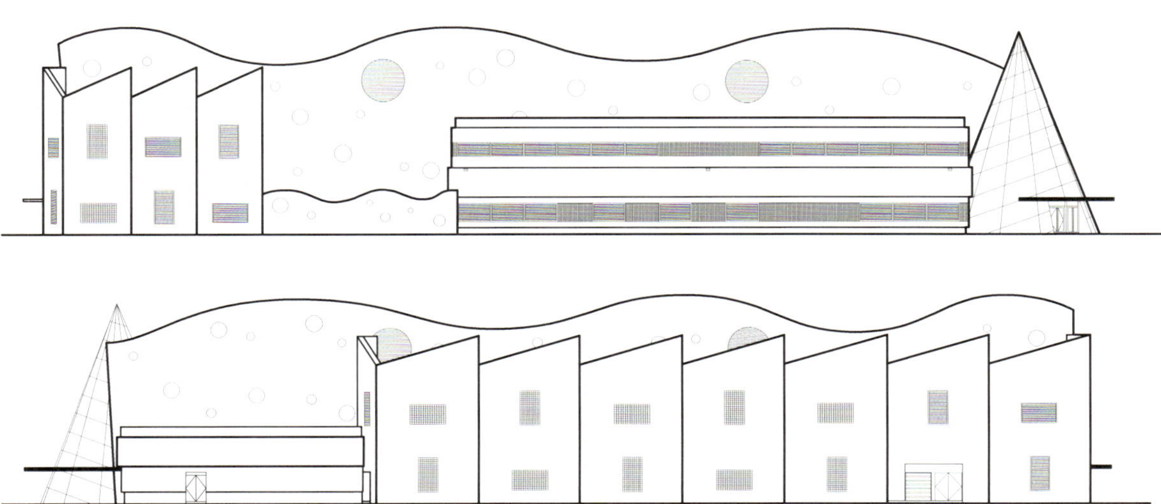

WILKIE D. FERGUSON, JR. UNITED STATES COURTHOUSE

MIAMI 1997 | 2007

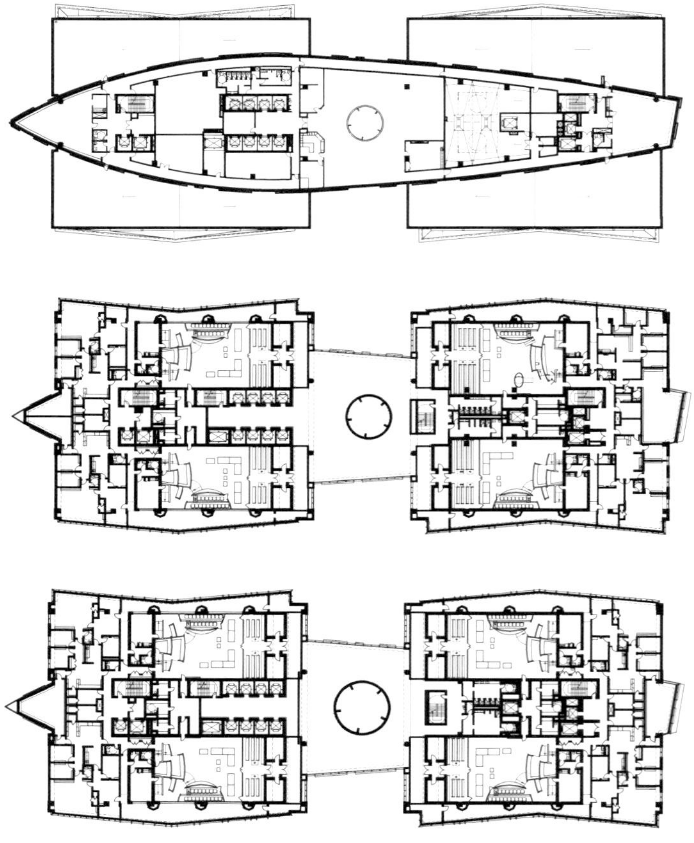

The Wilkie D. Ferguson, Jr. United States Courthouse is lifted 20 feet above its 6.5-acre lot by a colonnade of limestone pylons, hexagonal in plan, that reinforce the multifaceted, quartzlike quality of the building. "To us, this was a building that offered an opportunity to change the course of a neglected, undeveloped neighborhood, and serve as a catalyst," said Fort-Brescia of the building that is solemn, but also buoyant and unexpectedly airy. Arquitectonica developed a plan that would break up the primary mass of the 550,000-square-foot structure by splitting it into two equal parts: the south section, containing the main lobby, judges' chambers, U.S. Marshals Service, and eight courtrooms; and the north section, containing parking, six more courtrooms, and clerk of the court and administrative offices. Courtrooms and waiting areas are flooded with natural light. Judges' chambers have views of Biscayne Bay. One of the facades is convex; the other is concave. (One recedes, while the other protrudes.) They are further broken up by a variegated grid of mullions and specially laminated glass — tightly patterned and horizontal on the lower floors, and vertical and more diffuse on the upper floors.

The two halves of the courthouse are linked in the middle by a monumental seven-story glass atrium — a conical prism that tapers to a lesser radius as it nears the roof. It has a mesmerizing effect, and looking upward from the seventh-floor cafeteria, one sees a vortex of multiple reflections and changing patterns of light. It is a giant crystal oculus, skewering the very center of the building, and bringing natural light throughout its fourteen levels while creating both a spatial and symbolic armature. "We wanted to underline the concept of transparency for the process of justice, literally and metaphorically," said Fort-Brescia.

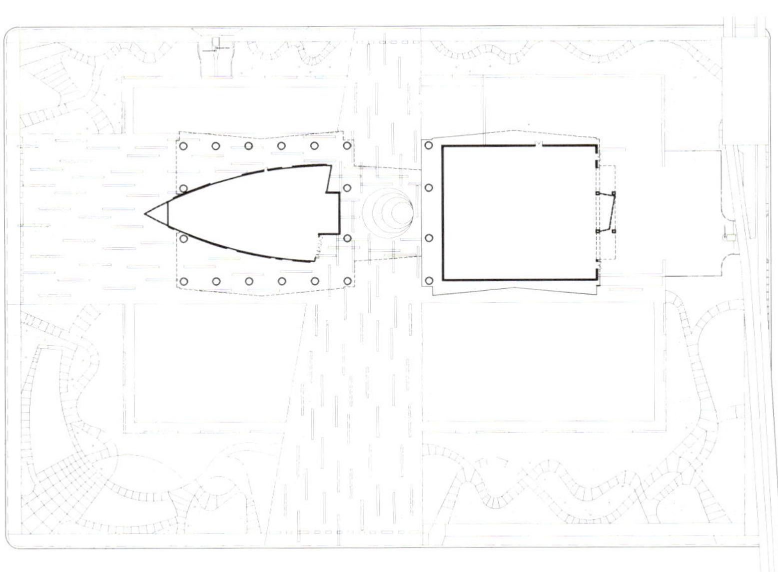

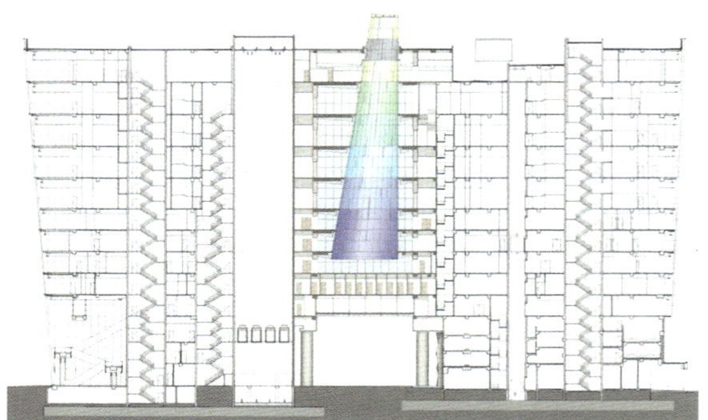

Solemn but buoyant, the quartzlike forms of the courthouse are split in two by a conical prism of glass.

Extrawide setbacks comply with blast-protection requirements and allow for a broad greensward to the east, which is landscaped with undulating mounds of grass by artist Maya Lin. The building rises above its parklike setting, a ship sailing south across Lin's Wave Field earthwork. A wedge of green-tinted glass projects from the south end between two limestone blocks as if it were cleaving the building in two with a dynamic, thrusting action.

The mosaic-like patterning of the facade is carried over to the interiors and surrounding plazas, with origami walls and multicolored tile work. Ceilings in the courtrooms are sculpted into prismatic contours. A three-story breezeway penetrates the center of the building and extends the pedestrian promenade that runs west to east, all the way to the edge of Biscayne Bay. On the opposite side, the courthouse makes a symbolic entry point for the new MiamiCentral transit hub, where the high-speed Brightline and light-rail Metromover converge.

A colonnade of limestone pylons leads out to the undulating mounds of turf by artist Maya Lin.

Prismatic facets animate both exterior walls and courtroom ceilings.

AVENTURA GOVERNMENT CENTER

AVENTURA, FLORIDA 1998 | 2001

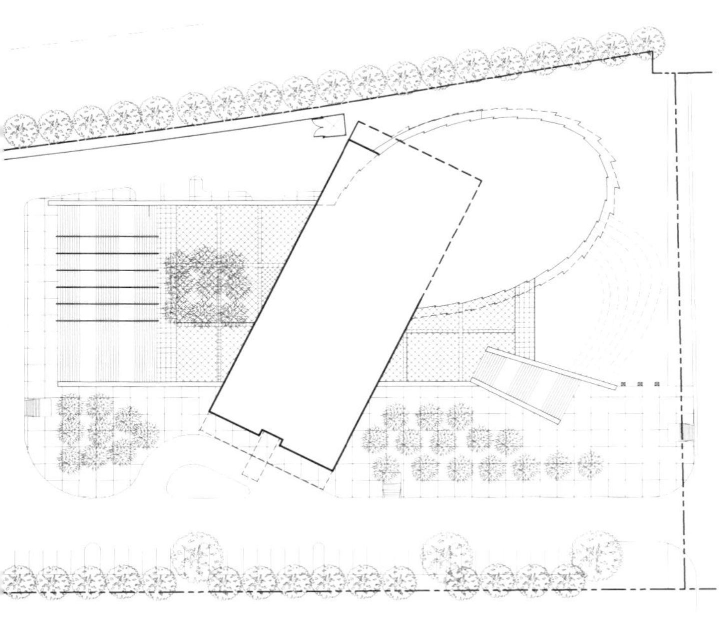

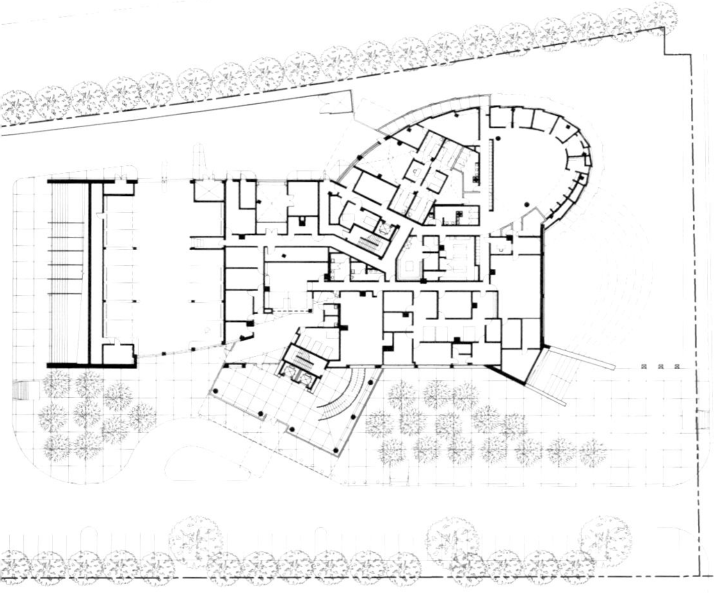

Arquitectonica's mission was to create a sense of center and civic identity for a municipality that had only been incorporated in 1995 with no perceivable history or cultural legacy. The 72,000-square-foot building is located on West Country Club Drive, a north-south thoroughfare that feeds into the sprawling Aventura Mall. Its true orientation, however, is toward the six-lane William Lehman Causeway that connects Collins Avenue to Biscayne Boulevard. "We needed to make a powerful and graphic building that can be seen from passing cars on the highway," said Fort-Brescia, who began by developing a composition of bold geometric forms: a contrast of square versus curvilinear, Euclidean versus organic. As with Arquitectonica's bank building in Luxembourg, an elliptical form intersects a larger block, and just as the forms in Luxembourg echoed the curving lines of an adjacent street, the primary forms in Aventura echo the curving movement of the 40-foot-high causeway. The building was raised on top of a grassy plinth to be clearly visible from that level.

The City Council Chamber is housed in a precast concrete ellipse that approximates the viewing radius of a passing motorist. The words "CITY OF AVENTURA" are carved, as in a classical frieze, into the upper part of the arcade. This part of the complex is earth-colored and hugs the ground, while the six-story block — the so-called "Crystal" — is clad with a reflective blue glass veneer that splays out toward the top and engages the sky. The prismatic form is striated with horizontal metal ribbing and canted at both ends. It houses various city departments, including offices for the mayor and city commissioners, while the police station is located on the ground floor. A grand staircase leads up to city hall.

CITY

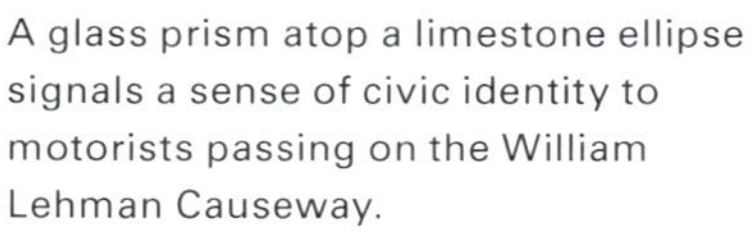

A glass prism atop a limestone ellipse signals a sense of civic identity to motorists passing on the William Lehman Causeway.

N T U R A

CYBERPORT TECHNOLOGY CAMPUS

HONG KONG 1999 | 2004

The long, serpentine extrusion — "a dragon-like chain of prismatic volumes" — wriggles across the reclaimed 59-acre site on Telegraph Bay. The key to Arquitectonica's master plan was the creation of a highly flexible environment that could accommodate multinational giants, such as Microsoft, IBM, Oracle, and Hewlett-Packard, and also provide nurturing space for start-ups and small tech incubators. From the air, it is a complex, multifaceted thing in gestation, breaking away from conventional parameters while anticipating new typologies. Several core structures — including Hong Kong University's main technology center, a transit hub, a conference hall, and a retail center — are linked by the narrow "IT" Street, a hyperextended atrium designed for collaboration, which is enhanced by state-of-the-art support technologies, multimode optical fiber systems, broadband cabling, with multimedia labs, webcast studios, and nodes of human interaction: meeting rooms, restaurants, cafés, a fitness center, and exhibition galleries.

In some places the structure follows the natural contours of the land. In other places it intersects with clusters of trapezoidal office towers, absorbing and then morphing into other programmatic functions, such as a hotel, and terraced housing blocks — before crossing the main access road and then terminating in a plateau with a park and an outdoor amphitheater. Interior lighting and decorative patterning on the multihued wooden floors and glass walls (blue, amber, and white) were designed to provide intuitive way-finding and to delineate one zone from another while helping visitors and tenants to map out the half-mile-long lobby.

A dragonlike chain of prismatic volumes follows the natural contours of the land. Decorative patterns provide intuitive way-finding throughout the half-mile-long lobby.

The challenge was to contain this sprawling, noncentered structure of 2.4 million square feet within a single contiguous skin. Exteriors are clad with multifaceted panels of laminated, heat-resistant glass —angled and dynamic — with tilting facades, cantilevered roof decks, and stainless steel fins to provide shading and break up the mass — all of it suggestive of something in a state of perpetual transition.

CULTU

SOUTH MIAMI-DADE CULTURAL ARTS CENTER

MIAMI 2000 | 2011

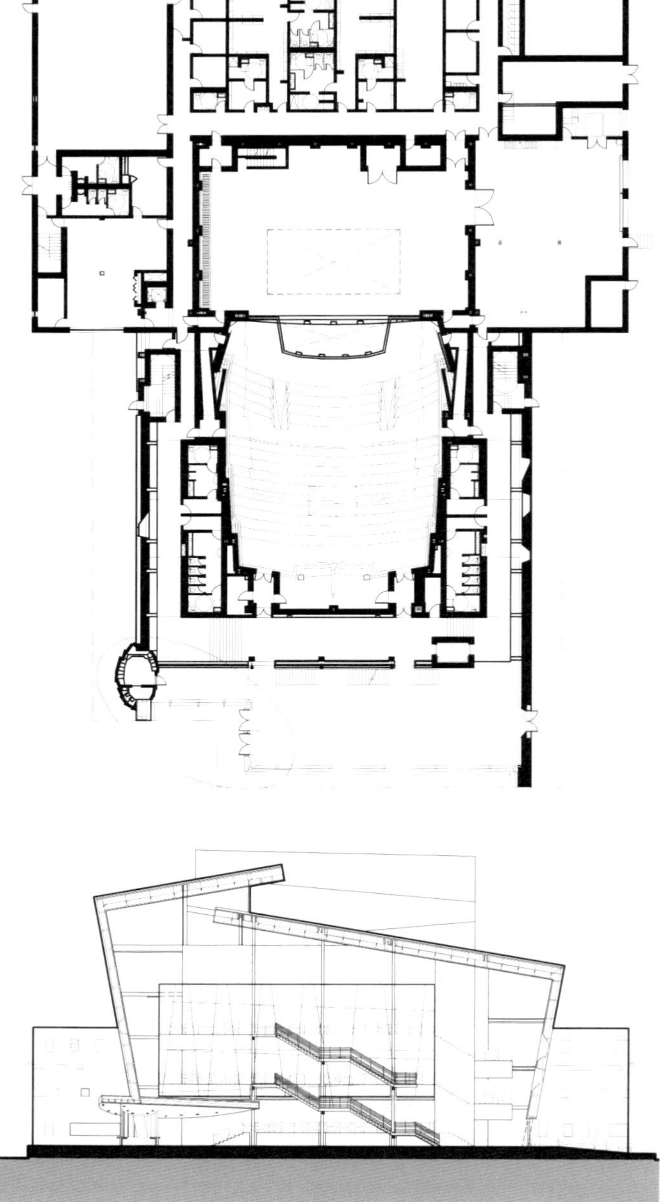

The South Miami-Dade Cultural Center is a puzzle of tilted walls, roofs, and skewed planes, evoking a theatrical sense of arrival and human interaction. The building was designed in sections, with two bracket forms, separate but interpenetrating, as if colliding, intersecting, and overlapping. Each part is offset in their geometries, but fused into a single object, with broad expanses of glass. Fort-Brescia compared the building to two hands clapping and called it an "homage to the act and art of performance." On approach, the main facade appears to expand and contract, while a circular slab penetrates the glass curtain wall and reaches out toward the entry plaza to create a welcoming overhang and entry to the main lobby. "All along, our concern was how it would feel to move from the street to the building," said Spear. "We wanted the building to reflect the spirit of movement, moving the patron through a visual as well as physical experience, turning the patron into a performer."

Windowless sidewalls feature a rainlike pattern, with long and short streaks — or "water drops" — in varying shades of gray. (Some of the smaller drops are actually windows.) A similar motif is carried inside, on the terrazzo floors of the lobby and the walls and grand curtain of the main theater.

Rainlike patterns on both exterior and interior surfaces celebrate the art of performance.

AMERICAN BANK CENTER

CORPUS CHRISTI, TEXAS 2001 | 2004

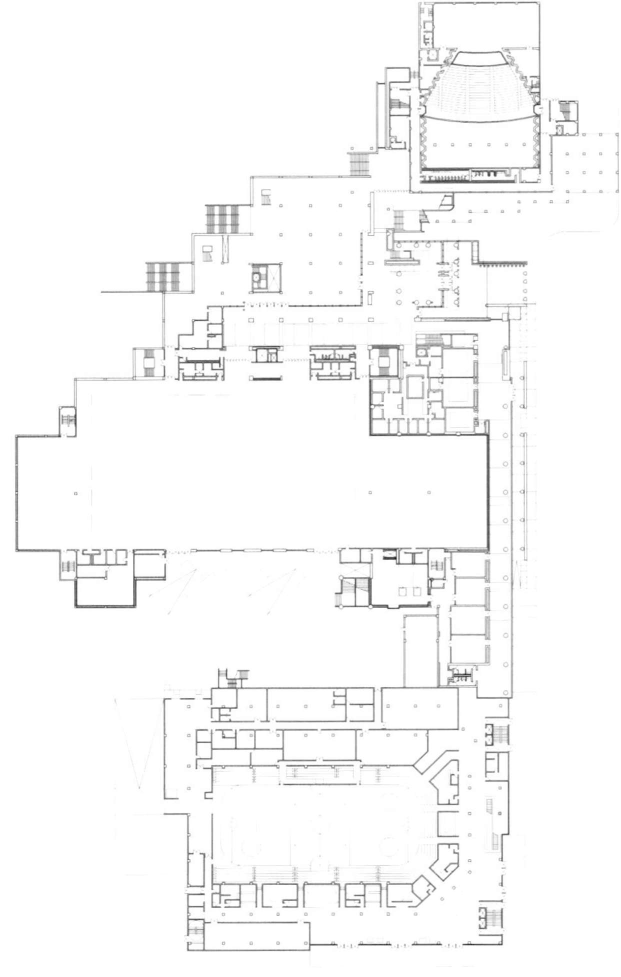

The overall idea was to encourage more people to visit Bayfront Park, an attractive but underutilized area just south of Nueces Bay in Corpus Christi. The zigzagging wall of glass establishes an immediate sense of identity for the American Bank Center and connects it to the waters of the Gulf that lie 50 yards to the east. Approaching from the south, the facade jumps out at you, a folded superstructure supported by steel framing that runs the length of the building and floods the atrium with natural light. The eccentrically shaped facade was intended as a metaphor for the winds that blow off of the Gulf of Mexico. It was also an ingenious way to masquerade a big-box arena and give it a sculptural presence, breaking down the scale and monotony of the large enclosed space that lies within. Arquitectonica had been commissioned to design a new 9,500-square-foot arena for sports (National Collegiate Athletic Association basketball and minorleague ice hockey) and entertainment. At the same time, there was a major renovation of the preexisting convention center located on the same avenue, just to the north. The 227,000-square-foot convention center was expanded, with an additional 129,000 square feet of ballrooms, exhibition halls, and a new entry lobby and facade to match the sports arena, but with slight variations. Instead of a double jag, the front of the convention hall features a single jag that extends over the sidewalk to create a protective arcade supported by seven sloping columns, further distinguishing the convention hall from the arena.

As metaphor for the winds that blow off the Gulf of Mexico, the zigzagging glass facade fills the atrium with natural light.

BRONX MUSEUM OF THE ARTS

NEW YORK CITY 2001 | 2006

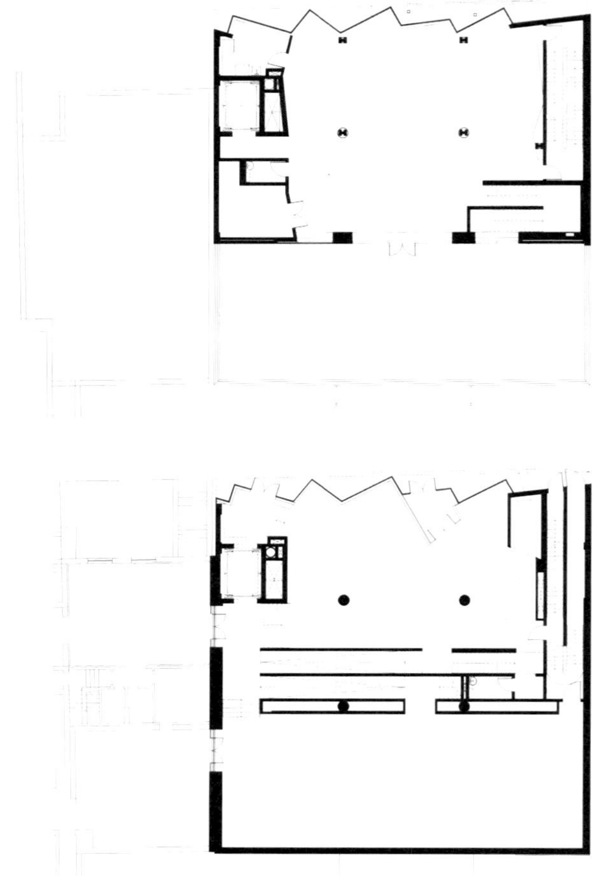

The Bronx Museum of the Arts makes an elegantly subdued statement of inclusion on the Grand Concourse, which runs north to south through the heart of the South Bronx. In comparison to Arquitectonica's other New York projects, it was a modest assignment, low scale and with a relatively low budget — a simple but memorable gesture for a community art museum that features a folded, accordion-style facade of Alucobond (aluminum) panels and fritted glass. "We wanted it to have more of a sculptural look," said Fort-Brescia. "It's a museum and should stand out from other buildings." The 16,700-square-foot addition not only doubled the museum's public space, it also gave the institution an identity that it formerly lacked. (The only other significant piece of modern architecture in the area is Rafael Viñoly's Bronx County Hall of Justice, just around the corner at East 161st Street and Morris Avenue.) The aluminum folds are not symmetrical or static. They tilt and lean and dance in the light, like a Richard Serra sculpture. As pedestrians walk past, the pleats appear to open and close like louvers, revealing the museum's inner spaces through vertical slits of semitransparent glass, and fostering a sense of interaction between the art inside and the public realm. "It's like an invitation," said Fort-Brescia. "Passersby get a sneak view inside."

THE BRONX MUSE

UM OF THE ARTS

Aluminum folds tilt and lean along the sidewalk, inviting passersby to peer into the galleries through vertical openings and interact with the architecture.

A horizontal slab of a canopy cuts across the zigzagging facade and cantilevers out over the sidewalk, supporting the museum's name in raised lettering. Upon entering, a light-filled lobby leads to a series of galleries with bare concrete floors and white walls. There is a café and a gift shop, and a ramp that leads up to a new 2,500-square-foot gallery at the back of the building, an auditorium and screening room on the second level, an education center on the third, and administrative offices above that. (A 2,000-square-foot sculpture garden is accessible from one of the upper galleries.)

Sidewalls on the north and south sides of the Arquitectonica addition were left relatively blank for future expansion. To break up the monotony, Spear designed a checkerboard pattern with interwoven bands of gray, black, and white brick. For a future phase of development, Arquitectonica designed a seventeen-story residential tower that will anchor the corner of 165th Street where the original museum, a former synagogue, now sits.

HIGH SCHOOL FOR CONSTRUCTION TRADES, ENGINEERING AND ARCHITECTURE

NEW YORK CITY 2001 | 2006

The school commands the corner of 104th Street and 95th Avenue, in Queens, with a distinctive, Lego-like collage of different shapes, materials, and colors. A red brick section with classrooms is cantilevered over the sidewalk and supported by a sloping black column. A projecting bay for the library is clad in yellow porcelain panels. The auditorium is covered in precast concrete panels inscribed with an irregular pattern, while the cafeteria and art room have corrugated metal walls, and the gym is sheathed in glass block.

"We wanted to treat it like a laboratory," said Fort-Brescia. "That was the idea." The 155,000-square-foot building accommodates more than nine-hundred students and includes a three-hundred-seat theater, a library, and classrooms, as well as specialized laboratories for mechanical drafting, model building, and computer-aided design.

HS
CEA

A Lego-type assemblage of colored concrete blocks becomes a pedagogical tool for high school students.

HS CEA

QUEENS WEST

NEW YORK CITY 2001 | 2013

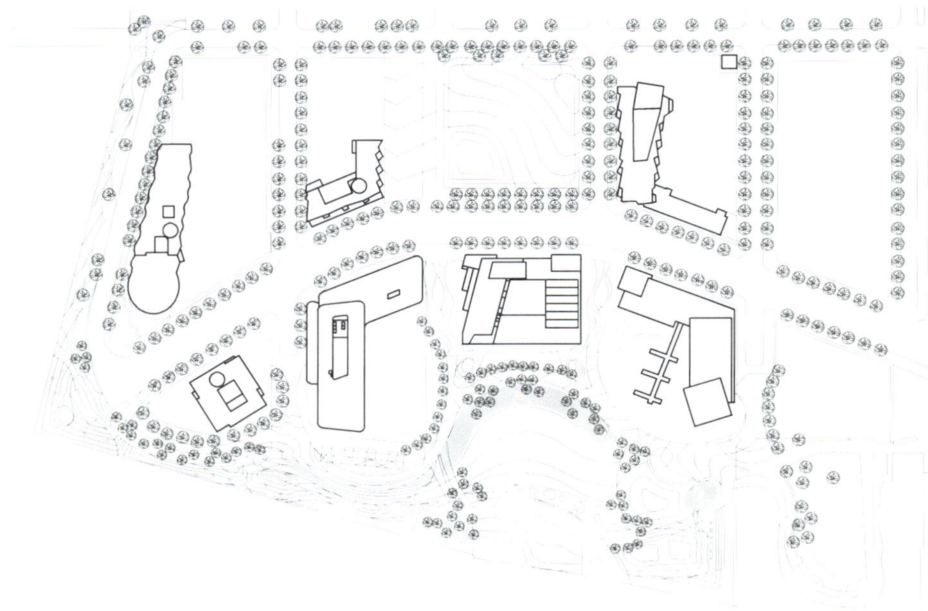

Arquitectonica devised a master plan for Queens West, a 3.2-million-square-foot development built on a former industrial area in Long Island City, directly across the East River from the United Nations Headquarters. The main road was moved inland to make it two-sided, with shops, a supermarket, a new public school, and other amenities. A curvilinear sequence of pocket parks, playing fields, and promenades skirts the edge of the river, rotating in and around the orthogonally positioned lots that branch off from both sides of Center Boulevard, the main axis of circulation. The residential towers range in height from twelve stories to forty stories .

A 10-acre park was moved to the edge of the East River and serves as foreground to the development, while the buildings frame specific view corridors across the river toward Manhattan. The northern end tapers to a ceremonial point with seating and viewing areas adjacent to the Anable Basin. The southern end features a contoured, earthen amphitheater surrounded by a series of open-air pavilions.

"The high-rises are abstract and project crisp geometries," said Fort-Brescia, who designed six of the seven completed structures. "We intentionally gave them individual identities; no two buildings are alike. We wanted it to feel like an extension of the existing city, not like a planned project with identical components."

The most iconic feature of the waterfront site is an eight-story-high Pepsi-Cola sign with swirling red letters and a giant bottle tilting seductively at one end. It has commanded the site since 1936, becoming a cherished landmark to New Yorkers who can see it from the Manhattan side of the river. At one point, the 147-foot-long billboard was threatened with demolition, but preservationists and executives of PepsiCo made every effort to restore it on the original site.

Pepsi-Cola

A "new city" of glass towers grows around an old Pepsi-Cola sign on the East River.

One of the residential buildings that Arquitectonica designed — an apartment tower at 4610 Center Boulevard — sits directly behind the Pepsi sign. Instead of moving the colossal piece of Pop art or altering it, the architects decided to recess the lower eight floors of the twenty-five-story building as much as 12 feet, in deference to the historic sign. "We chose to curve the corners so the facades seem to fade away," said Fort- Brescia. "We didn't want the sharp corners of a rectangle competing with the letters. The face of the sign ended up shaping the volumetrics of the building."

Shallow
water.

太古汇
PRADA

TAIKOO HUI

GUANGZHOU 2001 | 2013

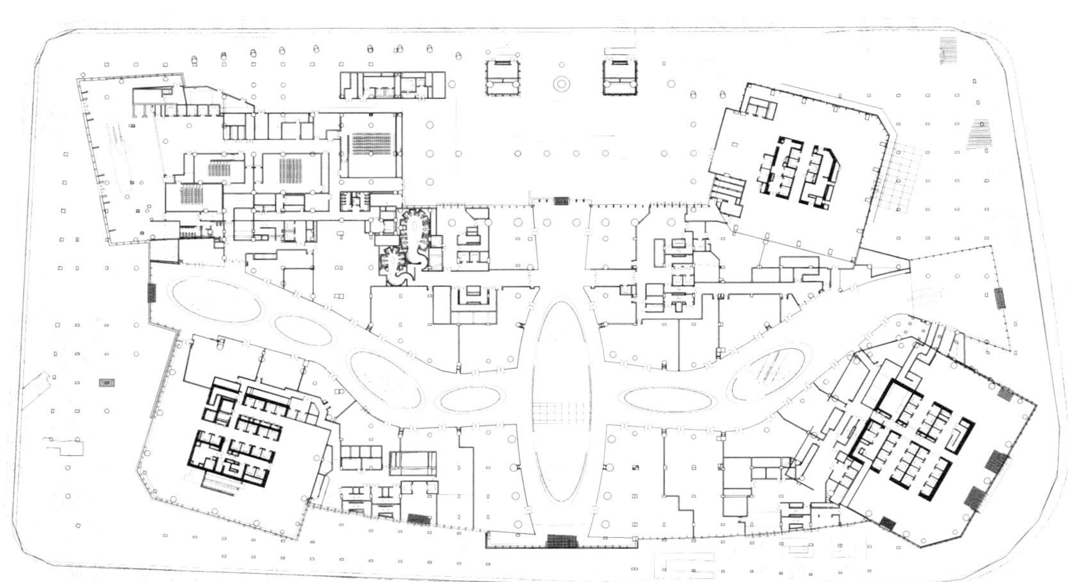

A 2 acre public park stands between three office towers and above a multilevel shopping center illuminated by elliptical skylights.

Taikhoo Hui is a dense, 5-million-square-foot cluster that includes three office towers, the Mandarin Oriental hotel, a four-level shopping mall, and a cultural center with a 1,000-seat performing arts center. Subterranean passageways connect all levels of the complex to a metropolitan station with inner-city metro and high-speed rail. Commuters and shoppers rise from an underground maze of transit connections and ascend through the shopping mall to a tranquil public space on the roof.

Three towers, with curving beveled edges, assume a relatively passive position around the periphery of the 12-acre property. They have been rotated away from the orthogonal to maximize views and allow light to penetrate the retail complex that sits at the center, its entry signaled by a prominent crystalline volume, cubic in form and clad with a transparent grid of glass. Architecture and landscape reinterpret the intimacy of a classic Chinese garden at a macro scale with green roofs, native plants, fully mature trees, and an interlacing pattern of walkways and parterres.

ArquitectonicaGEO designed the 2 acre garden on the third level that provides a human dimension and helps soften the urban impact with shaded seating areas, outdoor cafés, and restaurants. Lush arrangements of ferns, giant philodendrons, epiphytes, orchids, and begonias create a green buffer between city and man-made plateau. A long, eccentrically shaped skylight extends through the middle of the elevated plaza like a river running east to west, with overlapping panes of flickering glass. The undulating canopy of glass supplies natural light to the multi =level atrium below and amplifies the natural landscape metaphor, while two grand staircases provide access to the third-level plaza from the street, effectively turning it into a public park.

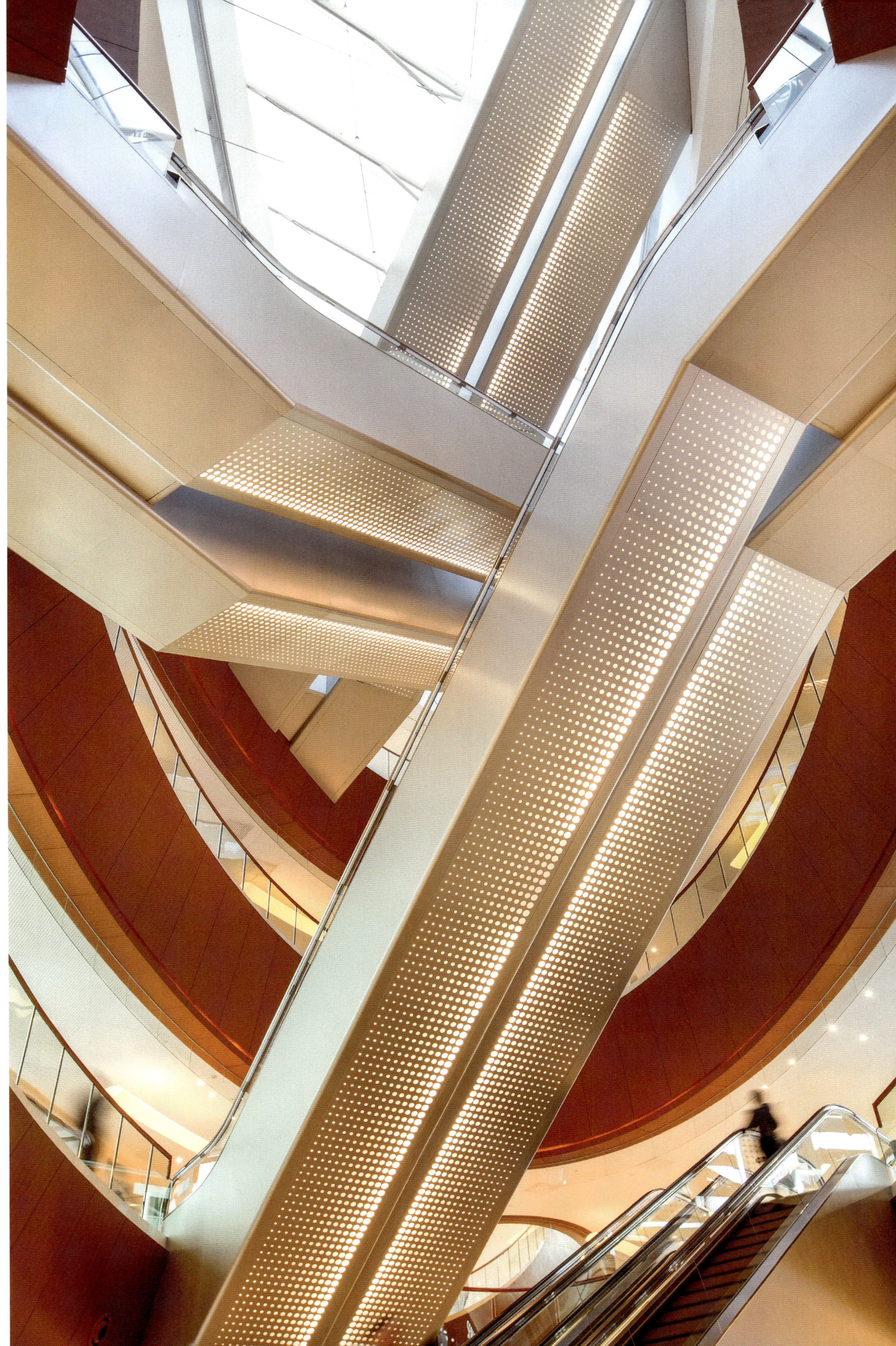

TRINITY PLACE

SAN FRANCISCO 2001 | 2020

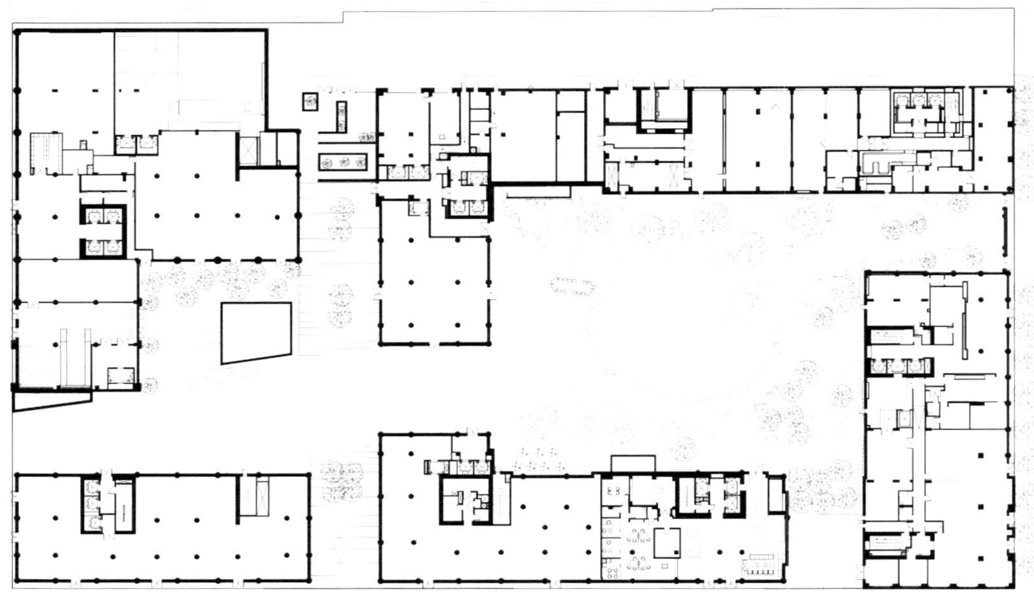

The first and second phases of Trinity Place were completed in 2010 and 2013, respectively, and they featured twenty-four and twenty-two story slabs built along Mission Street. The next phase was a ninteen story, L-shaped block with 540 apartments and a 960-car garage. The fourth and final phase is a seventeen story structure on Market Street with 503 apartments and 85,000 square feet of retail space, including a grocery store. In all, there will be more than 1,900 apartment units, making it the largest residential complex to be built in San Francisco since World War II. A good percentage of the apartments are below-market units, including 600 studio apartments, to help alleviate the city's affordable housing shortage.

"We wanted to start with something very graphic and pure, compared to the background of San Francisco," said Fort-Brescia, referring to the minimal, clean-edged massing of Arquitectonica's master plan versus the surrounding context of fragmented low-rise, suburban-scale buildings. The architecture itself reinforces the idea of a tightly formatted template of components with staggered setbacks, "cascading" shifts in roof height, materials, and types of fenestration, all to make the building blocks appear more complex and varied than they actually are. "The composition changes personality from one building to the next," said Fort-Brescia, who compared the design to a Cubist painting in which interlocking forms and colors create the illusion of separate blocks merging into a single larger structure. "I wanted to have an interaction between the buildings so that nothing looks separate or alone," he said.

The biggest innovation may not necessarily be the solid volumes of architecture, but rather the voids between the buildings and the introduction of significant public space into a privately financed development. There are portal-like openings on every side to let the city flow through and create a pedestrian experience for everyone, not just tenants. All four buildings are pushed to the perimeter of the site to allow the maximum space for a public, 1 acre plaza within. Named "Plaza Angelo" after the late developer, it features a surreal mix of rugged marble figures, seating areas, and an undulating greensward and public pathways. The centerpiece is a 92-foot-tall sculpture, a Venus de Milo in swirling stainless steel, by the artist Lawrence Argent. It is the tallest public sculpture in San Francisco and makes a fitting counterpoint to the geometrically taut grid-work of the four residential blocks.

Almost decades in the making, Trinity Place was the capstone on Angelo Sangiacomo's sixty-year career as a developer.

Interlocking forms and surface treatments create a "super-size urban collage" and the illusion of separate blocks merging into a single megastructure that surrounds a 1 acre plaza with a 92-foot-tall sculpture of Venus de Milo.

SARASOTA HERALD-TRIBUNE

SARASOTA, FLORIDA 2002 | 2006

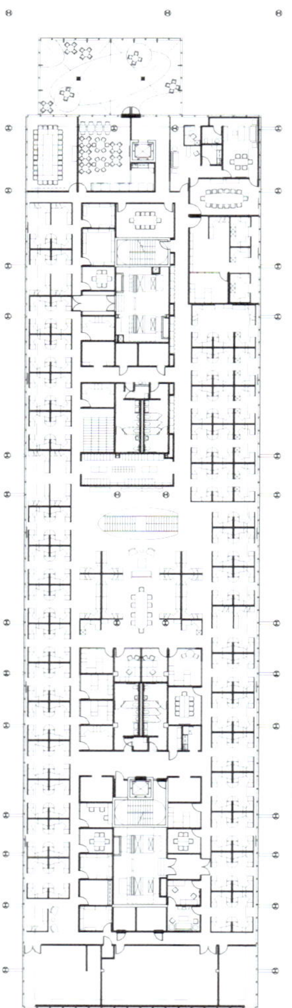

The city of Sarasota, on Florida's west coast, is known as much for its architecture as it is for its white, sandy beaches. A distinctive style of subtropical Modernism started in the 1950s with the work of Ralph Twitchell, Victor Lundy, William Rupp, and, most notably, Paul Rudolph. When the client, the *New York Times* (parent company of the *Sarasota Herald-Tribune* at the time) asked Arquitectonica to design a building, they responded with their own kind of homage to the small beach houses and pavilions that Rudolph and others designed in the 1950s, but upscaled it to meet the needs of a modern-day newspaper and local TV station: the Sarasota Herald-Tribune and SNN Channel 6. In the spirit of those early escape houses, the 71,253-square-foot building is open and breezy and conveys a casual sense of transparency and accessibility, qualities that are fitting for a modern news service.

The origami-like roof is the single most recognizable feature, supported as it is by a colonnade of 54-foot-high steel columns that set it apart from surrounding buildings. The support structure has been pushed out to the perimeter of the building, and the roof appears to float above a band of clerestory glass that fills in the triangular voids created by the peaks and valleys of the zinc-alloy folds. The deep overhangs create shaded points of entry at either end and allow enough space beneath the projecting eaves for an outdoor terrace.

A folded roof supported by slender pilotis evoke, the midcentury modern pavilions of this seaside resort. Glass is tinted in shades of blue and green to mitigate heat gain.

Interior spaces are left open to allow for flexibility and easy communication between departments. A staircase leads up to the expansive third-floor newsroom through a keyhole opening that creates the sensation of entering a secret inner sanctum. The continuous glass-curtain wall is tinted in shades of blue and green to help mitigate heat gain. As the building is in a hurricane-prone flood zone, the offices are raised to the second level and above, to avoid storm surge, and the glass walls are rated for 120-mile-per-hour winds.

PERFORMING ARTS CENTER

IRVINE VALLEY COLLEGE   IRVINE, CALIFORNIA 2003 | 2007

"The building needed to be expressive, theatrical," said Fort-Brescia. "It had to reflect its purpose." The 55,000-square-foot facility was built on the northwestern edge of a community college in South Orange County, about 35 miles south of Los Angeles. Somewhat isolated, the campus lies amid a former urban landscape of subdivisions, high-tech office parks, and orange groves. The Performing Arts Center was designed to create its own context and connect both to the immediate campus and the outlying community through a variety of performing arts events that would be open to the general public. It makes for an architectural marker, an invitation, sculpted with flat stucco walls that spiral around interior functions in a process of wrapping and folding that derives, in part, from the firm's earlier kind of collage process.

The outer skin encloses several different venues, including a four-hundred seat main hall, a one-hundred seat experimental "black box" theater, and a fifty seat recital hall. Each elevation is different, and the roofline rises or dips to reflect the internal workings of the theater.

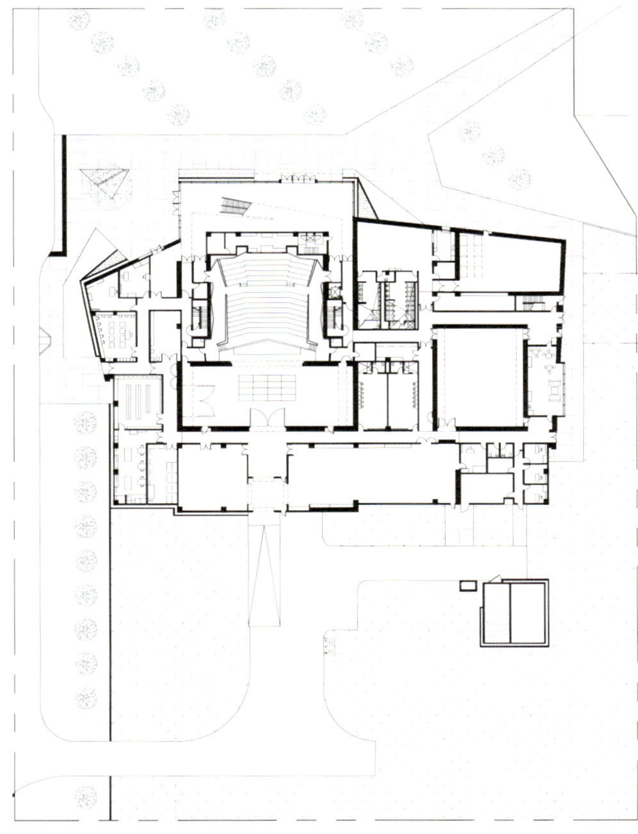

Facades are fractured with prismatic planes in alternating shades of terra-cotta red, gray and, blue. The lobby is exposed to an outdoor plaza through a high wall of glass on the north elevation, extending a sense of the theatrical, while an elongated balcony within the lobby acts like a free-floating proscenium. A red square rises more than five stories to signal the presence of the theater well beyond the confines of the college, and can be seen as far away as Jeffrey Road to the west and the Barranca Parkway to the south.

Facades are fractured with prismatic planes in alternating shades of red, gray, and blue. The roofline rises or dips to reflect the internal workings of the theater.

VINCENT PRICE ART MUSEUM

ARTS CAMPUS

EAST LOS ANGELES COLLEGE   LOS ANGELES 2003 | 2011

As built, the smaller of the three steel-framed structures took the form of a sharply angled trapezium and houses the 40,000-square-foot Vincent Price Art Gallery and student art studios. The L-shaped structure, at 42,000 square feet, has a 350-seat theater, while the flying wedge, the largest structure at 77,000 square feet, contains dance spaces, a large recital hall, and practice studios.

"It's an art quadrangle and we wanted to show students that architecture is also an art form," said Fort-Brescia, who clustered the buildings in a pinwheel rotation around a central green designed for cultural activities and student gatherings while creating a pedestrian quad and the semblance of "campus" within the sprawling circuitry of East Los Angeles. No two elevations are alike, and the sculpted facades are broken up with flaring, irregular openings and floor-to-ceiling windows that follow the same angular geometries as the master plan. Rooflines are beveled and sloped to provide another kind of topography — one that reflects the tectonic uncertainty of the nearby Hacienda Hills — tilted and planar, rising to a full four-story height in places, dropping close to the ground in others. In contrast to the industrial gray exteriors, interior spaces have been color-coded to promote intuitive way-finding and to distinguish the different departments: orange for theater, blue for music, and pink for art.

Three quartzlike buildings are clustered in a pinwheel rotation to create a central green and the semblance of "campus" within the sprawling circuitry of East Los Angeles.

STUDENT CENTER AND FATE BRIDGE

UNIVERSITY OF MIAMI **CORAL GABLES** 2003 | 2013

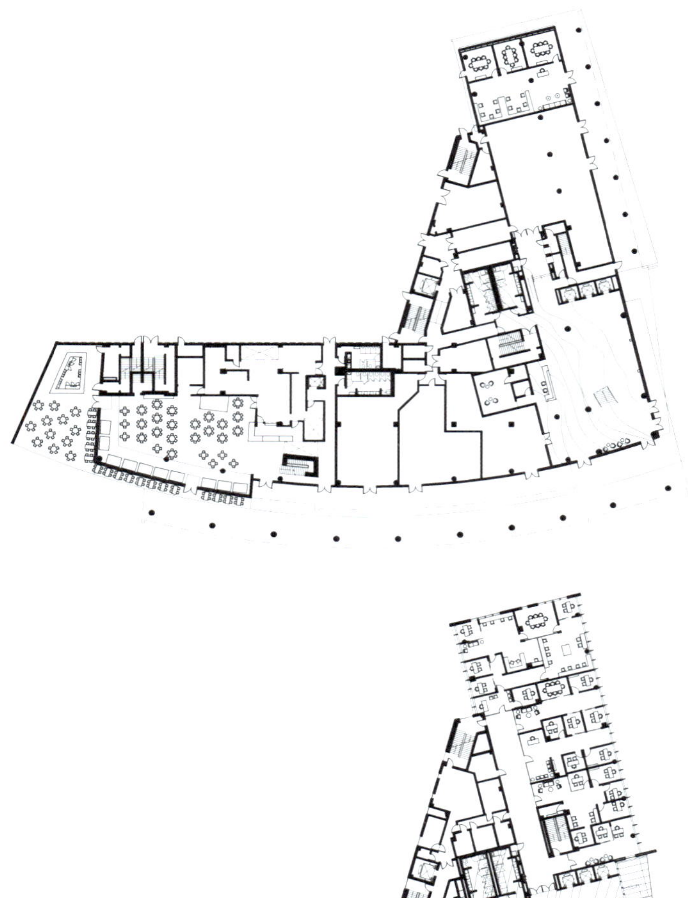

The Donna E. Shalala Student Center can be seen as the first part of Arquitectonica's ongoing master plan to transform the University of Miami's campus into a more cohesive and pedestrian-friendly environment. Its two-story elliptical, facade curves along the banks of Lake Osceola and assumes a central position where numerous cross-campus pathways intersect. The 119,000-square-foot building houses a twenty-four hour study lounge, a campus pub, and several snack bars as well as offices for student organizations, such as the school newspaper and yearbook. There is also a grand ballroom that can seat more than 1,000 people.

A second-floor balcony looks over the lake, and a curving glass curtain wall picks up on the reflective surfaces of the water. The most important feature is the center's prominent position at the nexus of campus activities and how it performs as a conduit for student movement. It serves as a kind of breezeway between the music school, a theater, and recital hall on one end and the Whitten University Center on the other, while wrapping around the back of the Maurice Gusman Concert Hall, effectively blocking the back-of-house loading docks and directing the pedestrian flow north toward the nearby law school and library.

Arquitectonica also designed a new pedestrian bridge to help create a greater sense of connectivity throughout the university grounds. The 210-foot structure connects the southeastern side of the campus (future site of the student housing village, also designed by Arquitectonica) to the student center, cutting short the longer way around via Stanford Drive. The Fate Bridge was finished in 2015 and plays a metaphoric role in campus life with the quotation — from the nineteenth century English poet William Ernest Henley "I am the master of my fate: I am the captain of my soul." — inscribed on the concrete walkway as a motivational message to students walking across the bridge on their way to classes.

An elliptical facade follows the curving banks of Lake Osceola and assumes a central position on campus.

ADARO ENERGY TOWER

JAKARTA 2004 | 2007

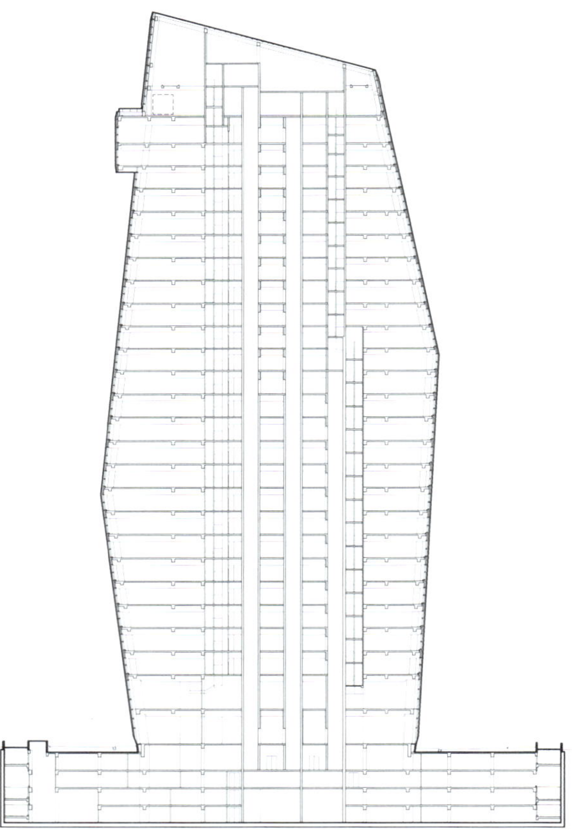

The twenty-six story office tower takes the form of a prismatic slab of steel and energy-efficient glass with no plinth or crown — something like a "chiseled diamond"designed to express the idea of prosperity — rising prominently within the "Golden Triangle" financial district of Jakarta. Early studies reveal a process of reduction, beginning with traditional Asian tropes — a two-hand greeting, Selamat, a broad-finned leaf, or palm frond — whittled down to their essence. The architects shaped the profile to express a singularly modern identity that would stand out from the neighboring corporate towers and urban clutter of the busy Jalan Rasuna district.

The building's sculptural integrity is further enhanced by the finlike ribbing that serves as a brise-soleil to break the equatorial sun while emphasizing direction and surface tension. The wider north and south facades have horizontal projections, while the narrower east and west facades have vertical projections. The main entry is marked by an indentation and a cantilevered canopy of fritted glass that signals arrival. The tautly applied outer skin is disrupted near the top with a two-story-high section that rotates away from the western facade, like a secret panel. It's a simple move, a subversion of the otherwise monolithic slab that retains a vestige of corporate hierarchy, containing as it does the corporate boardroom for the Bank of Central Asia and a private terrace with expansive views over the city.

LANDMARK EAST

HONG KONG 2004 | 2008

Landmark East was built as an anchor project, a "landmark" in the rejuvenation and continuing development of Hong Kong's Kwun Tong district, a former industrial zone and site of the old Kai Tak Airport. Designed in response to the long narrow lot on How Ming Street not far from the waterfront, Arquitectonica broke the mass into two separate towers with distinctive profiles that would signal financial leadership while activating the dense urban site and surrounding streetscape. The minimal shapes and tinted facades make the towers stand out against the clutter of East Kowloon's pale and mottled skyline. They are dynamic forms that appear to tilt and shift from afar, as if changing positions. "The idea was to differentiate the buildings from the static neighborhood," said Fort-Brescia.

The strength of the design is in the pairing. The twin forms are similar, but varied enough to create a subdued dialogue in place of a single statement. While they appear to be symmetrical entities — both tall and slender slabs of glass — that is only an illusion. Tower 2, at forty-three stories, rises three floors higher than Tower 1. Floor-to-ceiling windows give the office interiors unhindered views of Victoria Harbor and beyond to Hong Kong Island. The elegantly engineered fenestration features horizontal brise-soleil fins on the south and vertical fins on the narrow east and west elevations, which further accentuate the sculptural lines of the two towers.

Dynamic forms, cleaved and layered with interlocking slabs, appear to tilt and shift from afar, as if changing positions on their narrow urban lot.

500 BRICKELL

MIAMI 2004 | 2008

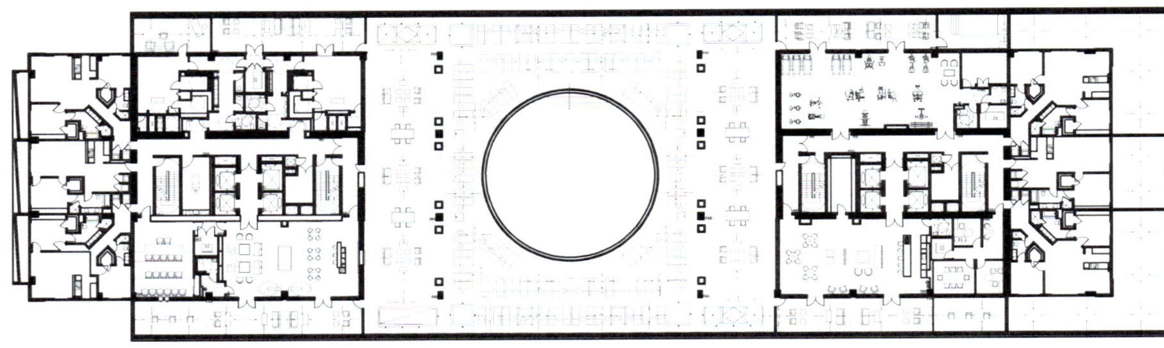

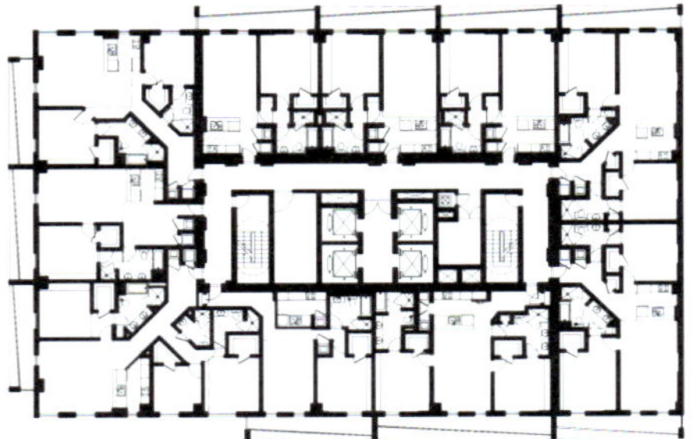

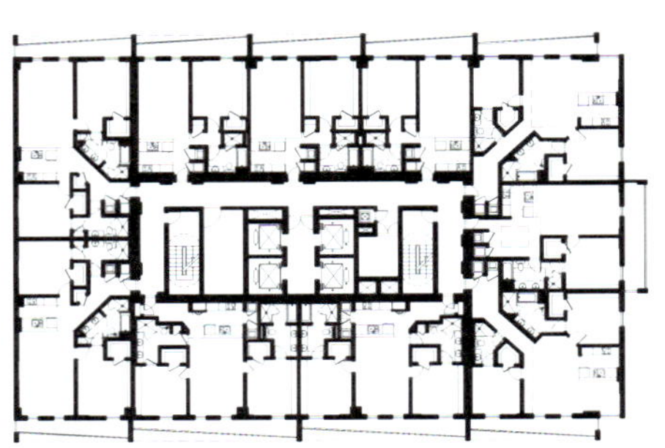

The "sky court" features palm trees and a circular swimming pool that aligns with a 75-foot-diameter oculus overhead. Rainbow-colored perforations turn the parking podium into a monumental work of art.

"It had to be monumental. It had to be big." — Bernardo Fort-Brescia

From the Miami River, 500 Brickell looks like a modern temple to the sky gods: twin towers, north and south, raised on a perforated plinth and connected across the top by a horizontal slab with a 75-foot-diameter oculus, a giant eye, at the very center. "Instead of a single building, we wanted to split it into two towers," said Fort-Brescia. "The oculus frames the Miami sky like a giant zoom lens." Between the forty-two story towers, Arquitectonica placed a "sky court," one of the biggest breezeways in the world, with palm trees and a circular swimming pool, which creates a mysterious alignment with the oculus above.

The vocabulary seems familiar. The sky court is an expanded version of Arquitectonica's earliest experiments — in particular, the Atlantis — complete with cutouts, bright colors, and palm trees at each corner of the courtyard. "We wanted to change the perception of the self-contained, over-air-conditioned residential tower," said Fort-Brescia. "In a tropical city, the dominant space should be an outdoor space."

The luxury high-rise tower was built on a narrow lot between Southeast 5th and Southeast 6th Streets, just off Brickell Avenue, overlooking the river on one side and Biscayne Bay on another. With 633 residential units and 20,500 square feet of retail stores on the ground level, 500 Brickell was the first new residential tower to be built in downtown Miami in fifty years.

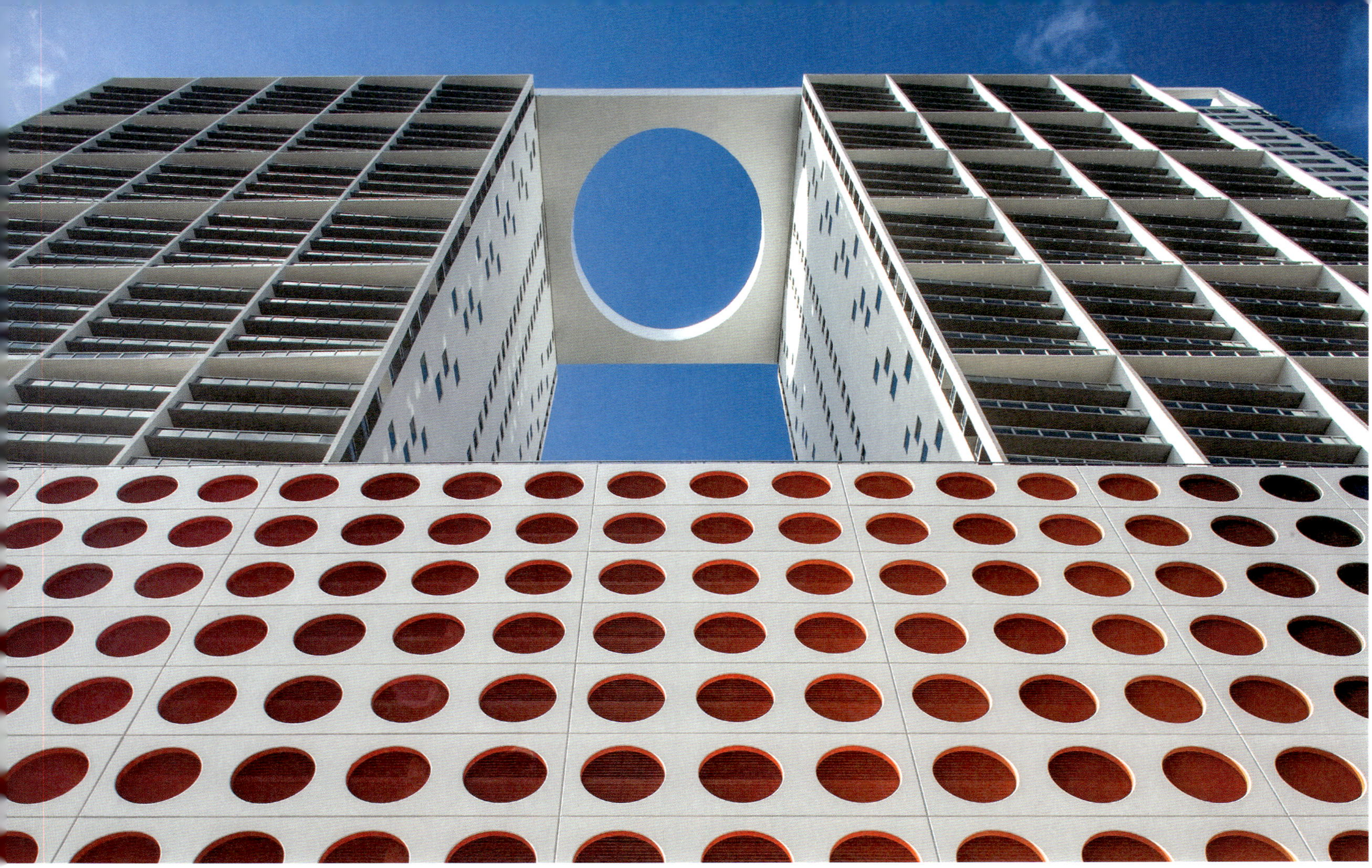

One of the biggest challenges was accommodating the city's stringent parking code. It called for ten levels of parking and the kind of ancillary structure that so often ruins a building with unrelenting walls and ramps. "The multilevel garage is a curse on all these cities that are dependent on the car," said Fort-Brescia. "Somehow, we had to turn it into an artistic expression and we chose to turn it into a monumental Pop art mural."

The "mural" in this case was made up of hundreds of multicolored openings on both the north and south facades that brought natural ventilation into the garage. Each opening was backed by mosquito netting painted in a different shade — something like a Pantone color chart — in stark contrast to the white surfaces of the exterior walls. Arquitectonica had effectively solved the parking problem and turned a negative into an asset. "The holes act like pixels," said Fort-Brescia. "The screening mesh produces streaks of color a block long." The overall effect was painterly, porous, and exuberant — like a rainbow-colored sieve.

MICROSOFT EUROPE HEADQUARTERS

PARIS 2004 | 2009

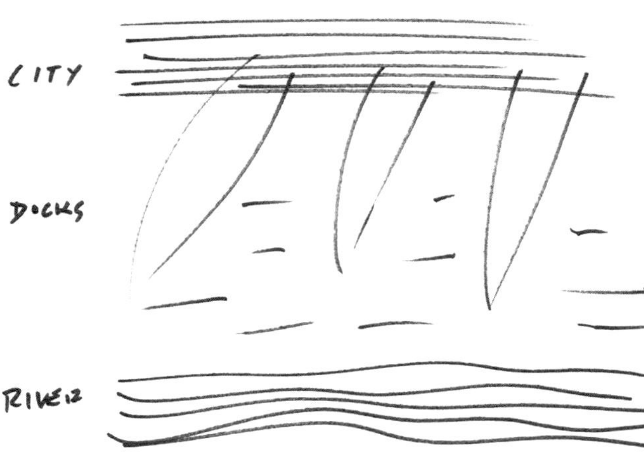

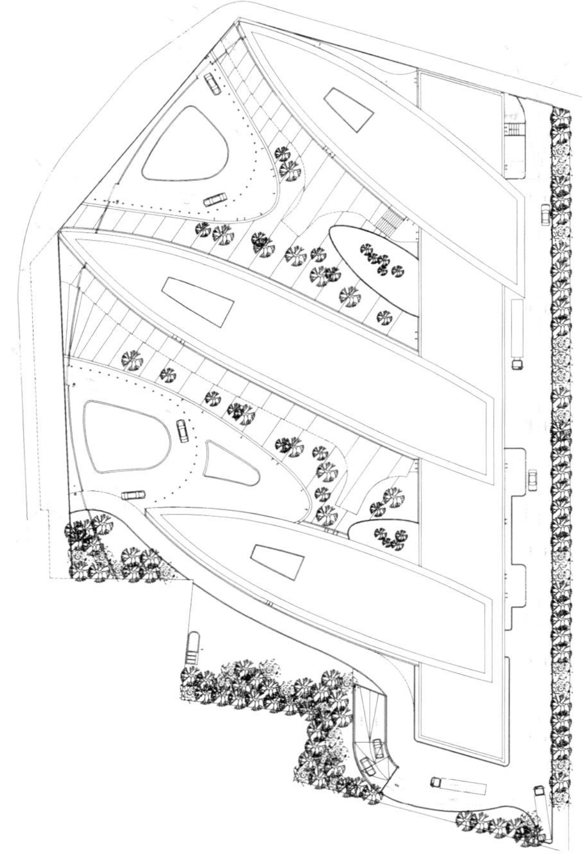

While the building rises high enough above the traffic and overpasses to signal the aspirations of one of the world's largest software companies, the three towers go beyond mere corporate branding. They are equal but separate entities — curving, elliptical, and pointed — each containing 160,000 square feet of office space, each aligned in a slightly different direction, as if ready to float downriver, but permanently moored to their site in Issy-les-Moulineaux, a semi-industrial hinterland that lies two miles south of the Eiffel Tower.

The three ellipsoid wedges appear to open and close as you pass, depending on your point of view or what mode of transportation you happen to be taking: from a car on the highway; from a commuter train on the RER; from a sightseeing boat on the Seine; or as a pedestrian strolling along Quai du Président Roosevelt, from which elevation the three sections loom above the sidewalk like sleekly tapered ocean liners.

While seemingly identical, the three elements are, in fact, slightly different in height, girth, and length, and this sets up a subtly descending hierarchy; the middle wing is eleven stories high; the south wing is ten; and the north wing is nine. They turn the corner from Rue Bara to Quai du Président Roosevelt, splaying and separating. The middle element acts as a pivot point, and is more pronounced than the other two, which appear to hold themselves back from the street.

Curving, elliptical, and pointed like the prow of a ship, each wing is aligned in a different direction, as if ready to disembark downriver, but permanently moored to their site in Issy-les-Moulineaux.

In this turning and splitting, there is something of Vauban's star-shaped fortifications — the projecting bastions and ravelins of medieval warfare — more than Le Corbusier or Mies, and this makes the in-between areas become more "defensible" in a modern urban sense, with an ephemeral lightness that only tempered glass can achieve. In late afternoon light, the wings turn into transparent chrysalides, absorbing light while revealing their inner workings: desks, partition walls, copy machines, and circulation cores. They move, converge, and expand in contrast to the rectangular bar that remains static, grounded and serving as a neutral base for the curving wings. It not only buffers the property from the noise of the adjacent railway line, but provides an extended gallery for circulation between different parts of the complex, and access to a multipurpose hall, a cafeteria, a spa, a VIP lounge, and retail shops, all under a monumental green roof.

The entire complex sits on top of a naturally contoured platform that conceals parking and mechanical services below, while carrying out the High Environmental Quality (HEQ) goal of introducing as much greenery as possible, expanding the immediate parklike setting, and connecting it to the river bank.

Microsoft

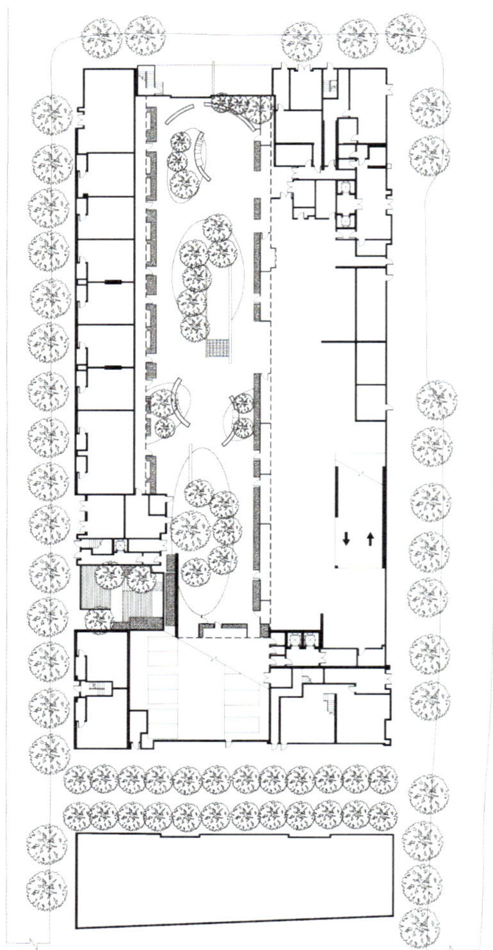

Townhouses and apartment blocks surround an elevated park with community gardens and playgrounds.

Built in the Mission Bay redevelopment district, the three-hundred unit complex is broken down into several parts, varied in height, color, and surface treatment. All of it is perched on a podium that provides parking below and a central 12,000-square-foot courtyard with community gardens, playgrounds, and outdoor movie screens. The ground level, along King Street, features a row of retail spaces that supports a nine-story slab, rising to seventeen stories at the eastern end, vaguely suggestive of something living, with a head and a tail — a horse, a snail. The anthropomorphic allusion is reinforced by alternating grids in red and gray that encase the underlying structure, revealing here or concealing there the white underbody, creating setbacks and a pattern of irregular openings, and turning what would otherwise be a prosaic block of apartment units into something dynamic and seemingly porous. It also helps to mediate the scale of the buildings in harmony with older, low-rise buildings in the immediate neighborhood. On the opposite side of the block, along Berry Street, is a row of low-rise townhouses with direct sidewalk access that back onto the shared community gardens. A grand staircase leads up from Berry Street to the courtyard.

AVALON MISSION BAY

SAN FRANCISCO 2004 | 2009

INFINITY

SAN FRANCISCO 2004 | 2009

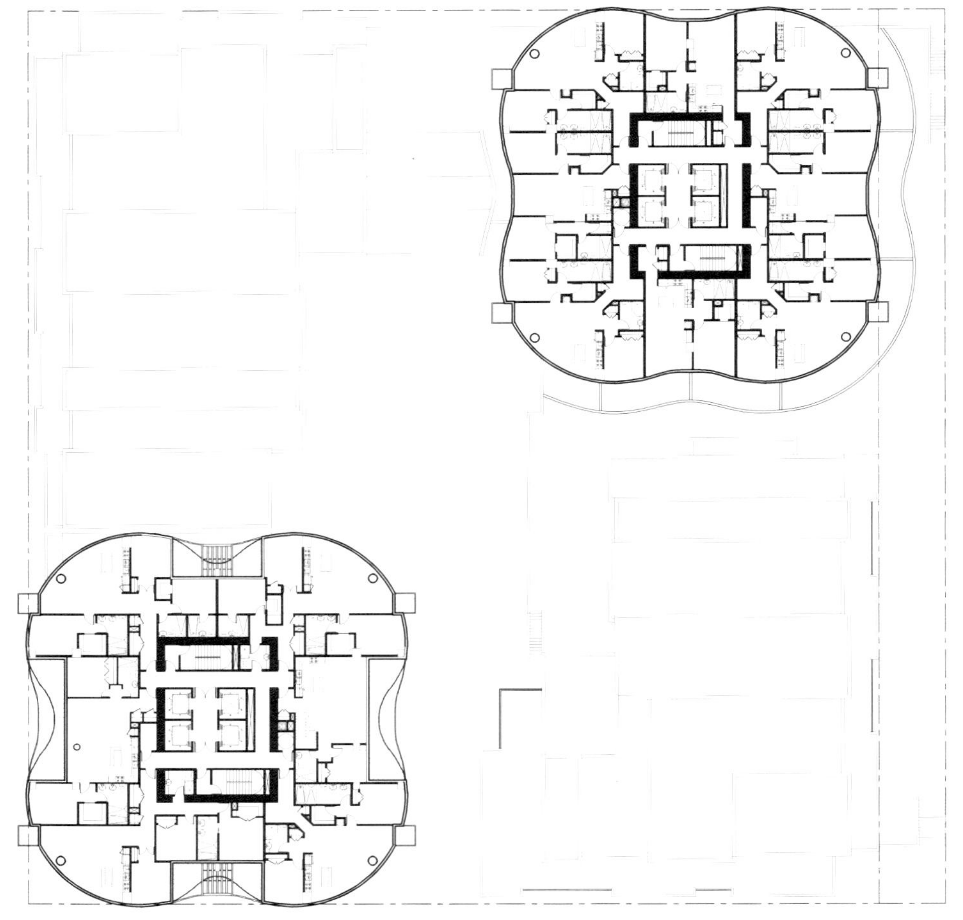

Tishman Speyer, the real estate company, hired Arquitectonica to redesign a residential property in the Rincon Hill area, only a block east of the Embarcadero and the Oakland Bay Bridge. The original footprint of two square towers was designed by a local firm, but Arquitectonica wanted to take another direction. "I thought it was bad feng shui in this city of Asian influence to have so many straight lines and sharp edges," said Fort-Brescia, who decided to move the two buildings closer together, push in the middle, and pull out the corners of each tower, giving them more perimeter. In contrast to the blocky buildings in the neighborhood, the towers are wrapped in curvaceously shaped curtain walls of green-tinted glass. In plan, they resemble four-leaf clovers. Two boxy orthogonal buildings take up the opposing corners — one at eight stories, the other at nine — in counterpoint to the curving facades of the high-rise towers. The lower structures anchor the project and bring the scale down to street level, while plugging into the city grid with variegated facades of cubic, push-pull fenestration.

The 1 million-square-foot project was designed for residential use (with 650 units), and there are 12,180 square feet of retail space on the ground level. The revised configuration also allowed for a central courtyard with public gardens and pedestrian throughways to help foster the feeling of neighborhood in a relatively peripheral urban zone. Loftlike interiors combine living, dining, and kitchen into a single generous space that commands unlimited panoramic views of San Francisco Bay and the downtown skyline through monumental bay windows that bulge from the corners of each building. "It's about the boundary of inside and outside disappearing, as if the owners were hovering in the middle of the sky, with no framed views," said Fort-Brescia.

BABSON COLLEGE
PROSPECT
FOLSOM

Two curvaceous glass towers rise in contrast to the lower, boxlike structures overlooking the Oakland Bay Bridge.

SM ARENA AND CONVENTION CENTER

MANILA 2004 | 2012

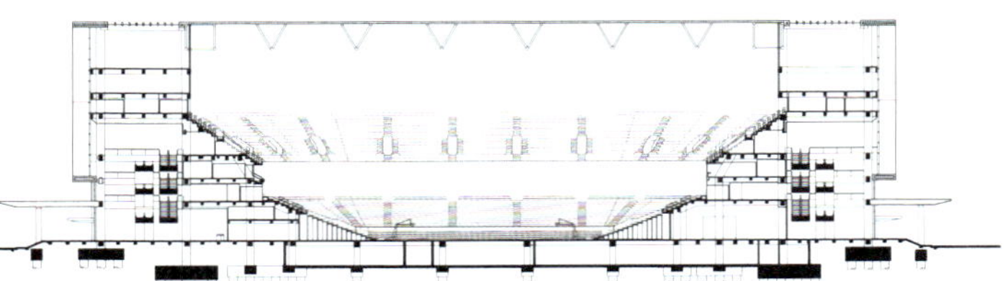

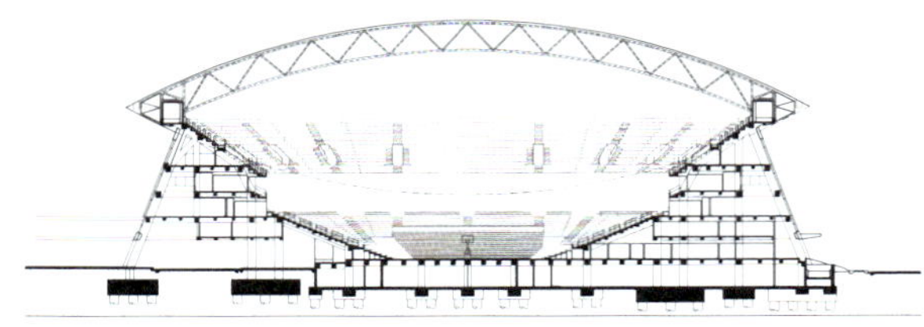

In their groundbreaking design for the Manila Arena, Arquitectonica made the entire structure into a symbol, not only for the surrounding Mall of Asia and the Pasay neighborhood, but for all of Manila, a point that was reinforced when Pope Francis visited the arena in January 2015 and performed holy mass there for more than twenty-thousand worshipers . What started as a vaulted roof over a 500,000-square-foot arena was mirrored by an upward curving vault, to form a pointed ellipse that suggests a lotus petal or a lens. But if there is a single operative metaphor, it is the eye — a giant, all-seeing eye that looks out over the bay. By day, it captures the passing clouds and changes character with different weather conditions. At night, it becomes a luminous beacon that can be seen from miles around.

The biconvex facade is buttressed by a podium of inward leaning trusses, and appears to extrude itself all the way to the back of the 3.9-acre lot where it connects to a 2,000-car parking structure via a pedestrian bridge. This wasn't just a box with a flamboyant lobby stuck on the front. It was an entirely sculpted environment designed for both entertainment and sports events. Inside, a ring of corporate suites — along with a VIP restaurant and a lounge — separates the lower seats from the balcony levels. The arena opened in May 2012 with Lady Gaga's Born this Way tour, and has held concerts by Madonna and the Miss Universe Pageant. It hosts regularly scheduled games of the Philippine Basketball Association and college-level basketball tournaments, as well as large-scale religious gatherings, such as the Pope's mass in 2015.

The Manila Arena is only part of a greater urban plan that includes a convention center and office buildings, as well as future residential towers and hotels, all designed by Arquitectonica and all built on reclaimed land facing Manila Bay.

Buttressed by inward-leaning trusses, the giant elliptical eye overlooks Manila.

INTERNATIONAL FINANCE CENTER

SEOUL 2004 | 2013

The 5-million-square-foot complex is an asymmetrical composition of vertical forms clustered around a parklike plaza in the heart of Seoul. Fort-Brescia and his design team turned to classical landscape painting for inspiration; in particular, rural scenes by the Korean court painters An Gyeon and Yi Gyeong-yun, from the fifteenth and sixteenth centuries, in which tall jagged mountains are drawn in shallow relief and rise through veils of mist. Here, the "mountains" became modern glass-and-steel towers that range in height from twenty-nine to fifty-five stories, all carved into distinctively sculptural forms, with multiple facets like "monumental crystalline outcroppings that have been shaped by the forces of nature, each with its own erosion pattern," according to the architect.

Sloping glass planes catch light and reflect the colors of the sky and passing clouds. At night, these same surfaces are illuminated by a crisscrossing filigree of lighting that creates a glowing landmark on the Seoul skyline. Iceberg-shaped canopies provide distinctive points of entry on the ground level, and lead down to a multilayered complex with luxury shopping, a nine-theater CGV cinema, and thirty-five restaurants. The subterranean mall is animated by an interplay of hovering escalators and staircases that link to a 1,050-foot moving walkway and lead pedestrians to Lines 5 and 9 of the Yeouido subway system. All three levels of the mall are illuminated by a flood of natural light through prismlike skylights above.

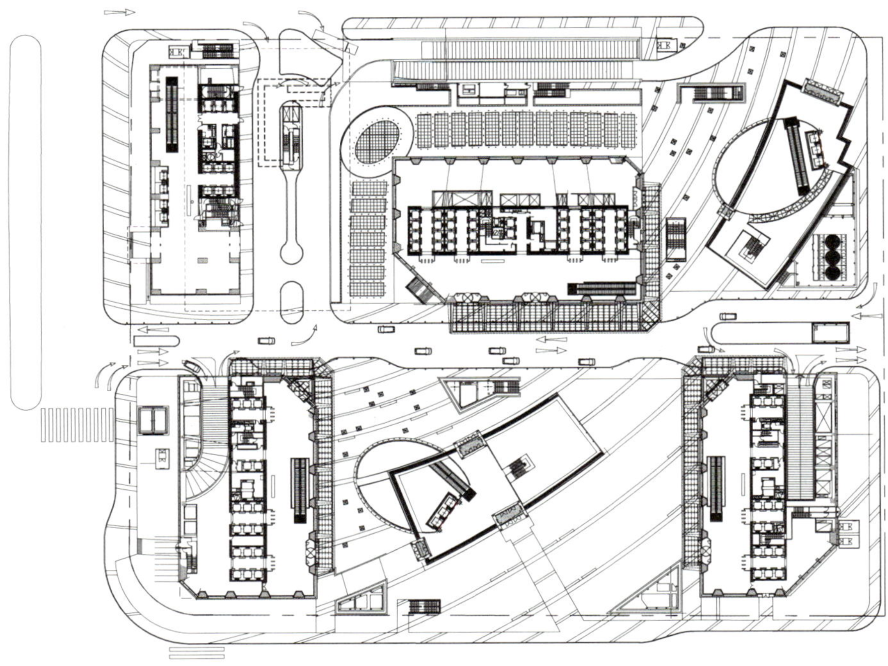

Three beveled glass towers rise into Seoul's skyline as "monumental crystalline outcroppings."

Several layers of luxury shopping descend beneath an iceberg-shaped skylight.

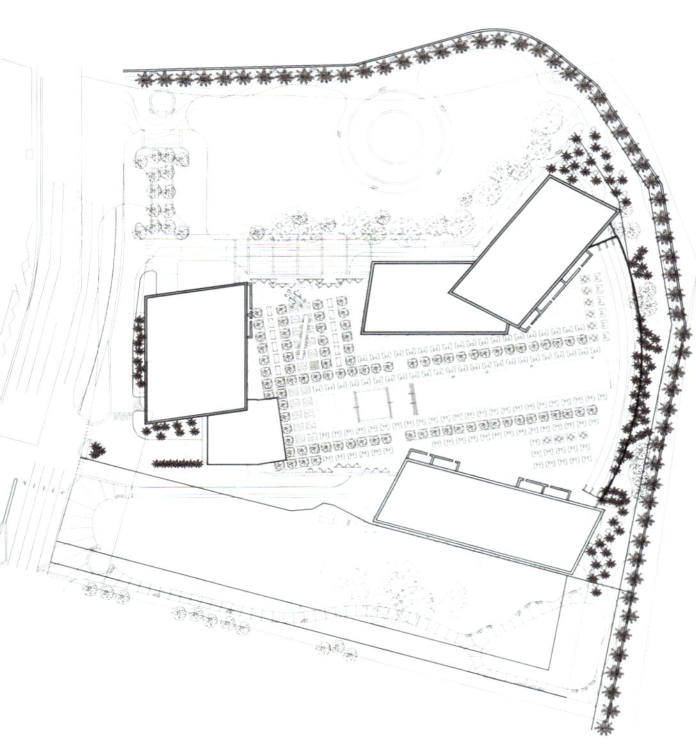

Built on one of Miami's most conspicuous locations, the Icon Brickell complex commands a site on Brickell Point, where the Miami River meets Biscayne Bay, just off the multilane Biscayne Boulevard, near a drawbridge, a sacred site of the Tequesta Native Americans, and across the channel from Brickell Key. Three towers — each a slightly different height, ranging between fifty and fifty-eight stories — are positioned around an elevated plaza that features a combination of formal alignments and casual indulgences. A series of pools, including a 300-foot long lap pool, create an elongated slash of blue (a "new river" according to the architects) while suggesting the alignments and forced perspectives of a seventeenth-century French garden, one that happens to hover twelve stories above street level. Surrounding the pool is a 2 acre sundeck, the largest in the city, with seating areas, an open-air café, and long allées of deciduous trees. It is a vertically giddy image, one that combines urban density with a parklike core. "It symbolizes the new Miami and its quest to have urbanization at its core," said Fort-Brescia.

The three towers turn away from the center, pinwheeling to the west, southeast and north, not only framing the central sky plaza but bringing spatial coherence to the irregularly shaped lot while leaving the eastern end open to unobstructed views of Biscayne Bay. The 4.6-million-square-foot complex includes 1,794 residential condominium units and a boutique hotel that rises above the western end of the plaza with 135 guest rooms and a 28,000-square-foot luxury spa. (Interiors are by French designer Philippe Starck.) The exterior is encased in structural veils of white steel, a birdcage of sun screens. "The idea transforms three large towers into eleven smaller prisms, creating a village of cubes," said Fort-Brescia. "The compositional approach counters the trend to make buildings look taller and more vertical than what they are. Here the design does the opposite. It breaks down the massing." The northeast tower is split into two sections that intersect at an obtuse angle and splay to the north and east, giving maximum panoramic views to the residential units, while serving as backdrop to the Miami Circle, the ancient archeological site that lies just to the north.

ICON BRICKELL
MIAMI 2005 | 2008

A city within a city, the three towers frame a central sky plaza and a 300-foot long lap pool.

ACCOR HEADQUARTERS AND EQWATER

PARIS 2005 | 2010

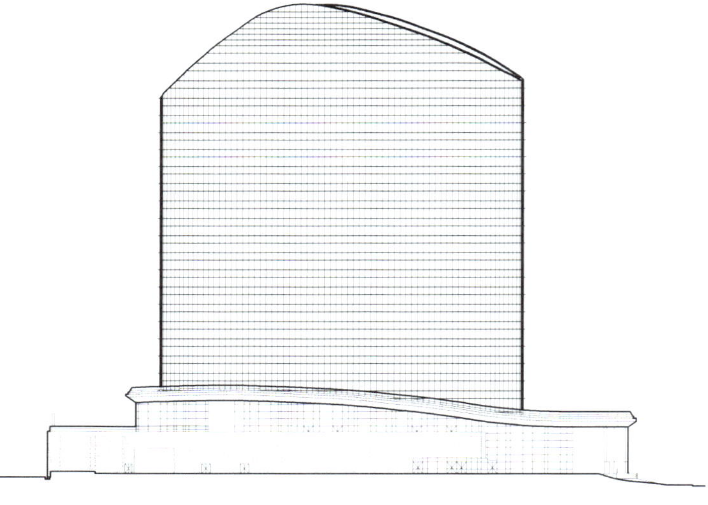

The lozenge-shaped tower serves as a recognizable logo for its corporate tenant; shiny and smooth, and rising twenty-four stories above the streetscape, it signals to motorists passing on the peripheral highway. (The shape of the tapered roof was determined, in part, by the glide path of a nearby helicopter route.) The tower's soft curving forms were intended to make the composition rotate in space, and the glass skin is articulated by a series of recesses that imply such a rotational force. The lower eight-story structure is more about speed and transitional vectoring than it is about historical notions of place or "center." One section slides alongside the other, interlocking but separate, more in the spirit of an off-ramp or train siding than a conventional piece of architecture.

"The design is inspired by a tree," explained Fort-Brescia. "It's a symbol of our green society, abstracted to its essence and wrapped in the modernity of glass and steel." There is no grand entrance or ceremonial lobby. The building can be entered from either end, reflecting the fact that some of the office workers arrive by train, while others come by car.

The tapered roof of the tower was determined, in part, by a helicopter glide path. The lower structure is about speed and transition, more in the spirit of a highway off-ramp than a conventional piece of architecture.

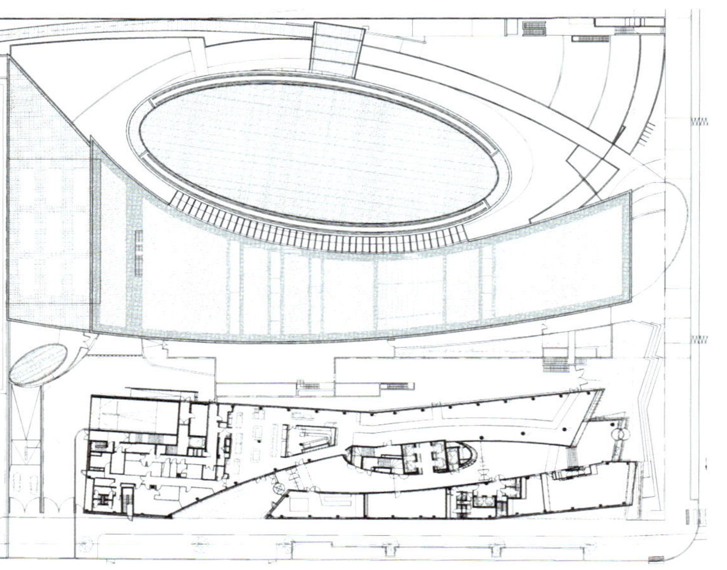

An east-to-west walkway expands into an elongated 4,123-square-foot hall that connects the two structures and creates a kind of public passageway, in the spirit of the glass arcades of nineteenth-century Paris, the "worlds in miniature" that Walter Benjamin memorialized in Passagenwerk. It is a highly activated plaza, containing the central circulation core, seating areas, and public art. The exterior is clad in a textilelike pattern of alternating panels; some are transparent, while others are opaque.

When completed in 2010, the project was awarded the highest environmental quality certification (HQE); it uses 20 percent less energy than the standard office complex. The twenty-four story tower has a photovoltaic roof and cantilevered brise-soleils that block the heat of the sun. A curving canopy structure between the two main buildings is covered with a sod roof and collects rainwater that is used for irrigation purposes throughout the complex.

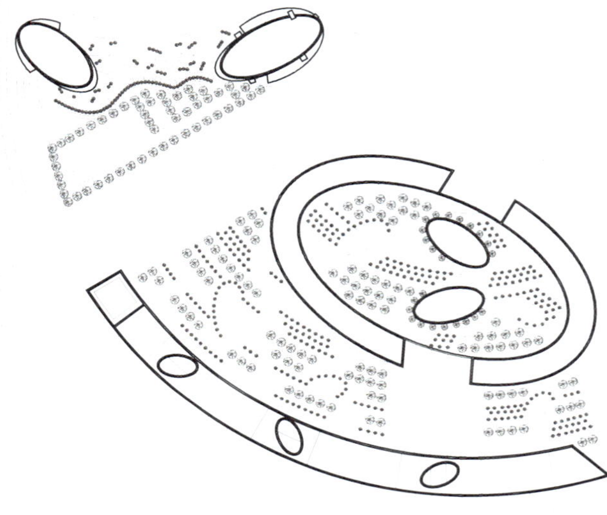

A symbolic gateway for a desert landscape that signals "arrival." The facades are clad in reflective glass interspersed with horizontal slabs of limestone to help absorb heat.

Seen in its entirety, the master plan for the Gate Towers on Al Reem Island in Abu Dhabi is a play of concentric ellipses in which buildings, gardens, and roadways converge in a new kind of urban synergy that could only make sense in the Arabian Gulf. The curving shapes of the buildings help to block desert winds, shield the sun, and create the feeling of a protected inner sanctum, a modern oasis. "I love the desert landscape," said Fort-Brescia. "It's the opposite of Florida. It's another world." Two major access boulevards pass through the middle, leading to a mixed-use development that was built on landfill in the waters of the Gulf. The idea was to create a symbolic portal, a gateway that signaled "arrival."

Rising from the outer periphery, the Gate Towers is made up of three sixty-six-story slabs capped with a horizontal bridge that links the towers at the top, creating one of the most recognizable features on the Abu Dhabi skyline, and offering panoramic views of the Arabian Gulf. Exterior facades are clad in reflective glass interspersed with horizontal slabs of limestone to absorb heat and reduce glare while creating a shimmering mirage effect. The horizontal transom contains sixteen penthouse apartments and a communal clubhouse with swimming pools, a spa, a fitness center, restaurants, and a movie theater. The grounds below are interlaced with tropical gardens, meandering promenades, and irregularly shaped swimming pools.

The semicircular "Arc" building, just to the south of the Gate Towers, is a twenty-three-story residential structure penetrated by large windowlike openings for air flow. Across the boulevard are two slender hi-rises, the "Sun Tower" at sixty-four stories and the "Sky Tower" at seventy-four stories. Both are elliptical in shape to reduce wind resistance. Panels of tinted glass — in white and shades of blue — create a speckled, abstract pattern suggestive of a Persian rug. Some of the interior spaces bulge out beyond the glass facades to break up the exterior surface with vertical bands on the Sky Tower, and horizontal bands on the Sun Tower. Giant bay windows become rooms in the sky. The two mixed-use towers contain offices, hotels, and residential units. The complex provides retail space and parking below, and allows for an expansive garden landscape above. It sits atop a six-story podium that connects to the Gate's podium by a slender pedestrian bridge.

SKY AND SUN TOWERS

ABU DHABI 2005 | 2014

SOLARIA AND ARIA

MILAN 2005 | 2014

"We designed houses in the sky," said Fort-Brescia, explaining how the Solaria and Aria project takes the form of three rectangular solids converging in such a way as to create a triangular void. This central core brings light and ventilation throughout the complex. "The abundance of light is magical," said Fort-Brescia. "Even the walk-in closets have natural light." Each apartment enjoys exposure on three sides, with views of the Duomo di Milano and the Alps. In an early conceptual sketch, Fort-Brescia drew a simplified vertical shaft with random horizontal markings. He called the sketch "tree trunk and branches," and that was the basic idea, expressed in its final form as branchlike balconies, half random in breadth, staggered and syncopated, slightly off-kilter, in such a way as to set up a contrapuntal rhythm up and down the height of the towers. Glass railings are fritted, fading from translucent white at the bottom to clear glass at the top. This gives the towers a smoky, ethereal second skin, almost as if pockets of fog had been suspended between the floors, contrasting dramatically with the black limestone walls and mullions of the main structure. At night, you see only the white railings, lit by recessed lighting, making for a ghostly, hovering illusion.

Projecting, branchlike balconies are staggered in such a way as to set up a contrapuntal rhythm. At night, the railings are illuminated to create a ghostly, hovering effect.

SCHOOL OF INTERNATIONAL PUBLIC AFFAIRS

FLORIDA INTERNATIONAL UNIVERSITY MIAMI 2006 | 2010

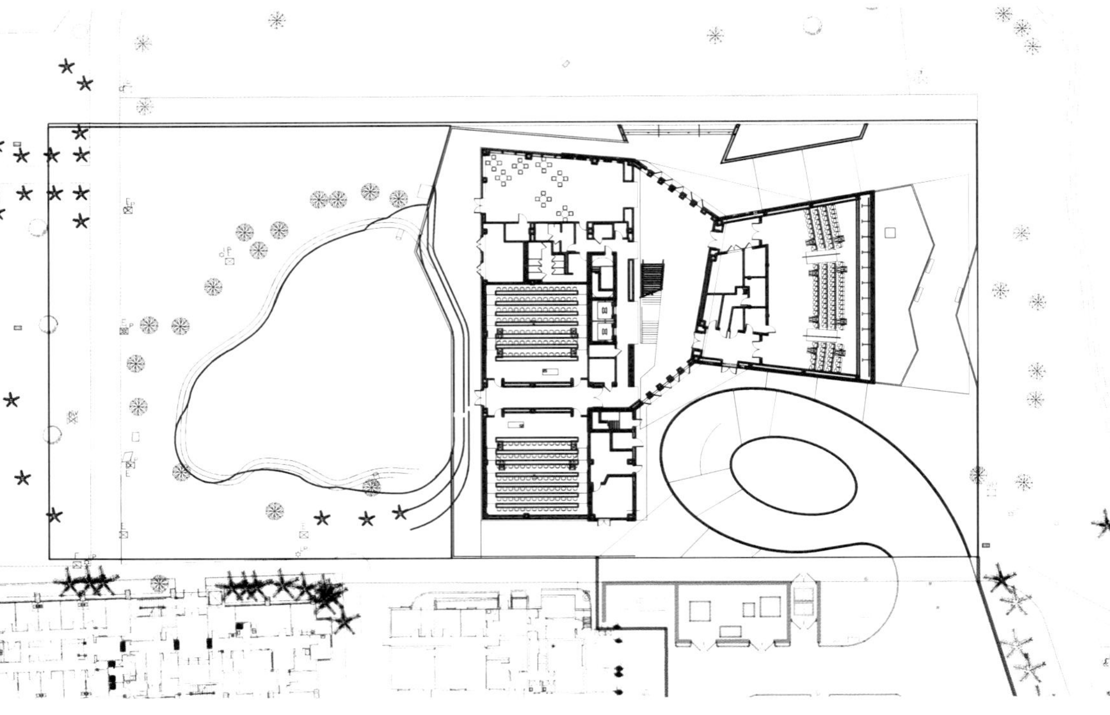

Florida International University's main campus lies just to the south of the Tamiami Trail in the town of Sweetwater and to the east of the Everglades National Park, a vast wilderness of wetlands that stretches 69 miles to the west. The majority of the buildings on the 570-acre campus are made up of a hastily built assortment of boxy buildings in tones of gray and buff stucco, laid out, hither and thither, within a web of interweaving roadways and parking lots, without much in the way of vision or master plan. For the School of International and Public Affairs, Arquitectonica's challenge was how to address such a flood-prone and largely nondescript landscape. The true legacy of the site is the watery Everglades themselves, of which the campus was once a part, and will no doubt return.

The operative trope was of a sixteenth-century Spanish galleon, abstracted and reduced to its most minimal components while making the earliest reference to international affairs that the architects could imagine. Instead of a crusty wooden hull, however, the 56,000-square-foot structure is more like a phantom ship — made from pale, smoothly cast concrete — set adrift on the soggy Sweetwater plain. The nautical theme is further enhanced by two man-made lakes that straddle the building.

The bulky mass of the "forecastle" rises off the ground at an angle, like the prow of the mythical galleon, crimped at the waist. One end of the building contains classrooms and faculty offices; the other features a large auditorium and lecture hall with a shared lobby in between. There is a pedestrian entrance from the campus green, while the automobile drop-off area lies to the west.

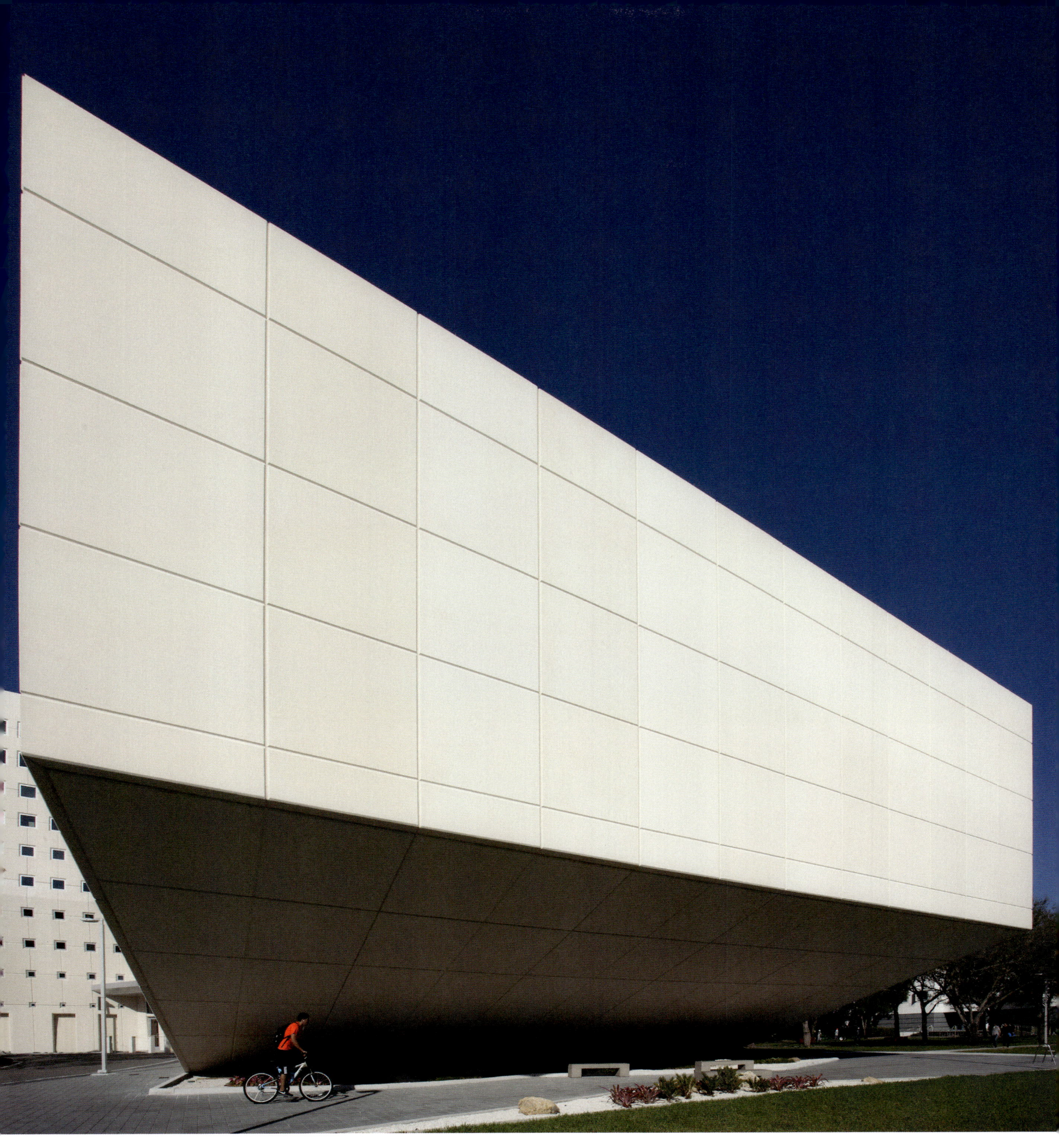

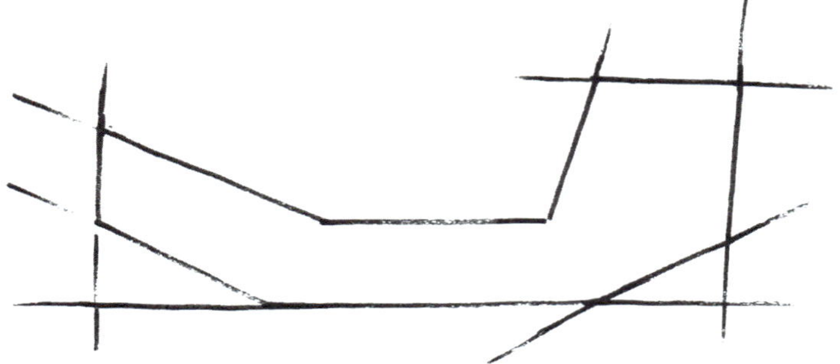

"The building calls attention to itself," said Fort-Brescia. "The angles on the outside tell you the story of what happens on the inside." While the lower, prowlike section is smoothly opaque and almost devoid of windows, the higher, eleven-story office block is punctured with a gridlike pattern of square openings, not unlike the cube-shaped cenotaph at Aldo Rossi's San Cataldo Cemetery in Modena, Italy (1971). There are smaller openings for the classrooms and language labs and larger openings for faculty offices. The variation in window size creates a kind of false perspective that makes the building appear to taper toward the bottom. Instead of a solid mass, the punched-out openings create the illusion of an exterior skin that has been stretched tautly over an armature. The resulting volumes appear more receptive to human interaction, light, and changing weather patterns. "Function and idea are all one," said Fort-Brescia.

A phantom ship made from pale, smoothly cast concrete is set adrift on the Sweetwater plain. Square, punched-out openings create the illusion of an exterior skin stretched tautly over an underlying armature.

FRANKLIN COUNTY COURTHOUSE

COLUMBUS, OHIO 2006 | 2011

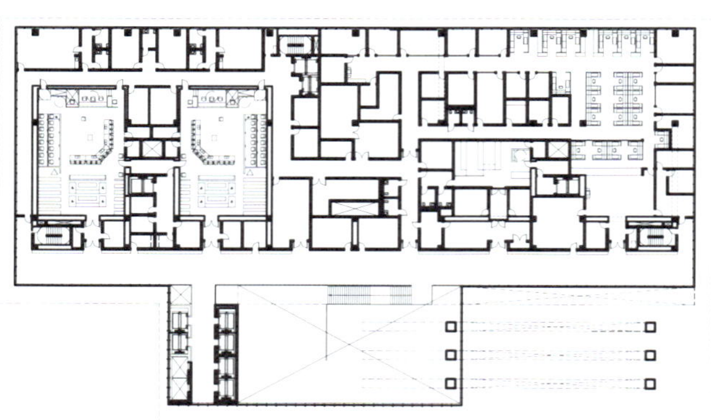

A cubic mass picks up on the city grid, harmonizes with the existing urban context, and reinterprets the traditional role of public courthouse in a way that signals civic accountability. The pronounced horizontal strata are emphasized by a painterly pattern of sun-shading screens that filter summer light, while the elevator core stands out as the dominant vertical element, counterpoint to the largely horizontal composition.

Altogether, the architecture creates a landmark presence on Mound Street. It is a contemporary symbol of justice that is at once transparent and open, yet grounded by a precast framework that brackets the glass walls and turns the corner onto High Street. A limestone arcade reaches out as a welcoming kind of proscenium, leading the public into a spacious lobby that features a green roof. Upper floors house twenty trial courtrooms, ten magistrate courtrooms, judges' chambers, and settlement suites. Public waiting areas and courtrooms are oriented east to west, and are flooded with natural light through the seven-story glass curtain wall. The building is set back with a broad forecourt stepped for seating and landscaped as a public plaza, with a recessed lawn and monumental stone benches. A rain garden on the corner of Mound and Front Streets harvests rainwater for irrigation purposes. The complex includes a new tunnel that connects the courthouse to the existing government center and jail on the opposite side of Mound Street.

ENTER HERE
ENTER HERE

345
Franklin
County
Common
Pleas
Courthouse
345

03
04
02

The horizontal strata are emphasized on the exterior by sun-shading screens that filter summer light. The elevator core serves as the dominant vertical element, while circulation to courtrooms is naturally illuminated through the all-glass facade.

AGRICULTURAL BANK OF CHINA AND CHINA CONSTRUCTION BANK

SHANGHAI 2006 | 2013

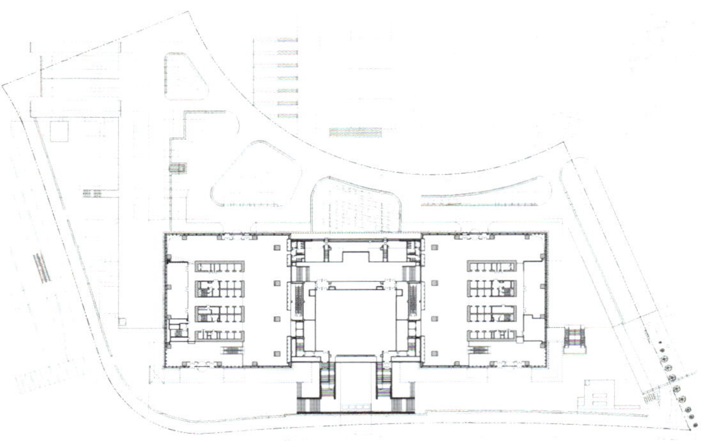

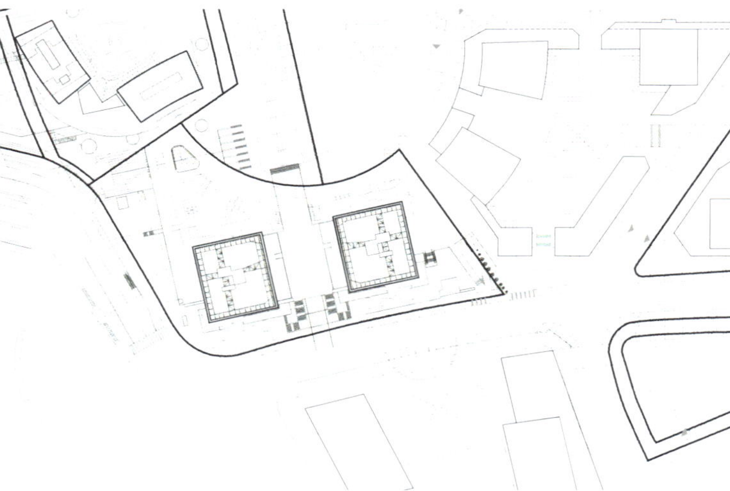

Two symmetrical, forty-nine-story towers rise between Yincheng Road and the east bank of the Huangpu River, assuming a key position in Shanghai's rapidly expanding skyline. Built on the former site of the two-hundred-year-old Shanghai Shipyards, Arquitectonica picked up on the lines of the river and the original slipway that slopes through the property and into the river. The slipway has been preserved and restored as the central axis of a new urban park, while the shipyards themselves were moved to a new location.

As with most of Arquitectonica's Asian projects, there is a single signature move, but one that is subtly restrained, conveying the principal message of "gateway" (*wang guan* in Chinese) while offering a new architectural trope for this booming city of twenty five million, one that looks to the future while acknowledging the past. The figure-ground relationship is reversed and, in this case, the elliptical space between the two towers becomes the "figure," while the solid buildings become, in effect, the "ground." "The void rules over the solid as the defining form," explained Fort-Brescia. In a sense, the space between the forty-nine-story towers takes the form of the missing hull of the former shipyard, and the maritime metaphor is extended to two smaller glass buildings that house the Mandarin Oriental hotel, spa, and residences."Their transparency and undulating forms recall the wake generated by a passing ship," suggested the architect. At the same time, the slender towers might be seen as bamboo stalks bending in the wind, and the greenish tint of the glass, as well as the irregularly alternating brise-soleil fins, reinforce this illusion as they create a naturalistic rhythm to the facades, not unlike the scaffolding that is still used on many Asian construction sites. As an antidote to Shanghai's urban sprawl, the towers express autonomy within a spacious, parklike setting that leads down a popular promenade that straddles the banks of the river.

The elliptical void between two forty-nine-story towers rules over the solid as a defining form.

REGALIA

MIAMI 2006 | 2015

"We were seeking to make a soft building with sensual layers," said Fort-Brescia of Regalia, the forty-three-story oceanfront condominium tower that rises into the Miami skyline like a slender stalk, airy and drifting with rippling surface effects that not only echo the ocean waves and patterns of beach sand, but complement the softly contoured cloud clusters that drift overhead.

The Regalia commands its site on the northern-most edge of Sunny Isles while straddling the border with Golden Beach, an affluent beachfront community of low-lying residential properties. There is enough open space around the perimeter of the tower to make it stand apart and it is a freestanding sculptural object in contrast to the clutter of architectural statements directly to the south. Each unit takes up an entire floor, with wide, 2,000 square-foot wraparound balconies that provide shade and cross-ventilation for the interior. Glass balustrades allow for uninterrupted water views and set up the rippling effect that gives the building its unique outer shell. Shared amenities on the lower levels include an infinity pool set among a lush tropical landscape, beachfront cabanas, a library, a media room, and a lounge. The double-height lobby features a blown-glass sculpture by Dale Chihuly and a waterfall.

A stack of fluctuating balconies echoes the patterns of ocean waves and softly contoured clouds that pass overhead.

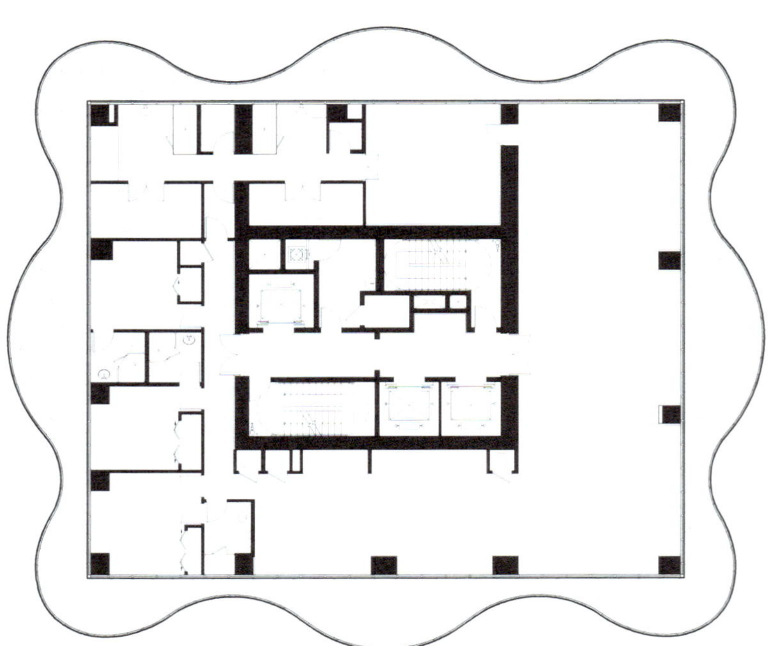

BANCO REAL SANTANDER | JK IGUATEMI

SÃO PAOLO 2007 | 2012

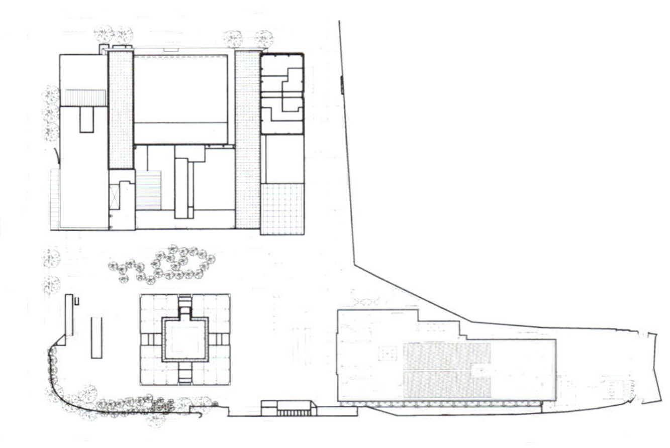

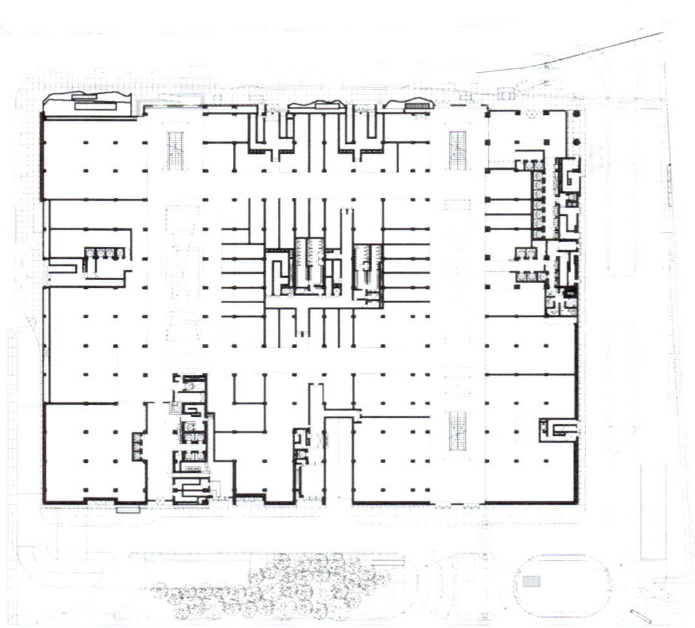

Arquitectonica's first major project in Brazil was a series of mixed-use buildings for the WTorre Plaza in São Paulo's burgeoning financial district. The 4 million-square-foot complex was built along the banks of the Pinheiros River, adjacent to the six-lane Avenida das Nações Unidas and a municipal train line. It includes bank headquarters, three office towers, and a major retail-shopping complex. One of the towers was built around the skeletal core of a preexisting structure, the former headquarters of Eletropaulo, a Brazilian power company. Arquitectonica realized that it would be cheaper to recycle and repurpose the old, twenty-eight-story structure than tear it down and start from scratch, thereby cutting the cost of all-new construction, reducing the carbon footprint, and saving as much as twenty-four months in work time.

The original structure —squat, and of rather undistinguished design — was transformed with a few simple moves. Floor plates were extended to the perimeter for additional square footage. Center bays were removed to create vertical cutouts on all four sides. This streamlined the profile and created the illusion of a cluster of four sleek towers. Each corner has a slightly different angle around its roofline in a sloping pinwheel pattern, further accentuating the multitower illusion, and creating the protective perimeter for a rooftop helipad. The recycled tower became the headquarters for Banco Real Santander, with more than 947,000 square feet of space over twenty-eight floors. Two additional office towers — one at twenty-two stories, the other at nineteen stories — were built to match the sleek profile and surface treatment of the first tower with vertical aluminum ribbing and striations of gray-tinted glass.

An older, twenty-eight-story structure was repurposed and given a sleek glass veneer, saving on material and construction time.

The JK Iguatemi shopping mall lies at the bottom of the taller tower as a kind of extended base, with glistening white crystallite bays that project toward a public plaza. "We wanted the tower to be floating off the podium," said Fort-Brescia. "The building rejects the gravitational effect." The interior of the 712,387-square-foot mall is an elegantly restrained study of white ceramic cladding and transparent glass. More than two-hundred luxury shops and restaurants are positioned around a four-story atrium, with clifflike balconies and cantilevered shading systems. Together, the towers and shopping mall create a sense of unity in an otherwise discordant part of São Paulo's financial district.

Two hundred luxury shops and restaurants are positioned around a soaring, four-story atrium with hovering, clifflike balconies and cantilevered shading systems.

freddo
GOYARD
GOYARD
Ermenegildo Zegna

BRICKELL CITY CENTRE

MIAMI 2008 | 2016

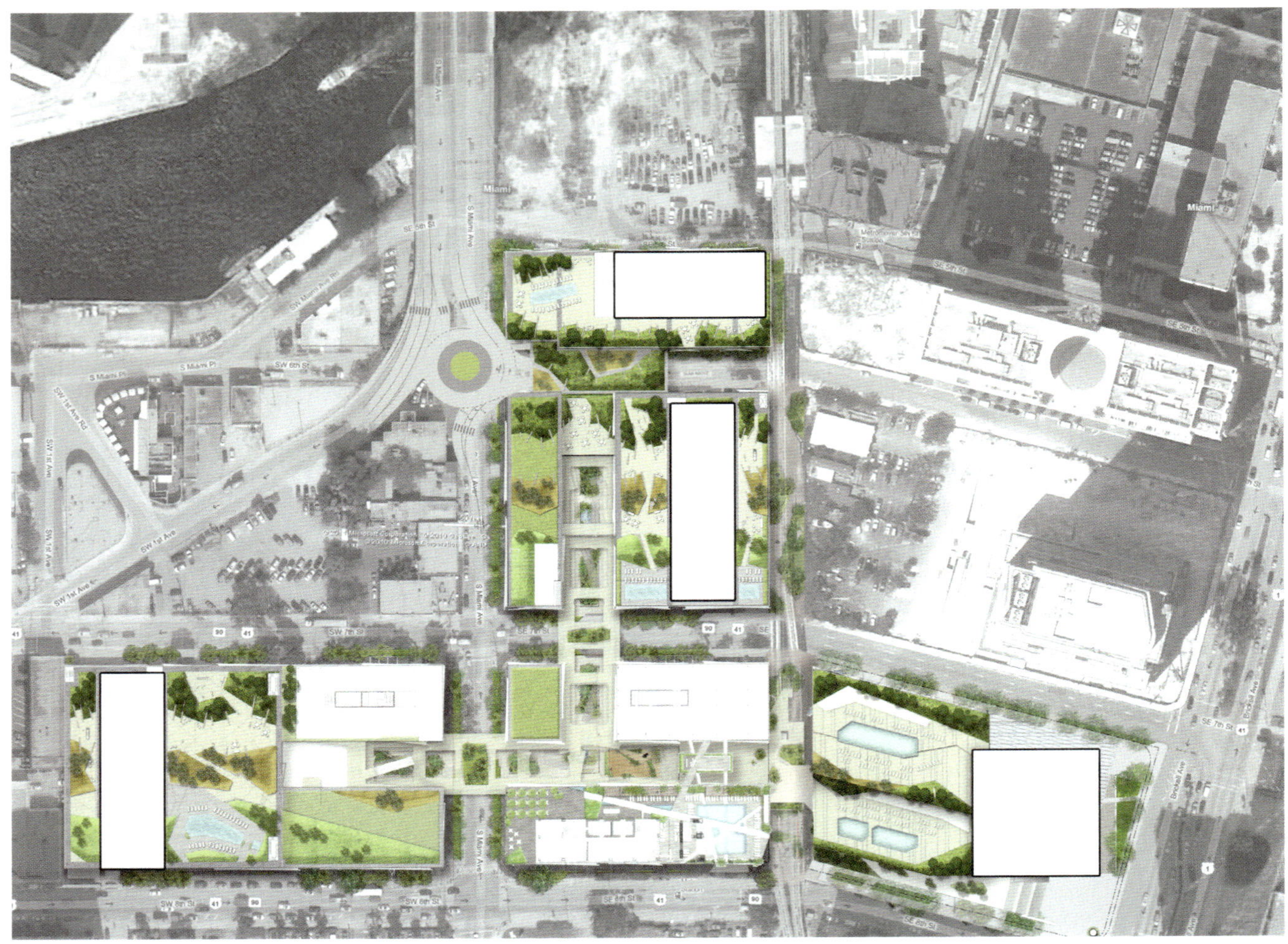

The most ambitious of all of Arquitectonica's downtown Miami projects is Brickell City Centre (BCC), a 5-million-square-foot complex that spans more than five city blocks and includes three levels of shops, office towers, and a 352-suite hotel. The master plan includes a new transit station for the Eighth Street Metromover and a vast underground parking garage, all jumbled together with a sense of what Dutch urbanists call "messy vitality," or what architect Fort-Brescia calls a "true jigsaw puzzle," one that weaves in and around the existing streetscape, and merges with the city itself. "We didn't want to disrupt the urban fabric so we chose to keep the blocks and the existing streets in place," he said. (The concept was inspired, in part, by the nineteenth-century glass-covered arcades of Paris and Milan.)

There are balconies and trestle bridges that offer views over SE 6th Street, and out toward the Miami River. Curious pedestrians wander in and out. People shop, and meet friends.

Blocky volumes hover and bulge from the Euclidean grid. In some cases they appear to shift and slide to one side like shoji screens, leaving openings, glimpses of interior spaces, while corner transparencies reveal the merchandise on sale. The architecture does not shout for attention, but the lighting ranges from moody shadow to dramatic chiaroscuro to bright sunlight. There is a cinematic vision at play — something out of Fritz Lang's *Metropolis* — with crossovers, suspended walkways, metallic canyons, skewed lines of sight, and cascading escalators, a feeling of density, complexity, and porosity. This is exactly what saves it from being yet another soulless shopping mall. "We are not seeking a shape," said Fort-Brescia. "We are seeking an experience that is an extension of the city."

The Climate Ribbon, a "corridor for wind", flows above and between the buildings with ten parallel fins made from PTFE synthetic resin that channel breezes into the open-air mall and captures rain water.

PANDORA
PANDORA

Walls are made up of narrow horizontal panels — aluminum coated with metallic automobile paint — like clapboard siding but slightly skewed, and this gives them a rippled, reptilian texture, absorbing light in some places, deflecting it in others. The asymmetry and apparent randomness of the cladding were intentional as it served to break up the bulky regularity of the structures. The tropical colors of Arquitectonica's early work have given way to a more restrained palette, with shades of neutral gray, ranging from dull pewter to mercury, slate, and silver.

Unlike most malls, the shops face the street, further punctuating the perimeter, as well as inward to naturally cooled, lushly landscaped esplanades. Walkways are staggered back so that you can look down and see the many levels. (Loading docks for delivery trucks are concealed within the interior of the complex.)

The spatial glue that helps to pull BCC's different parts together is the patented "Climate Ribbon" that flows above and between the buildings like a pale river, with ten parallel fins sculpted from curvaceous fiberglass, turning and dipping in places, catching and filtering the light and giving the elevated plazas a kind of underwater luminosity. The blades of the Climate Ribbon cover an area of more than 100,000 square feet as they zig and zag, leaping across South Miami Avenue, and continuing on the opposite side. They shade and shepherd the trade winds that blow off Biscayne Bay, channeling breezes throughout the length of the mall so that no centralized air conditioning is needed.

"I envisioned our canopy as a corridor for the wind," explained Hugh Dutton, the French artist-engineer who developed the $30-million ribbon in collaboration with Arquitectonica. The ribbon also collects rainwater that is filtered and recycled to irrigate the planted terraces.

An upper-level landscaping plan by ArquitectonicaGEO features native grasses and wildflowers to create a feeling of elevated meadows in and around the different towers.

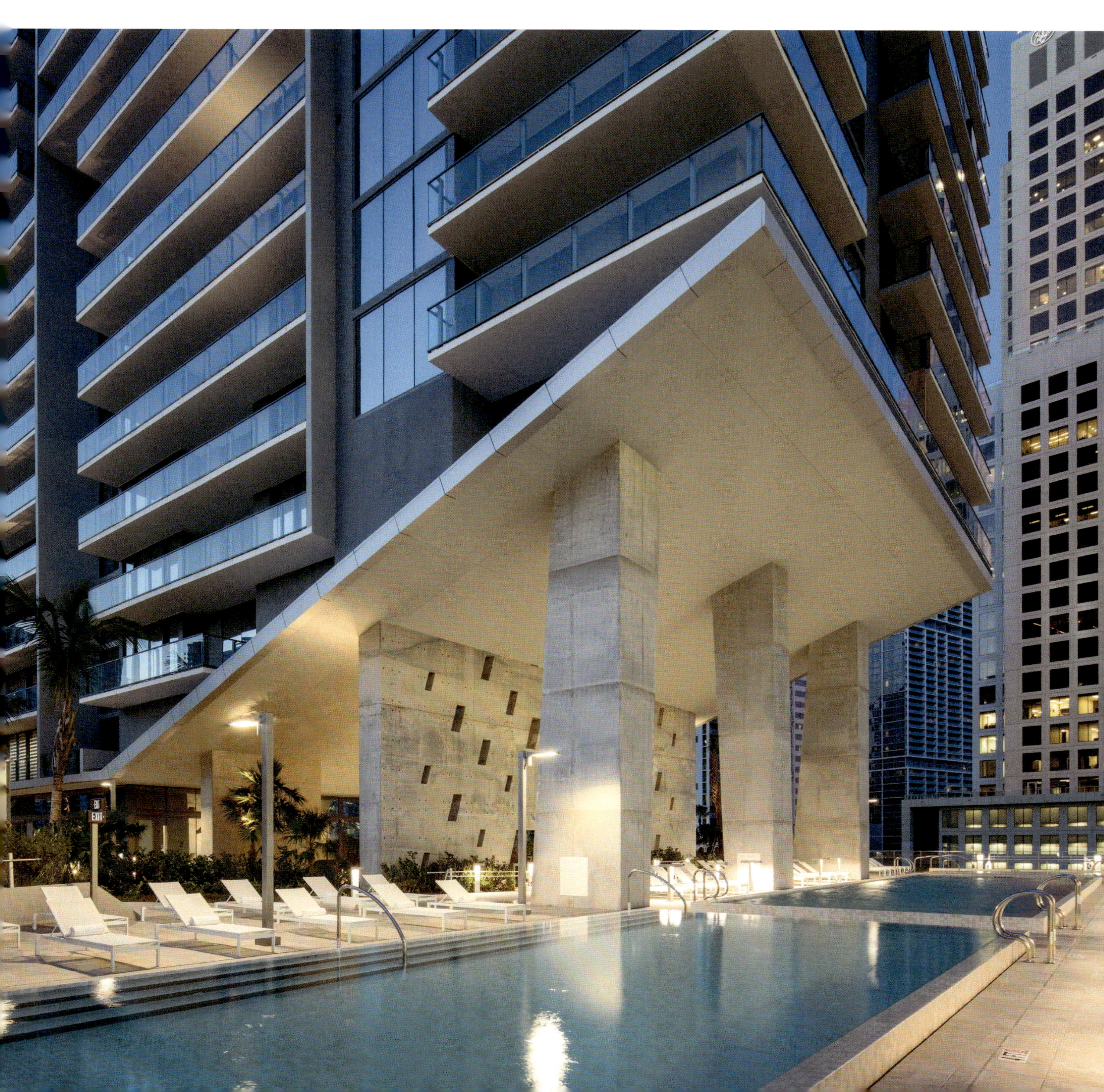
EXIT

Upper decks are landscaped with natural grasses and wildflowers to create the feeling of elevated meadows in and around the towers.

COLE HAAN
BOSS
BOSS
ONE WAY

SAN ISIDRO FINANCIAL DISTRICT

LIMA 2009 | 2011

Arquitectonica began to develop a master plan for this new "campus of commerce" in 2008. It will eventually feature a park and seven glass towers, including the Westin Lima Hotel at thirty stories, and the Banco GNB (also known as Torre Begonias) at twenty-six stories. They face each other across Calle Las Begonias, a central location beside a major new subway station and just off a cloverleaf interchange, where two of the city's most important expressways — Avenida Paseo de la República and Avenida Javier Prado Este — intersect.

"We began with a square footprint then started to give them different edge conditions," said Fort-Brescia, who looked to ancient Incan textiles for inspiration. Ancient weavings from Nazca have both zigzag and serpentine patterns. All are strikingly geometric and pure, seemingly modern, with abstract forms to represent natural elements used in Incan culture, such as sun, mountain, fire, sky, lightning, river, snake, and bird. "I felt that this was an appropriate source to draw from," said Fort-Brescia.

The towers set up an architectural dialogue — similar in form, but with slight deviations from a common theme. One tower is planar and hard-edged. The other is sensuous and swelling. The Westin features angular "fractures" down each of its four corners that create a prismatic effect, a recessed triangulation that appears to open and close as it descends from the roof. "The glass used in the corners captures light that seems to cascade all the way to the main lobby," explained Fort-Brescia. "I wanted it to look as if it had been made by the blowing wind."

In contrast, the walls of the Banco GNB tower bulge slightly, stretch upward, and flare at both top and bottom. Elliptical facades of reflective glass appear to pull apart at the edges, as if the corners were delaminating themselves from the rest of the structure, bowing out, and leaving long, tapering gaps. "The towers are intimately related," said Fort-Brescia. "They create a sisterhood of forms, and the vertical lines on their exteriors — the mullions — are like hand stitching in the Inca textiles."

For a new "campus of commerce" on the outskirts of Lima, one tower features angular fractures, while another has elliptical facades that appear to pull apart at the edges, as if the corners were delaminating themselves from the rest of the structure.

A lower, four-story section branches from the base of the Westin and provides a ceremonial entry to the hotel's main lobby. Angular, glass-encased wedges and a broad, cantilevered balcony project toward the street. From its upper floors, the hotel offers panoramic views of the Pacific Ocean and the surrounding peaks of the Andes mountain range. At night, the corner shafts of both buildings are illuminated with ribbon lighting and become vertical beacons shining across the new city center.

Lima is prone to earthquake activity so the towers were structured to withstand significant seismic shock. Central cores were made from structural steel plates that extend out and connect to a single row of perimeter columns. This provides maximum resistance to tectonic shifts while also providing an open layout for more flexibility for interior planning. The curtain walls of both towers have 30 percent reflectivity, which helps to save on air conditioning costs. Both are oriented to take full advantage of natural light, while all their artificial lighting is sensor-activated. Water usage has been reduced to a minimum, with low-flow bathrooms and the use of recycled gray water for irrigation purposes. Lima has a desertlike climate, with little annual rainfall, so all terraces and outdoor areas have been planted with native species that require little or no watering.

The Westin and Banco GNB towers are the first components of a larger urban plan. "From the beginning we were thinking of the future totality and how all of these different structures were going to work together," said Fort-Brescia. "We wanted to create a kind of Rockefeller Center condition with consistent, sympathetic elements."

MOUNT PARKER RESIDENCES

HONG KONG 2009 | 2015

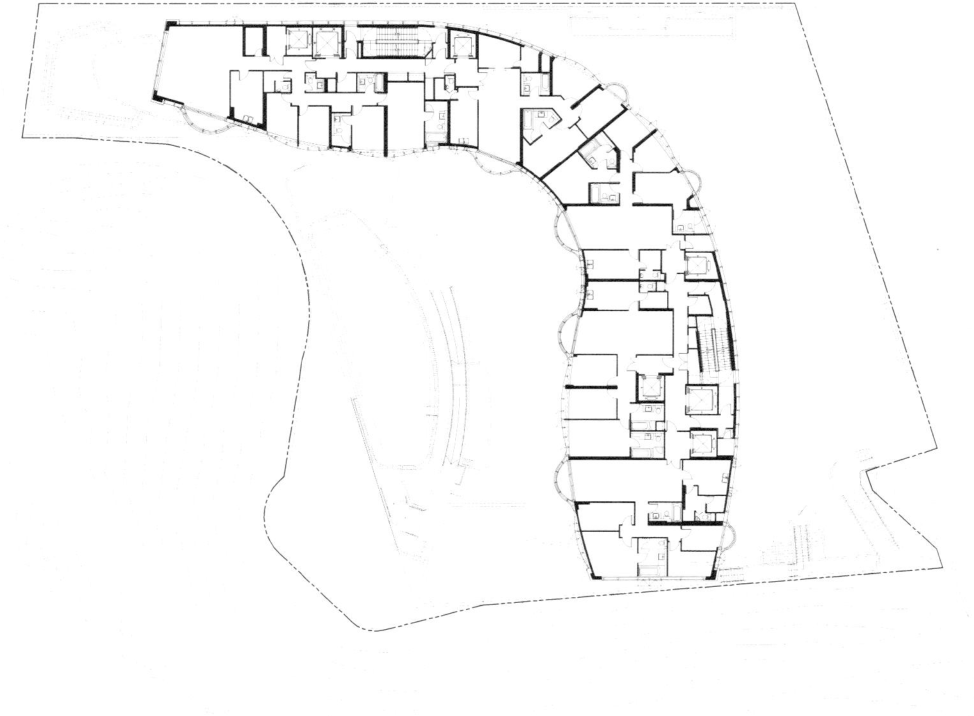

Arquitectonica designed the Mount Parker Residences as counterpoint to a densely developed neighborhood in the Quarry Bay district of eastern Hong Kong Island. The folding, curvilinear shape of the twenty-one-story structure was generated in part by the unusual site: a steeply inclined outcropping, thick with vegetation and surrounded by multilane roadways. "The form is organic rather than geometric," said Fort-Brescia, who once again chose to play off the poetically rich traditions of Chinese landscape painting. "It appears as if it were shaped by nature rather than man." Indeed, the building is a cloudlike object, perched on slender columns as to hover atop the ancient rock formations of Mount Parker.

Glass panels alternate with metallic sheathing. Balconies bulge to create undulating surface rhythms, further accentuating a sense of the organic in contrast to the urban clamor of Quarry Bay and the busy, looping byways of King's Road and Kornhill Road that surround the site like concrete rivers. The boomerang-shaped plan was choreographed to give every apartment cross-ventilation and maximum view lines over Eastern Bay and beyond to Mainland China.

A gently contoured shape was generated by the steeply inclined site. Balconies bulge to create an undulating surface that further accentuates a sense of the organic in contrast to the urban clamor of surrounding roadways.

BEACH HOUSE 8

MIAMI BEACH 2010 | 2017

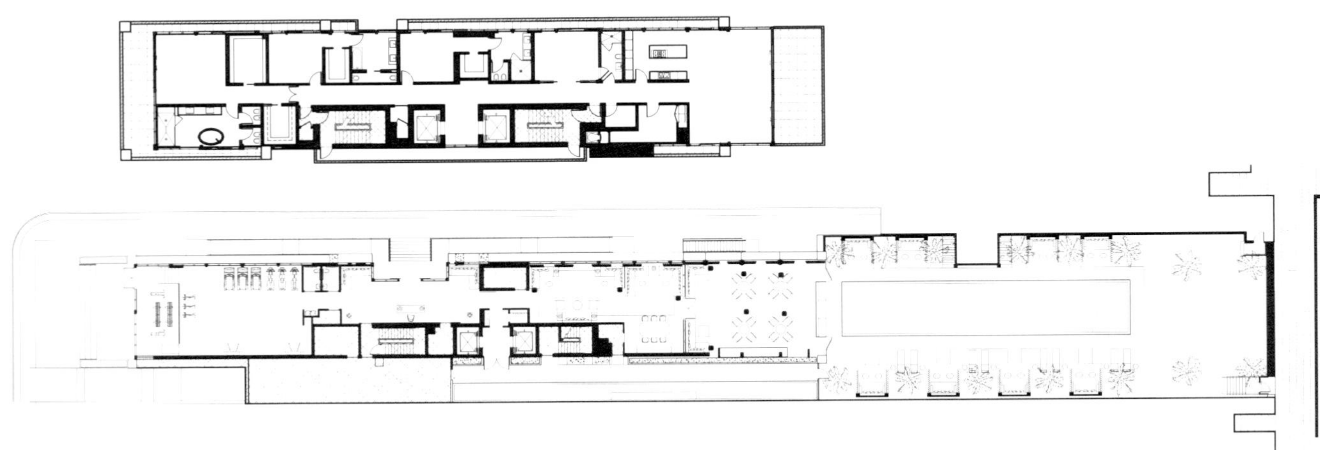

Beach House 8 addresses the narrow beachfront lot with eight tiers pushing and pulling east to west like so many drawers stacked on top of one another. "We decided to exaggerate the thinness of the lot and create a sense of movement from the city to the ocean," said Fort-Brescia, who worked closely on the project with Italian developer Valerio Morabito. "We gave it a speed and a direction, a certain dynamic that most beachfront architecture lacks." It can be seen as a series of abstracted dwellings, separate beach houses stacked on top of one another on eight levels — hence the name. Each floor contains only one unit, so that the residents enjoy full, 360-degree views. Balconies are over 1,000 square feet in size. (The 6,000-square-foot penthouse is a duplex with a private pool.) The skeletal framework — horizontal brackets in white aluminum — is not there just for aesthetic or structural reasons, but serves as a brise-soleil system for blocking the harsh afternoon light. "Nothing is superfluous here," says Fort-Brescia. "Everything has a reason."

Skeletal brackets of white concrete encase a stack of extended balconies that push and pull towards the beachfront.

LINEA

SAN FRANCISCO 2011 | 2014

A cluster of intersecting cubes turns the corner from a busy thoroughfare to a quiet residential street.

Linea, with 115 residential units, was designed in response to the immediate context and multilayered complexities of the Hayes Valley section of San Francisco. The building rides a sharp corner between Market and Buchanan Streets with a cluster of boxlike forms, stacked and interlocking, pushing out from the triangular property, enlivening the street, and creating a more user-friendly sense of community. Linea faces the long straightaway of Market Street, with 5,700 square feet of retail shopping. A grid of exaggerated steel framing is broken up by arrhythmic variations that help to diminish the bulk of the nine-story structure. (An irregularly shaped courtyard opens up the center of the complex, bringing natural light and interior views to the rear of every apartment.) The building opens up and comes to life as it turns onto Buchanan Street, a much narrower one-way incline. Some sections push forward, while others collide, intersect, or step back in an interchange of prismatic volumes that energize the bend with recessed terraces and projecting overhangs.

The facade becomes more subdued as it makes the transition from busy four-lane avenue onto a quieter pedestrian setting with traditionally proportioned fenestration and a limestone elevation that better suits the low-rise scale of Buchanan Street.

OUTFRONT
EAST SOUTH
80 101
Oakland
San Jose
Healthy, Holistic Pet Foods & Supplies
Self-Service Solar Pet Wash
cat adoptions today!
pet food express

ICON BAY

MIAMI 2011 | 2015

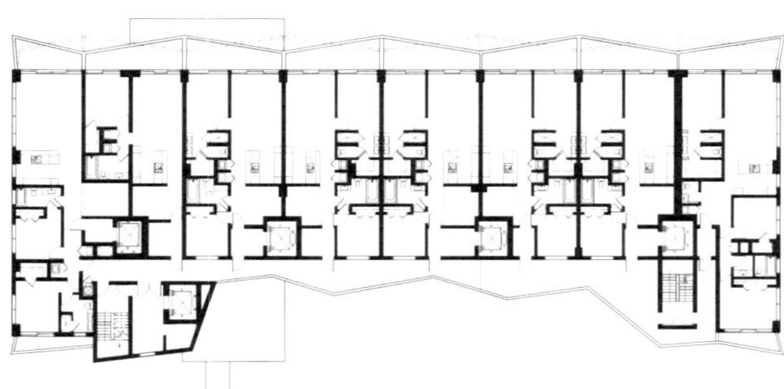

A 500-foot-high slab was relieved by propping the building on slender pilotis and creating a sculpted facade: a folded pattern of zigzagging balconies and overhangs that breaks surface tension while serving as a foil for the flickering hues of watery, bayfront light. This configuration also provides deeply set terraces on each level, as well as 180-degree vantage points that protrude like the bow of a ship.

Icon Bay is part of a larger master plan intended to connect the disparate parts of the Edgewater neighborhood and connect them to the waterfront. "This is not just a building," said Fort-Brescia. "It is a planning and landscape project intended as a catalyst for the new bayfront park." Private development meets public access at ground level, where a small park merges with a linear bayfront walkway that, when complete, will skirt the periphery of Biscayne Bay.

The 1-acre pocket park was designed by ArquitectonicaGEO, inspired in part by Henri Matisse's *Jazz* cutouts of 1947, with elliptical parterres and looping pathways that play in counterpoint to the crystalline facade and the otherwise orthogonal relationship between building and bulkhead. The landscape features native grasses, oaks, and palms planted in informal clusters, interspersed with pathways, benches, murals, and sculptural installations. The terrace and swimming pool are also elliptical in shape.

A folded pattern of zigzagging balconies and overhangs creates a kind of three-dimensional Navajo weave that breaks surface tension while serving as foil for the watery, bayfront light.

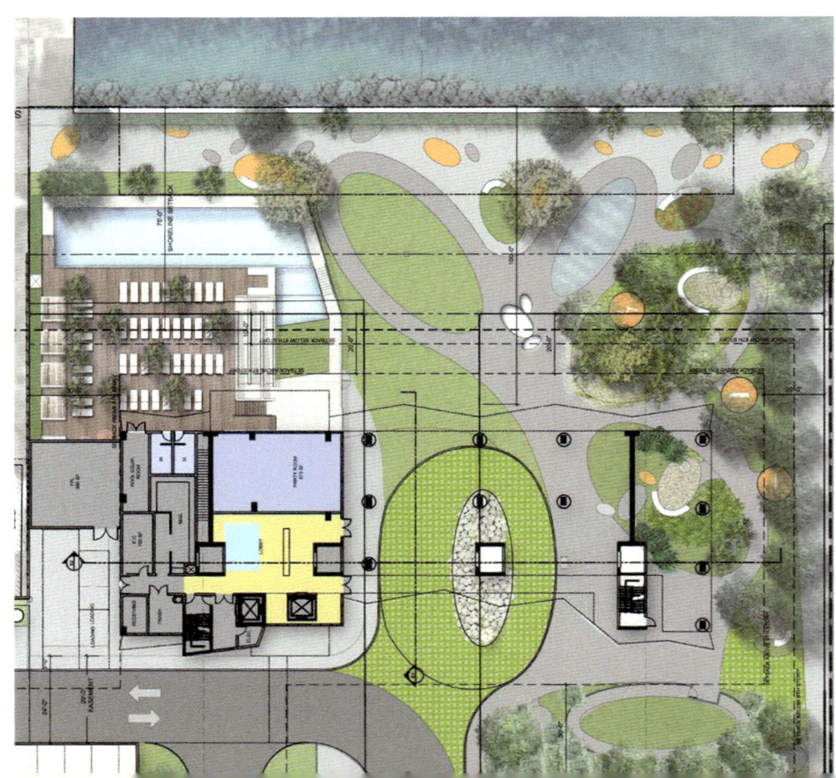

BBVA TOWER

BUENOS AIRES 2011 | 2017

The ground floor of the BBVA Tower is like a greenhouse with cafés, a landscaped Eden under glass, with fullygrown trees, bamboo thickets, and long native grasses. From here, the building rises another thirty-two stories to the roof, where the sense of refined nature is repeated and reciprocated with two penthouse levels that feature private, open-air courtyards linked to a series of corporate boardrooms. The pasturelike sky gardens are surrounded by glass screens that block the wind and allow for spectacular views of the Río de la Plata and beyond to Montevideo.

The building's true architectural identity, however, takes place between the two green extremities. "I was looking for something distinctly Argentine," said Fort-Brescia. "Buenos Aires means 'good winds' and it's a very windy city, so I began with a pure square at the bottom and returned to the square at the top. But what if we made the square appear to twist in the wind?"

On the way up, the building pivots with a subtle rotation, and its prismatic corners spiral and twist, like a splayed deck of cards, creating highly sculptural effects along the edges, and catching the light and reflections of neighboring buildings. These flaring facets change shape and character as the passerby circumnavigates the base. "This gave it life and created a sense of movement," said the architect.

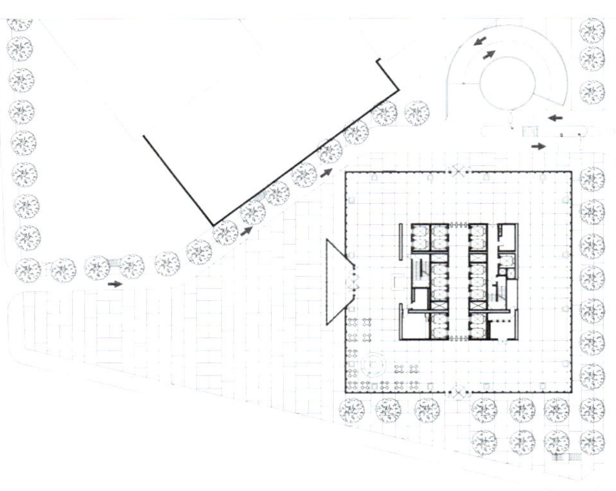

The building appears to pivot with a subtle rotation, its beveled glass corners twisting, like a splayed deck of cards, creating a sculptural effect along the edges, and catching reflections of the neighboring buildings.

BBVA

PORT MIAMI TUNNEL

MIAMI 2012 | 2014

Eighty-foot-high portals stand like ancient monoliths midway down the causeway that connects downtown Miami to Miami Beach. The soaring portals are not mere architectural follies, however. They were designed to contain and conceal a set of mechanized floodgates that can be lowered during a hurricane emergency to block the entries to the two 4,200-foot-long tunnels. A graphic treatment of bas-relief lettering breaks up the monotony of the cast-concrete facades with variations of the Latin word for "navigate" — *navigo, navigas,* and *navigatis* — and this further underscores the maritime nature of the project. The letters are deeply set into the concrete surface and catch sunlight within their chiseled cavities. The narrow sides of the portals are open to reveal bands of orange metal mesh and are back lit to create the impression of volcanic action splitting the portals from within. At night, the openings cast an enigmatic orange glow across the concrete facades.

NAVIGATIS
444-4444

NAVIGAS
NAVIGATIS
NAVIGAMUS
NAVIGATIS

children's

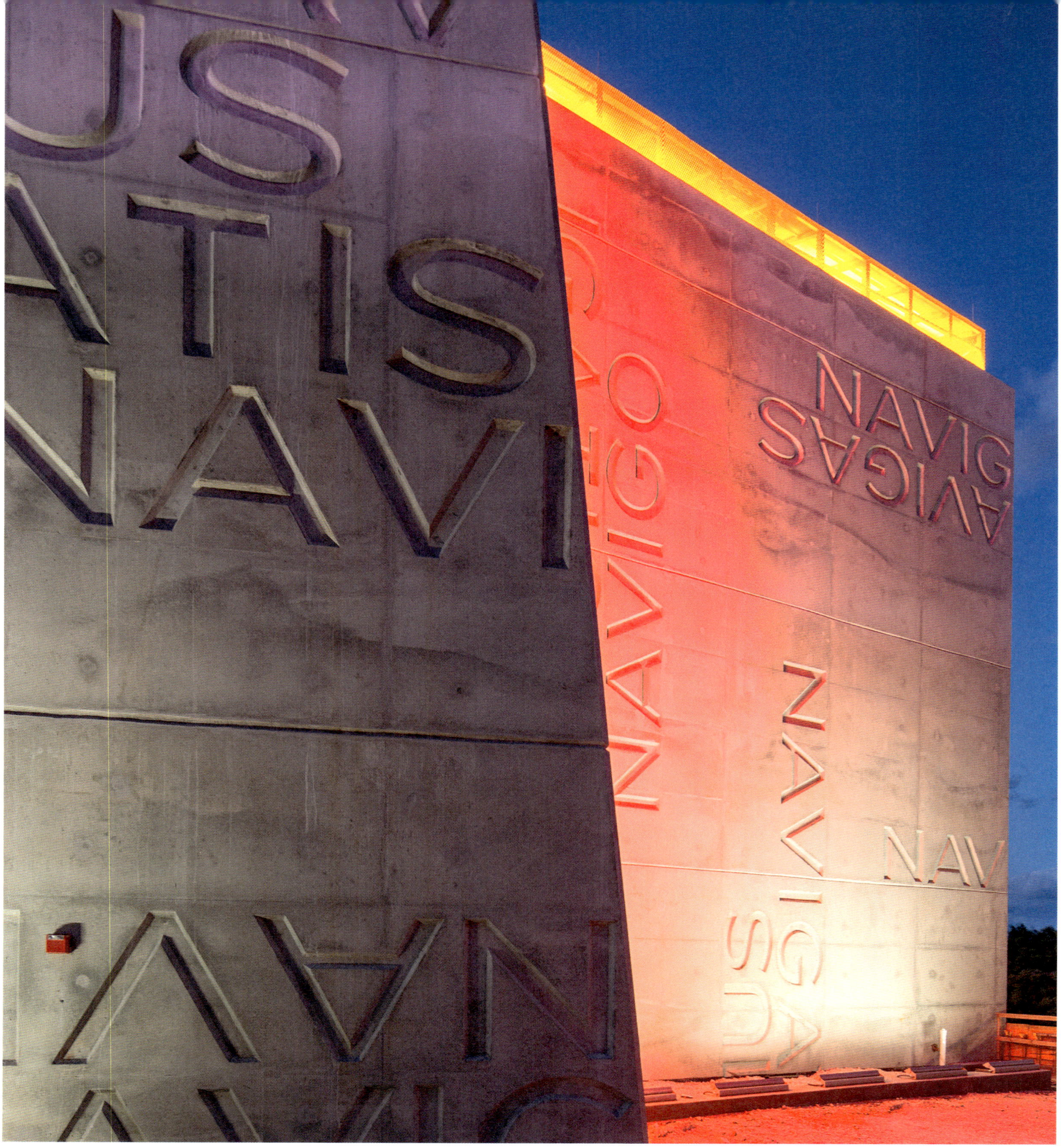

The graphic treatment continues inside, with colorful, cartoonlike murals that depict sharks, swamp grass, and sea turtles in an underwater narrative — a kind of high-speed animation up and down the walls of each tunnel. The shades of aquamarine, purple, green, and yellow grow darker as the roadway dips farther under the water, and then lighten as the roadway rises to the surface again. Running human figures, painted in black, show where the emergency exits are located.

In addition to tunnel interiors and concrete portals, ArquitectonicaGEO also developed an extensive landscaping plan for all approach roads, ramps, drainage swales, and meridians. A 6-acre buffer area that surrounds the tunnel entrances was designed to echo the natural ecosystem of Biscayne Bay and the not-too-distant Everglades.

Eighty-foot-high portals stand like ancient monoliths, concealing mechanized floodgates that can be lowered during hurricanes to protect the tunnels from inundation. Variations of the Latin word for "navigate" are inscribed into the cast-concrete facades.

BG GROUP GLOBAL TECHNOLOGY CENTRE

RIO DE JANEIRO 2011 | 2016

A glass cube is wrapped in a crisscrossing shading device made up of broad aluminum fins calculated to block the sun at every possible angle. "It's Brazil," said Fort-Brescia. "We wanted to make it more organic, a soft geometry. We were trying to 'Brazilianize' the box and humanize a very technical solution." The brise-soleil fins are made from perforated aluminum panels to lighten the load and allow for wind to pass through. It is not a static Euclidean grid, however. The porous fins undulate in and out and intersect at a variety of angles, all according to computer analysis. The matrix of sun-and-shade data creates an irregular outer casing — an almost living, breathing contour, like the protective shell of an underwater crustacean.

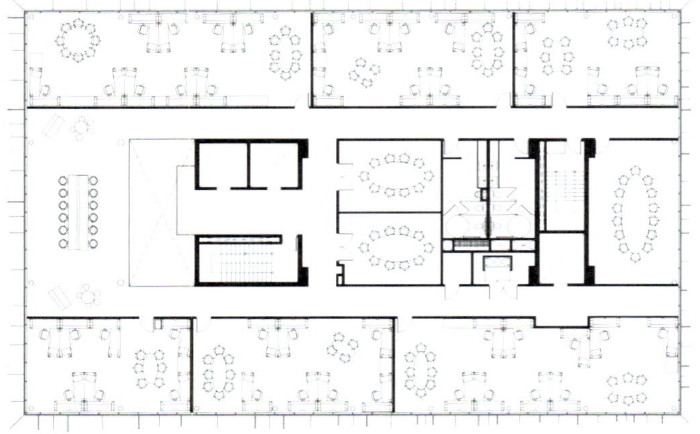

"It's almost like a natural sponge, expanding, swelling, absorbing the direct rays of the sun," said Fort-Brescia. "There's something exuberant about it, like Carnival."

Interior spaces are closely integrated, with flowing connections between the six floors, multiheight spaces, open planning, interlocking volumes, and a series of mezzanines designed to foster creative thinking, flexibility, and interactivity among the different offices and research laboratories. Floors were made from recycled material and sustainably harvested lumber from local forests.

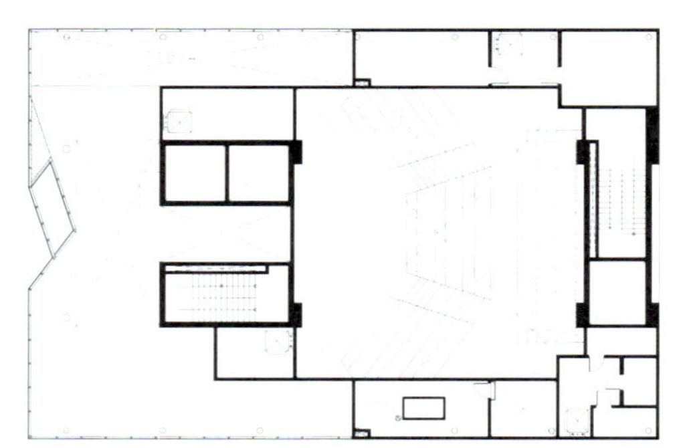

A broad staircase leads to a communal roof terrace that features native plantings and a system of cisterns for collecting rainwater used to irrigate plants both inside and outside the building. The grounds are planted with native shade trees, flowering hedges, and exotic bromeliads. The surrounding pathways and parking areas are paved with pale grasscrete to diminish the effects of reflected heat.

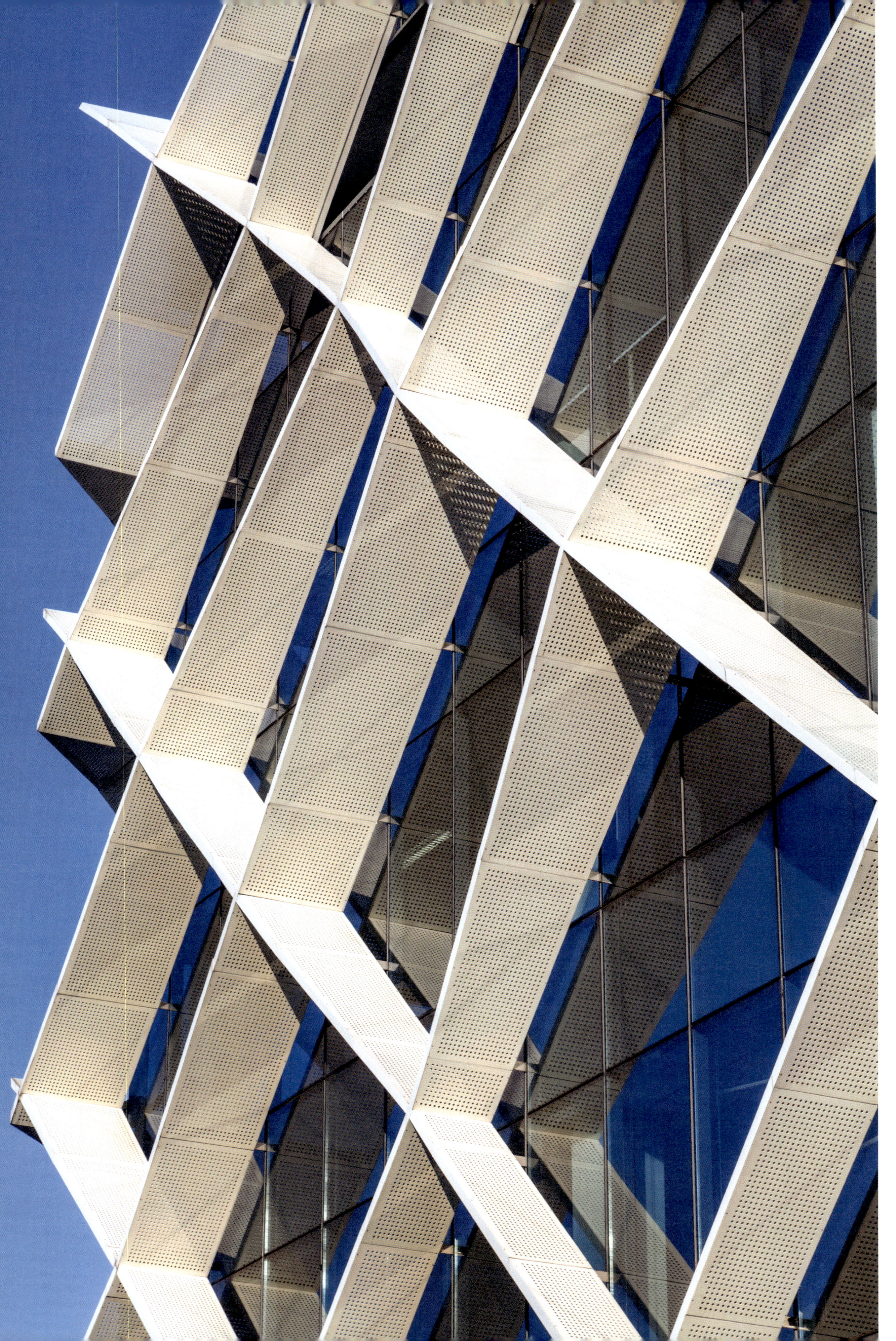

Perforated aluminum brise-soleil encase a six-story glass cube and filter out the direct rays of the Brazilian sun.

FENDI CHATEAU

MIAMI 2012 | 2017

In ancient Egypt, a mastaba —meaning "house for eternity" — was a structure with a flat roof and inward sloping sides, usually made from mud bricks. The Fendi Chateau, at 9365 Collins Avenue in Surfside, is an updated version of the mastaba, with similarly sloping sides, but clad in rolling swathes of glare-resistant glass. The twelve story chateau is lower, more anchored to its site than most of Arquitectonica's other glass structures. With twelve stories and only sixty units, it has the appropriate scale for Surfside, one of the last remaining low-density residential areas along Miami Beach.

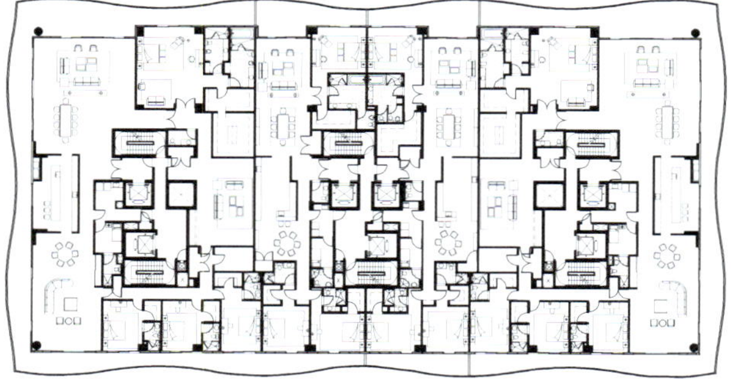

For a structure that bears so much transparency, it doesn't exactly hover above its sandy site. It has a certain stolid presence that breaks free and comes to life at the corners, especially in the evening hours when towering cumulonimbus clouds mount over the Everglades and the building gathers an interlacing of reflections. The balconies and all-glass safety railings project several feet from the sloping body of the building and undulate in the rhythm of the beach itself — like overlapping waves or windblown sand — and these elements appear to converge at the corners as they catch the gold-and-purple radiance of the setting sun. The outwardly sloping sidewalls allow ample wedges of the sky to break through on either side, a relief in a beachfront area that has seen oversized buildings blocking out the sun.

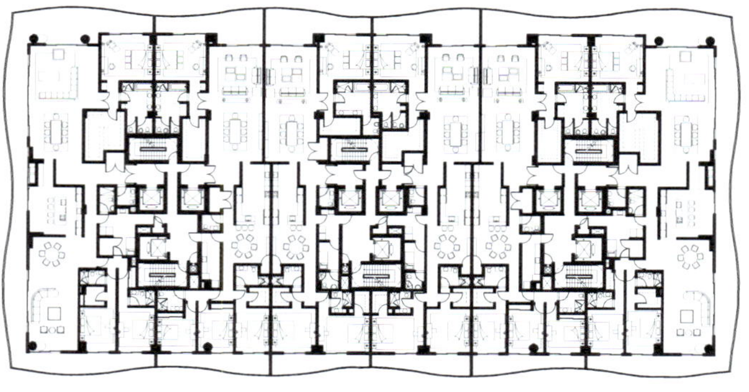

Wavering balconies wrap around the twelve story building and come to life at the corners where they overlap, catching reflections and ocean breezes alike.

ELLIPSE

JERSEY CITY, NEW JERSEY 2012 | 2017

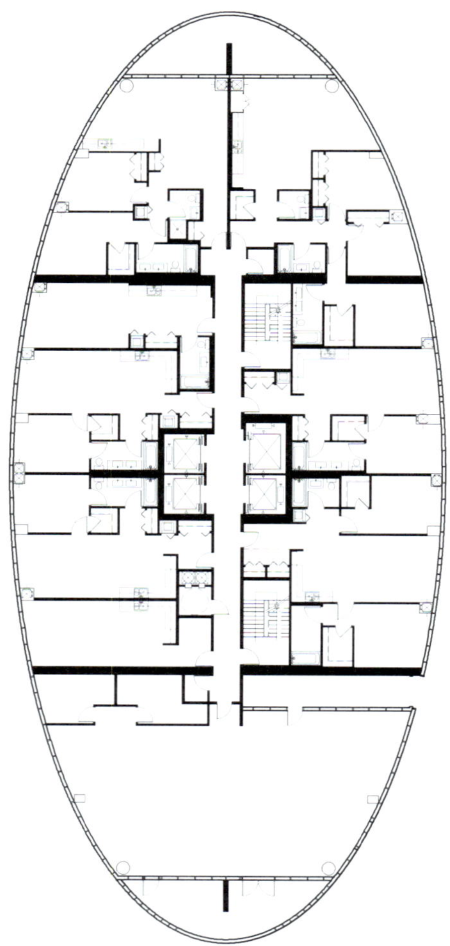

The site is a narrow promontory that juts into the Hudson estuary directly across the river from 42nd Street, with unobstructed views of Manhattan, the harbor, and the Statue of Liberty. It is a part of a 600-acre planned community, known as Newport, that is being developed by LeFrak, a family-run company based in New York City.

The Ellipse tower stands out from other waterfront buildings that are, for the most part, boxy, rectangular structures with little or no architectural distinction. It beckons across the Hudson River to the more refined high-rises of Manhattan's West Side.

"We wanted a nautical shape — something for multidirectional viewing — in the middle of this watery world," said Fort-Brescia. "A circle wouldn't be able to fit on the narrow site, so it became an ellipse."

Suddenly, the area has an identity it never had before. The oval tower sits on a pier of steel pylons that extends into the river. It catches the evening light in the sensual curves of its translucent surfaces. It is further anchored to the waterfront site by a 271-car parking structure clad with a veil-like screen of steel-mesh panels, which echo the elliptical shape of the building. The garage roof supports parklike landscaping, swimming pools, cabanas, a fire pit, and other recreational amenities.

The narrow east and west elevations of the tower are pierced by recessed balconies that create a wavering imprint down the full length of the forty-three story tower. At the same time, the wider north and south facades feature curving swaths of darker framing and fenestration — like subtle watermarks that might represent a vertical river or waterspout. Together, the recessed balconies and surface patterns give the building a liquid, saturated quality that liberates it from the land and marries it to the river.

A forty-three story lozenge rises on the edge of the Hudson River, beckoning across to Manhattan with recessed balconies and wavering, watery imprints.

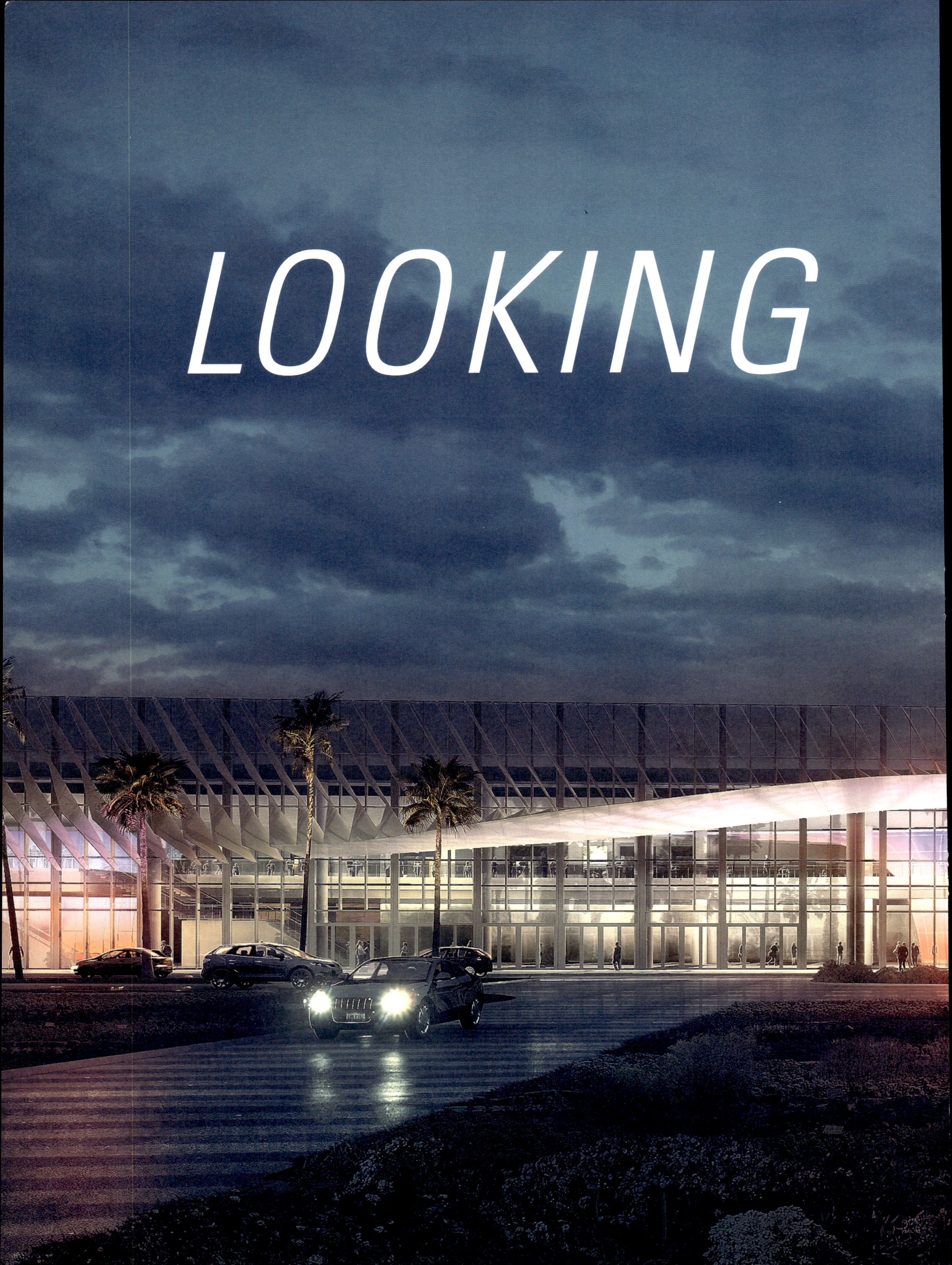
LOOKING

AHEAD

LOOKING AHEAD

IAN VOLNER

Cut a month-wide slice out of Arquitectonica's output in any year in the current decade, put it in a book of its own, and what you would have is a reasonably good primer on the state of architecture, and indeed of urban culture at large, during that thirty-day interval. Is the media abuzz with talk of mega-towers in Manhattan? Arquitectonica is there. Is China looking to tourism to diversify its economy? Ditto. Miami real estate market on the upswing? One firm is leading the charge.

This last section, devoted to ongoing projects begun in the last decade, really could be a stand alone book: the sheer quantity (to say nothing of quality) of projects; the diversity of type and locale; and above all the extraordinary ductility of the design approach manifest in commission after commission. All of it seems to demand a treatment at least as expansive as the practice itself, capable of accounting for all its various moods and modes. Of course, to attempt that kind of summing-up would be somewhat superfluous, since — as the reader may have surmised by now — the whole essence of Arquitectonica is its insistence that the firm's work stands for itself. What motivates the designers today, as it has from the beginning, is the making of architecture for its own sake, and the making of it in the most imminent sense possible, as realized projects bearing an immediate impact on the built environment. In the 2010s, Arquitectonica is busy projecting itself into the unknown every place they can find it, be it around the world or around the corner.

MIAMI DOLPHINS HARD ROCK STADIUM

MIAMI 2009 | 2019

One part clear-cut geometry, one part surprising trusswork, and one part conceptual rethinking of what a sports stadium could be, Arquitectonica's design for a renovation of the Miami Dolphins stadium became an aggressive reconsideration of customary stadium-design strategies. Pragmatically, the project includes a new roof; renovation and redesign of the stadium; the addition of new concession stands; and a new master plan for the surrounding area, as well as the addition of an exterior amphitheater. Conceptually, it's a whole new ballgame: the rubberized membrane roof, a 622,000-square foot canopy, becomes a perfect square, with cantilevers that stretch out past the boundary of the current stadium. From the air (a frequent perspective in television broadcasts), the aperture in the center of the stadium makes the entire building look like a picture frame in plan — a nuanced critique and celebration of the way in which professional sports have become our culture's art. Structurally, the project appears to hang from the sky, with columns tapering as they rise, hiding their hard work in a visual rhetoric of anti-gravity. The low roof amplifies the sound of excited crowds, turning the fans into their own aural spectacle.

SPIRIT OF SAIGON

HO CHI MINH CITY, VIETNAM 2010 | 2019

As if ready to leap off the perimeter of Ho Chi Minh City, the mixed-use Spirit of Saigon crouches like the dragon it's meant to evoke (if not explicitly represent) and waits: for change, for progress, for shifts in boundary and meaning. Writing into architecture an abstracted image of two intertwined dragons — the symbol for the former colonial capital — the structure rises from an eight-story plinth containing a convention center and parking. Above it, the West Tower holds offices and a Ritz-Carlton hotel; the East Tower contains luxury residential apartments. Each tower's "head" twists, the two dragons operating in constant relationship and constant tension — an expression of the city's complex history, as well as the way in which Arquitectonica simultaneously took on both the most deeply pragmatic needs and the most evocative metaphor. Between them, the twinned forms buttress a cubic glass volume, its delicate form suspended as much by the physical strength of the towers as by the opposing symbolic forces they represent. The project is building-as-history and building-as-future, staking out new territory from a global perspective, steeped in the past and bending towards the future.

CONCORD CHONGQING

CHONGQING 2010 | 2022

A base-and-tower skyscraper of the kind that has become all but ubiquitous in fast-growing Asian cities, Arquitectonica's combined retail, office, hospitality and residential tower in southwestern China attempts to soften the sometimes harshly synthetic typology through key enhancements to both its program and its aesthetic. In the base structure, a giant winter garden alive with plant life gives users an all-weather indoor park; the rooftop observation deck is likewise dense with greenery, turning the whole building into a vertical oasis in the middle of the teeming metropolis. Structurally, the tower stands out for its near-total lack of standard floors, each floor plate being slightly different in size, resulting in a wavering outline that seems almost to diffuse into the air at its peak. As impressive as the form itself is what wraps around it: the cladding system that creeps up the serrated frame of the spire is a multi-faceted patchwork of glass tesserae, each deflected at a discrete angle. This glittering, crystalline facade sets up a clear dialogue with the similarly wrought envelope of the winter garden, lending some rarely seen unity to the base and tower halves of the popular urban type. Even better, the two together strongly suggest a distinct romantic image — a rocket readying for takeoff, leaving behind it clouds of smoke — truly putting the "boom" into China's building boom.

THE PIERCE

BOSTON 2011 | 2018

In the heart of the historic Fenway district in Boston — a town not known for its skyscrapers, and a neighborhood that's never had one to begin with — The Pierce makes a strong but sensitive case for verticality as an urban imperative. Rising sheer above a two-story base to a 30-story summit, Arquitectonica's first building for New England's de facto capital sits on a key salient in its famously jumbled cityscape: on the outskirts of Boston proper, near the border of adjacent Brookline, only steps from Fenway's storied baseball stadium and from the park (part of Frederick Law Olmstead's celebrated "Emerald Necklace") that also bears the area's name. Given the prominent site, local planning authorities recognized The Pierce as a prospective gateway to downtown — an entrée to the denser business district beyond — and gave a green light both to its considerable size and to its multi-use zoning, allowing for 349 residences combined with 20,000 square feet of retail space. Arquitectonica stepped up to the brief with a building that's equal parts bold and welcoming: conforming to its triangular lot, the tower is wedge-shaped in plan, narrowing to a crisp point along its western front; to the east, it does precisely the opposite, opening into a butterfly formation with an elevation divided into multi-story blocks, each angled slightly differently. This segmentation does double duty, picking up sunlight and refracting it into a jewel-like array, while simultaneously breaking down the scale of the high-rise to that of the surrounding mid-rise buildings, and turning to face them, as if in gracious acknowledgment.

606 WEST 57TH STREET

NEW YORK, NEW YORK 2011 | 2018

Incredible as it may seem, in a city practically synonymous with bigness, Arquitectonica's 1.1-million-square-foot tower on Manhattan's West Side will be the single largest residential structure by area in New York City history. The 42-story behemoth housing 1,028 apartments occupies a site stretching much of the distance between 11th and 12th Avenues; however, since by law no single building in the area can exceed 175 feet in length, the firm engineered a creative solution, dividing the tower into a sequence of volumes, some of them turned ninety degrees to take advantage of the site's partial through-block depth. This, in a fortuitous turn, developed into the project's signature massing strategy: the various volumes are piled together in an irregular stack — something like oversized volumes on a bookstore display table — with each connecting to the other by way of sunlit corridors and skybridges with stunning views of Manhattan and beyond. While the quasi-modular approach does provide some scalar moderation, Arquitectonica reasserts the building's overall bulk by making the individual modules larger as they reach the top, lightening it just slightly with an increasingly glazed facade on the uppermost floors. Snaking through the block, slipping at one point behind older commercial frontage, the massive building is a ready-made urban neighborhood all its own, with 40,000 square feet of street-side retail, its own onsite laundry and valet service, a package room larger than that of many public post offices, and a gymnasium that would be the envy of any suburban high school.

AQUALINA AND AQUAVISTA

TORONTO 2011 | 2018 | 2013 | 2018

Though directly adjacent to one another — and similarly named — Arquitectonica's two mixed-use high-rises on the shore of Toronto Harbour are intended as discrete but complementary design solutions tailored to their respective sites. The East Bayfront district, where both are situated, is being

transformed from a former shipping hub into a thriving urban community; the 13-story Aqualina occupies a parcel running perpendicular to the waterfront, while the 12-story Aquavista runs parallel to it, giving each a distinct role within the broader East Bayfront scheme. Accordingly, Aquavista addresses itself southward, toward Lake Ontario, with a curvilinear footprint that guarantees optimal views for its 412 units (including 72 below-market residences), while the highly-rectilinear Aqualina encloses its 363 condominiums within a sequence of projecting and receding boxes, all perched on a base containing 30,000 square feet of retail space. Rather than the stylistic consistency typical of many pre-planned developments, the desired effect of two such dissimilar structures is that of a naturally occuring urban agglomeration, one where the architects' identity takes a back seat to the visual and functional diversity of the streetscape. There are, nonetheless, commonalities that connect the pair: in particular their shared observance of strict environmental standards. In keeping with East Bayfront's ambitious goal of attaining Canadian LEED Gold certification, both Aqualina and Aquafina are replete with bicycle parking spaces and lushly planted terraces, and both afford easy access to regional and national transit networks through Toronto's Union Station, which is only a few minutes' walk to the north.

TESTIMONIO II

MONACO 2011 | 2019

Despite its luxurious appearance, the bulk of the 195 units in Testimonio II (the name technically denotes the site, not the building itself) are in fact subsidized apartments, just one of the many perks enjoyed by the small but prosperous population of Monaco. The latest phase of Arquitectonica's project for the principality is an elaborate civic enterprise aimed at keeping residents of Monaco at home and stemming the brain drain that has drawn many of its younger citizens abroad. Along with the residential component, the project includes daycare facilities and a new home for the École Internationale Monaco, as well as parking for 1,200 cars. The design divides the complex into two parts: a tower, containing a majority of the social housing, which will be one of Monaco's tallest buildings; and a mid-rise structure with a sinuous facade that affords sensational views of the Mediterranean from multi-tiered terraces and balconies. More sensational still is the way the design negotiates the topological complexity of the site: the two structures are built into a steep escarpment, with an eleven-story drop separating the thoroughfare above the ensemble from a central roadway passing through it, and then a further six-story drop to the waterfront. Reminiscent of Barcelona's Park Güell or New York's Brooklyn Heights Promenade, Arquitectonica's solution activates its tricky cliff-side locale and turns a challenging constraint into an architectural opportunity.

UNIVERSITY OF MIAMI SCHOOL OF ARCHITECTURE

CORAL GABLES, FLORIDA 2012 | 2018

Extending a longtime association with the institution (both Bernardo Fort-Brescia and his son Raymond have taught there), Arquitectonica's commission for the University of Miami School of Architecture cements the firm's commitment to its hometown with a one-of-a-kind design laboratory for the city's and the country's next generation of architects. Fully stocked with studio spaces, digital fabrication facilities, exhibitions areas, and ample room for social and public functions, the scheme synthesizes every aspect of twenty-first-century design pedagogy into a cogent whole, packing them into a deceptively simple envelope: the building is in essence a single oversized shed, featuring a vaulting roof suspended 18 feet over a floor with few load-bearing columns and few fixed walls. The roof itself, fashioned of improbably thin concrete, becomes a moment of high visual drama, the slab warping slightly (melting, as it seems, in the Miami heat) to form a gentle arc that adds a touch of complexity to the silhouette. Besides affording effective shading over the glazed east and west fronts, the bowed roof also sets up the design's primary formal swerve — a single curved wall, also in concrete, facing the nearby public transit entrance and a nearby turreted structure by architect Leon Krier. In addition to softening the building's rectilinear plan, the curve invites students to walk up to the building and marvel at their friends' work pinned up inside, acting as a symbolic gesture of welcome.

Furthering a connection between dense interior spaces and the expansive campus is the activation of the surrounding area landscape through an emphasis on continuing the lush greenery native to the Coral Gables area.

HOBHOUSE

LONDON 2012 | 2019

In this narrow street just off London's Trafalgar Square, Arquitectonica inhales a deep and abiding sense of local history and exhales a playfully cubist take on the British urban scene. The building, the firm's first in London, is a mixed-use project slated to contain nineteen residences, retail, and an art gallery. Scale, material, and style create a *trompe-loeils* effect here, ripping themselves apart and sewing themselves back together in a conceptual loop made visually palpable. Purposeful shifts and slips introduce a feeling of subtly powerful deformation; the smoothness of a brick becomes jagged, the long pane of a window creases. Arquitectonica blends old and new not only conceptually but also practically: pre-existing walls have been incorporated into the final design, surfaces textured with a combination of extremely old and all-new masonry. The five-story facade ripples and breaks on its way from the street to the sky and back down again; it shifts vertically and horizontally, breathing life into this historical street through the careful manipulation of basic architectonic elements — floor plate, brick wall, rectangular window. The project is as allusive as it is elusive, loaded with both invention and historical reference.

33 TEHAMA

SAN FRANCISCO 2013 | 2018

A thin geometric meander crawls its way up the facade of 33 Tehama, the tallest residential project under construction in the rapidly growing SOMA neighborhood of San Francisco, itself a rapidly growing and constantly changing urban center. A residential project developed in concert with artist Yayoi Kusama — whose plaza installation is her first major west coast public art project — 33 Tehama slips its way into the San Francisco skyline. The meander is both a formal move and a conceptual one, linking the building both inward to itself and outward to the larger context, the compacted urban landscape of the nearby (and under-construction) Transbay Terminal and the swiftly developing city. The skyscraper becomes at once a legible form — the vertical delineations of the ribbon drawing the eye to the horizontal floor plates and the clarity of the sweeping glazing. Within the envelope of the structure are 403 residential units, augmented by a rooftop retreat, wellness spa, solarium, bocce court, and sun deck.

1061 WEST VAN BUREN

CHICAGO 2013 | 2019

Zig zags appear throughout the firm's oeuvre, often as a means of dividing a large mass into smaller chunks while adding an element of graphic interest. Rarely however has the effect been as dramatic, or the context more fraught, than in this residential tower in Chicago's West Loop neighborhood that marks Arquitectonica's first project in America's Second City. A formerly neglected but now fast-gentrifying corridor adjacent to the Eisenhower Expressway, the site is so close to the highly trafficked east-west artery that anything built there must possess some aspect of an architectural billboard, apprehensible by hundreds of thousands of drivers streaming at speed to and from O'Hare. As in other Arquitectonica buildings adopting the same motif, the zig zag cutting through the facade gives it almost the appearance of two separate buildings, one a stepped-back tower and the other an inverted partial ziggurat, the two interlocking like complementary Lego bricks. Here, it goes a step further: the cut is recessed several feet behind the main skin of the building, making space for functional amenities in the form of terraces and private balconies along the length of the divide. More significantly, the jagged line seems to have an easy-to-grasp symbolic import, communicating an almost Futurist sense of movement and speed that rhymes perfectly with the freeway next door.

ONE BRICKELL CITY CENTRE

MIAMI 2013 | 2020

Arquitectonica's transformation of Miami's Brickell district is already well under way, following the completion of the phase-one Brickell City Centre commercial complex in 2016. Yet that project was only the beginning: One Brickell City Centre will be among the tallest towers in the region, an eighty-story advertisement for the revitalization of the area and its economic and cultural status in the city. The tower — linked directly to the retail bloc via an undulating, sheltered walkway equipped with a patented climate-control system — hosts an unusual array of functions, including not only a hotel and residences but also office spaces and three shopping levels.

Declaring itself the prime access point to Brickell City Centre (and, by extension, to the city itself), the building orientation reflects the logic of the site: its footprint rotates slightly, following the movement of traffic as the street grid begins to turn towards downtown and highway drivers enter it from the nearby interstate. Taking up the theme, a pair of cutaways at the southeast and northwest corners act as gestural greeting for the approaching visitors; they also furnish much-coveted outdoor space for the high-value units surrounding them. With a facade treatment that partially reveals and partially conceals the glazing around the terraces, the building's slices make for an atypical but legible hierarchy, one in which edges become fronts, turning an imposing skyscraper into an urban entryway.

PARAISO BAY

MIAMI 2014 | 2018

Distilled to its typological essence, the postwar Miami apartment building could be summed up as a slender, foursquare slab with all-white finishes and a balcony-raked facade. In their project on the bayshore perimeter of the Wynwood arts district, Arquitectonica — rarely content with the typical — has come along to burst the bubble, almost literally: Paraíso Bay, four 54-story towers with a total of 1,200 units, takes the familiar outline of the area's resort condominium towers and introduces an uncommon bit of formal mischief, in the shape of large swelling projections along the eastern front. Resembling nothing so much as bubbles rushing to the surface from an underwater swimmer (an image the design team actually deployed in making their case to the client), the domed geometry disrupts the regularity of the grid of the towers' facades; it then becomes a geometrical motif of its own, appearing in the rounded water features and circulation elements of the landscape plan. Impish as all of this may seem, the building's apparent departures from orthodoxy masks a much deeper fealty to the architectural origins of the Miami high-rise. In a fulfillment of the early-modern ideal rarely found in South Florida, every apartment in the building has more than one exposure, an organizational feature made possible through the use of multiple private elevators rather than the usual centralized core leading to double-loaded corridors. The resulting cross-ventilation renders air conditioning all but superfluous, and the abundant light and views of sun and sea are straight out of the classic Corbusian playbook.

MIAMI BEACH CONVENTION CENTER

MIAMI BEACH, FLORIDA 2014 | 2018

Since its debut in 2002, Art Basel Miami Beach has helped convince the world that Arquitectonica's hometown is precisely the cultural hotbed the designers had always argued it was. Yet the convention center that hosts the show (to say nothing of dozens of other national and international events every year) has never quite lived up to the same lofty standard — a problem that the current $65-million renovation project, and the selection of Arquitectonica to lead it, is plainly aimed at remedying.

The existing building, first constructed in the late 1950s and augmented and retrofitted in the late 1980s, suffered not only from aesthetic awkwardness and inconsistency, but also from a curious disregard for the abundant sunlight that so many conventioneers flock to Miami to enjoy. Eliminating the surface-level parking that had long cluttered the adjoining sites, the firm's plan moves parking to the roof, which will also feature a richly landscaped outdoor terrace.

Inside the building, fairgoers will no longer have to walk through miles of airless corridors: sunlight will flood the perimeter thanks to new curtain walls on the north and south facades, the glass sheathed in creamy aluminum louvers that reduce thermal load while providing a rhythm and materiality to the exterior that are picked up in the rooftop sunshades. This "tropicalization" of the Convention Center is complemented by an expansion in its capacity of a quarter million square feet, proving once again that Miami can more than keep pace with Basel.

ELYSÉE

MIAMI 2014 | 2019

Biscayne Bay, the scene of so much of the Arquitectonica story, is once again the setting for a residential project that works to upend expectations for what a Miami high-rise can be. In this instance, the shift is fairly explicit: for reasons of self-evident financial interest, the client for the 100-unit Elysee informed the designers that the apartments toward the top of the reed-thin, 57-story tower should be larger than those toward the bottom. Acting on this suggestion, the designers hit on a way of conveying it to would-be buyers through the building's immediately recognizable silhouette — an inverted ziggurat that fattens as it ascends, seemingly in defiance of gravitational necessity. The thickening occurs in two successive bulges, with cantilevers projecting above a pair of glass-enclosed service floors halfway and two-thirds of the way to the top. Perhaps best appreciated from the very base of the tower looking straight up, this act of structural daring also makes its mark on a skyline already spiked with Arquitectonica landmarks.

INFINITY

LUXEMBOURG 2014 | 2019

Familiar territory for Arquitectonica since the days of its European debut, Luxembourg is one of Europe's smallest countries — a condition that sits uneasily alongside its rather brisk growth. To relieve the ensuring pressure, the government of the tiny city-state has been drawing development away from the old city, towards a broad plateau separating the historic core and the airport. Already home to several EU office buildings, the area is now becoming a major business district, and Arquitectonica's mixed-use complex will help make it a fully-functioning 24-hour urban center.

Comprising a residential volume and a shorter office block, the scheme highlights the firm's planning know-how with a unique ligature connecting the two main components — a glazed public corridor, topped with a pair of green roofs that crisscross in a dynamic figure eight. Creating a fluid passage through the complex (as well as out of it, to the adjacent European Court of Justice), the lofted park also provides shelter for a small plaza to the south, protecting it from the occasionally severe winds blowing off the nearby Alzette River. The adjoining buildings, meanwhile, take up the entwined geometry of the connector between them: the west-facing facade of the office block, which greets Luxembourgers as they approach the area, crimps in the middle and is cut by a diagonal marquee, anticipating the X of the corridor; the residential slab is organized as a pair of conjoined twins, each linking directly to one or the other of the landscaped strips.

WYNDHAM AVENUE OF THE ARTS

COSTA MESA, CALIFORNIA 2014 | 2019

Arquitectonica faced two challenges in their hotel project for the central commercial neighborhood of upscale Newport Beach: first, to introduce a tall building into the traditionally small-scale urban fabric of Southern California; and second, to avoid slipping into the static, boxy expression that seems to be the default setting of commercial hospitality projects the world over, particularly in smaller cities. The site has an especially important cultural dimension in the region — located directly across the street from a major performance venue, Cesar Pelli's 1988 Segerstorm Center for the Arts, and hard by the prospective future home of the Orange County Museum of Art — giving the designers a special responsibility to live up to the aspirationally titled thoroughfare in the hotel's name.

The chief feature of their parti is the articulation of the facade, a zippered diptych of two angled faces with a sculptural presence. Containing 150 rooms, the 15-story high-rise is certainly taller than its neighbors, yet it hardly imposes on its surrounds, sitting in contextual counterpoint to an existing low-rise hotel directly next door — becoming, in a sense, a diptych within a diptych. With a dose of aesthetic sophistication more akin to an urban boutique hotel than a national brand, the Wyndham is poised to help Costa Mesa realize its ambition to become a regional arts destination.

THE CARLYLE ALEXANDRIA

ALEXANDRIA, VIRGINIA 2015 | 2020

Three slipped cubes, modernist in their gridded facade and postmodern in their playful take on the straight modernist skyscraper, make up this 34-story residential structure developed as part of the much larger Carlyle Plaza Two development. Four towers comprising office and residential space will rise at this former railyard. The slipped tower is slated to contain 370 residential units, while low-rise townhouses — a stark formal and spatial contrast to the iconic tower — provide another twelve. The whole project rests almost directly on top of a D.C. Metro station, its existence linked to the nearby metropolis in its overt aesthetic reference to iconic architecture and, more practically, through its infrastructural accessibility.

The Carlyle will be the tallest tower in Alexandria, and offers a multiplicity of angles both visual and conceptual. From one side, the three slipped boxes introduce a sense of playful levity to an often-formal typology. From another, the sense of slippage retreats, replaced by a much subtler visual move as the masses begin to line up: a moment of delineation and articulation that invites the eye into a subtler and more evocative reading of the volumes. Floor plates between stories become visible, as do the separations between each volume, while the separate windows become newly articulated.

CONCORD SHANGHAI

SHANGHAI 2015 | 2020

Two towers, all residential, linked at the top and bottom, the Shanghai Concord takes a novel formal conceit — something between a flattened loop and a stretched-out window — and puts it in the service of contemporary urban living. Staggered back and away from each other, the twin high-rises are separated by a wide aperture that gives all the apartments maximum access to light and air, which residents can enjoy (along with the striking prospect down the Nanjing Road, one of Shanghai's prime commercial strips) from the ribbon-like balconies that run around each tower and give both their regular, terraced rhythm. No less stunning are the views, stretching as far as the Huangpu River, that can be seen from the observation deck located in the building's bridge-like crown — a structure almost as exciting to look at as it is to look out from: gazing upward, passersby on the street will see the narrow strip connecting the two towers high above, a seemingly perilous span suspended in the sky. Only from a bit further back will the building's real visual gamesmanship be evident, as the twisting legs of the two towers and their horizontal connections come together to form an unusual geometric figure, a skewed picture frame for a real-life portrait of sky and city.

UNIVERSITY OF MIAMI STUDENT HOUSING

CORAL GABLES, FLORIDA 2016 | 2019

The primary intent of this project was connection: between the school of architecture and the dormitories, between the new student housing center and a pool, between a place to learn and a place to live. Referencing the 60s-era Biscayne Bay structures of Stiltsville, Arquitectonica arranged the residential cubes into a necklace of forms strung together to produce a single undulating structure containing a theater, bicycle center, post office, residential administration office, and a sand volleyball court. The residential building itself is large, with multiple core lobbies that touch the ground underneath what becomes essentially a canopy; the architecture traverses sky and ground, at once ethereally floating and connected to the ground. Four types of facade designs — wood, metal, concrete and stucco — add visual interest on the vertical plane, a sense of demarcation and separation that lends itself to the idea of individuality and autonomy presented in the overall design. Using every opportunity to question the typical "dorm" anti-style, this 1,100-bed project is part of a major push by the University of Miami's to increase the cohesion of the student body, providing a sense of community through the adoption of careful and consistent architecture.

Furthering a connection between dense interior spaces and the expansive campus is the activation of the surrounding area landscape through an emphasis on continuing the lush greenery native to the Coral Gables area.

LAKE NONA RESORT

ORLANDO 2017 | 2020

Arquitectonica's sprawling hospitality complex in central Florida's most famous resort city has to compete with an unusually eye-catching next-door neighbor — a fifteen-acre crystal-clear lagoon, one of the largest of its kind built to date using a proprietary non-chlorine technology. But this condition also represented an opportunity: artificial inland beach resorts being relatively new under the sun, there was no pre-existing typological norm, Arquitectonica, as usual, felt free to invent one of its own. The main volume of 250 guestrooms and 80 condo units is cast as a highly irregular "groundscraper," its horizontality emphasized through continuous balcony registers but vexed by a double-curved plan and its sideways-hourglass elevation. A terrace with bars and restaurants sits atop the middle point, while below it — where the hourglass thins at the hip — the building pirouettes over the lagoon and lands on a peninsular spit of beach before continuing back to the mainland. In part this configuration was determined by the relatively limited size of the footprint, obliging Arquitectonica to fold the structure back on itself; in part it was simply to create a stunning pictorial moment, with guests arriving to discover the lagoon neatly framed by the leaping arch as though issuing forth from a natural grotto.

PORT OF XIAMEN

XIAMEN 2017 | 2021

A major port city adjacent to the Taiwan Strait, Xiamen is the focus of a concerted effort by the Chinese government to attract cruise-ship traffic to the country's southern coast. Arquitectonica was tasked with designing a complex that could at once accommodate large-volume traffic and maintain an appropriately festive air, a mood that would appeal to seagoing holidaymakers. Due to the height of modern ocean liners, arriving passengers' first encounter with the facility will be looking down on it; Arquitectonica therefore topped the structure with a series of abstracted visual motifs based on dolphins and clouds. The alighting crowds are conducted through the arrivals hall past various attractions, with the decorative devices above acting as shading, finally moving toward a high-rise group straddling the axis of the main arterial route.

Containing hotels and office spaces, the high-rises were part of a separate commission also won by Arquitectonica. Yet they operate as part of an integrated functional unit with, and narrative complement to, the arrivals area: considering the port as a metaphorical "threshold," the architects conceived the vertical buildings as a "window" and a "door," with the wavy glass facade surrounding the latter a "curtain" apparently billowing in the wind. The window structure is especially felicitous, opening up the volume to the scenic hillside beyond, drawing visitors onward and upward toward the upper-level sky lobby from which they can take in views of both the forested uplands and the scenic coastline.

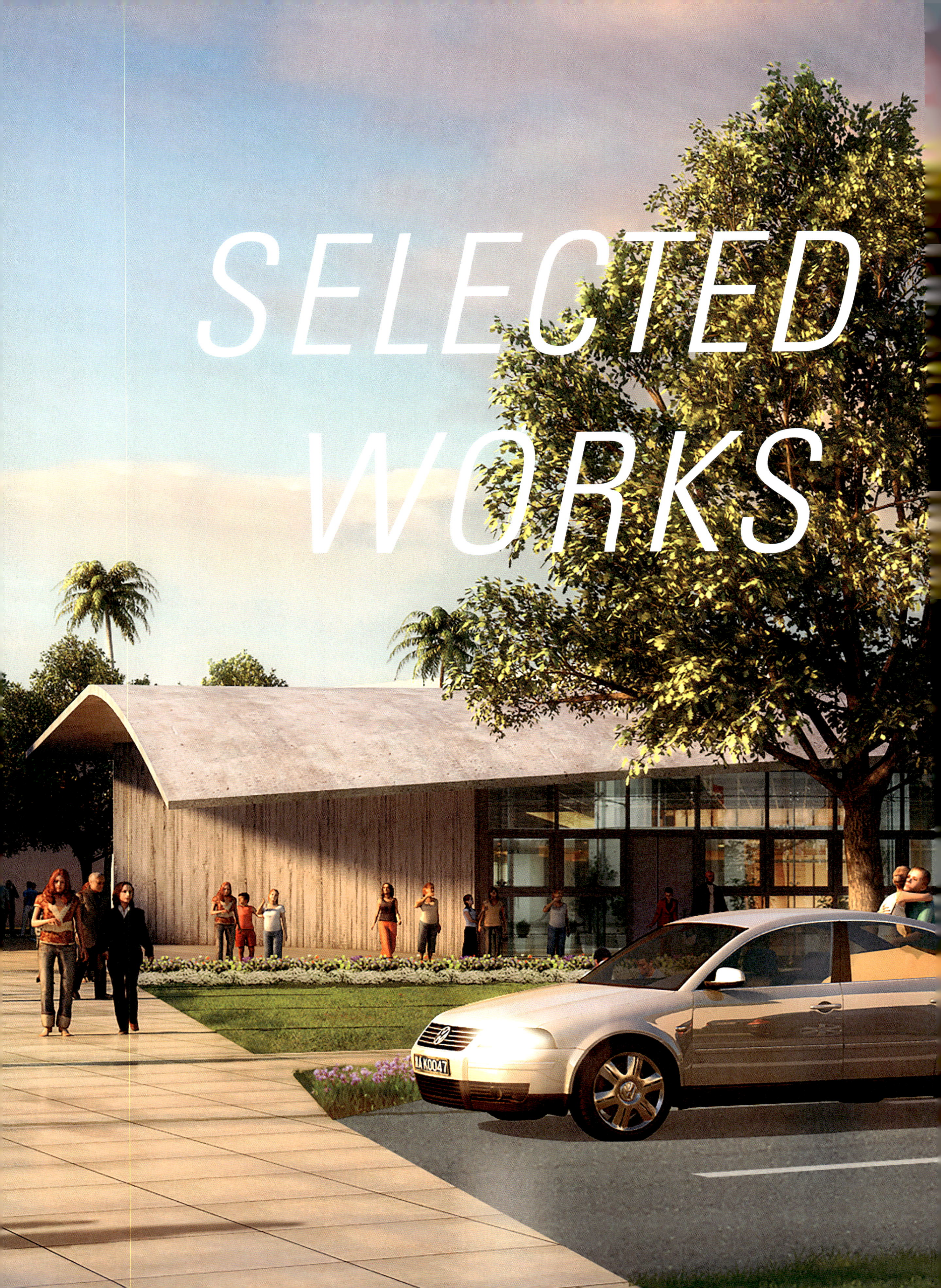

SELECTED WORKS

SELECTED WORKS

Lorem ipsum dolor sit amet, consectetur adipiscing elit. Morbi cursus ac elit et eleifend. Morbi mattis vitae dui non efficitur. Vivamus scelerisque, urna at molestie viverra, sem eros dapibus odio, ut aliquet libero justo et tellus. Aenean imperdiet maximus aliquet. Nam vehicula hendrerit urna sed vulputate. Nulla finibus a lectus hendrerit imperdiet. Ut vitae viverra arcu, convallis aliquam nunc.

MIXED USE

HELMSLEY CENTER, Miami, Florida, USA, 1981

HORIZON HILL CENTER, San Antonio, Texas, USA, 1982

MESA WEST BETTER HOME LIVING CENTER, Austin, Texas, USA, 1983–1984

HANNA WINERY, Alexander Valley, California, USA, 1987–1988

THREE PALMS CENTER, Jupiter, Florida, USA, 1988–1990

FOUR SEASONS HOTEL & RESIDENCES, Caracas, Venezuela , 1992–2001

FESTIVAL WALK, Hong Kong, China, 1993–1998

KOWLOON CANTON OFFICE AND LNTERMODAL CENTER, Hong Kong, China, 1994

CANYON RANCH LIVING, Miami Beach, Florida, USA, 1995–2008

THE ROYAL PALM RESORT, Miami Beach, Florida, USA, 1996–2002

EXCHANGE SQUARE OFFICE AND RESIDENTIAL TOWERS, Manila, Philippines, 1996

ORLANDO CITY CENTER, Orlando, Florida, USA, 1996–2002

VISIONCREST, Singapore, 1997–2008

MIRANOVA CONDOMINIUM AND OFFICE TOWERS, Columbus, Ohio, USA, 1997–2001

DIJON CHAMBER OF COMMERCE & INDUSTRY AND IBIS HOTEL, Dijon, France, 1997–2005

GALLERY PLACE, Washington, DC, USA, 1997–2004

CYBERPORT TECHNOLOGY CAMPUS, Hong Kong, China, 1999–2004

RITZ-CARLTON HOTEL AND RESIDENCES, Fort Lauderdale, Florida, USA, 1999–2005

MECA CARIBBEAN STUDIOS, San Juan, Puerto Rico, 1999–2001

EL COMANDANTE AMPHITHEATER AND MULTIMEDIA ENTERTAINMENT COMPLEX, San Juan, Puerto Rico, 1999–2000

MECA AMPHITHEATER AND MULTIMEDIA ENTERTAINMENT COMPLEX, Miami, Florida, USA, 1999–2002

MILLENNIUM CITY PLAZA, Hong Kong, China, 1999–2001

TAIKOO HUI, Guangzhou, China, 1999–2013

AVENTURA PLACE, Aventura, Florida, USA, 2000–2004

AVALON CHRISTIE PLACE, New York, New York, USA, 2000–2005

Z OCEAN HOTEL SOUTH BEACH, Miami Beach, Florida, USA, 2000–2005

SEWARD PARK MIXED USE DEVELOPMENT, New York, New York, USA, 2000

LONGEMONT HOTEL AND OFFICE TOWER, Shanghai, China, 2000–2005

OMNI MALL SHOPPING CENTER RENOVATION, Miami, Florida, USA, 2001–2002

MARRIOTT PRAGUE HOTEL & LUXEMBOURG PLAZA OFFICE BUILDING, Prague, Czech Republic, 2002–2005

RENAISSANCE SHANGHAI ZHONGSHAN HOTEL AND CLOUD NINE SHOPPING MALL, Shanghai, China, 2002–2004

DOUGLAS STATION, Miami, Florida, USA, 2002–2006

WILSHIRE VERMONT STATION, Los Angeles, California, USA, 2002–2006

BEIJING FIFTH SQUARE, Beijing, China, 2002–2007

ZENDAI FORUM, Shanghai, China, 2003–2005

MARINA BLUE, Miami, Florida, USA, 2003–2008

ZHONGGUANCUN AVIATION & SCIENCE PARK, Beijing, China, 2003

LATITUDE ON THE RIVER AND ASSIST CARD TOWER, Miami, Florida, USA, 2003–2005

500 BRICKELL, Miami, Florida, USA, 2004–2008

COSMOPOLITAN RESORT AND CASINO, Las Vegas, Nevada, USA, 2004–2010

MARQUIS AND ME MIAMI, Miami, Florida, USA, 2004–2008

INTERNATIONAL FINANCE CENTER, Seoul, South Korea, 2004–2013

MIMA AND YOTEL, New York, New York, USA, 2004–2011

LUDI HE CHUANG TOWER, Shanghai, China, 2005–2008

SHANGHAI MEILONG CENTRE, Shanghai, China, 2005–2007

ICON BRICKELL RESIDENCES AND W HOTEL, Miami, Florida, USA, 2005–2008

GRAND HYATT SAN ANTONIO CONVENTION CENTER HOTEL AND ALTEZA CONDOMINIUMS, San Antonio, Texas, USA, 2005–2008

THE GATE AND ARC TOWERS, AND BOUTIK MALL, Abu Dhabi, UAE, 2005–2013

SKY AND SUN TOWERS, Abu Dhabi, UAE, 2005–2010

TRINITY PLACE - PHASE 1 - 1188 MISSION STREET, San Francisco, California, USA, 2006–2010

W SQUARE RETAIL AND OFFICE TOWER, Hong Kong, China, 2006–2008

CONCORD CITY, Shanghai, China, 2007–2022

BANCO REAL SANTANDER HEADQUARTERS, JK IGUATEMI MALL AND WTORRE PLAZA, São Paulo, Brazil, 2007–2012

BRICKELL CITY CENTRE, Miami, Florida, USA, 2008–2016

HUDSON LIGHTS, Fort Lee, New Jersey, USA, 2009–2017

TRINITY PLACE - PHASE 2 - 1190 MISSION STREET, San Francisco, California, USA, 2009–2013

CONCORD WORLD FINANCIAL CENTER, Chongqing, China, 2010–2022

POLY DONGRUI PLAZA, Foshan, China, 2010–2018

BANCO DE ORO TOWER AND SM KEPPEL TOWER, Manila, Philippines, 2010–2019

SPIRIT OF SAIGON, Ho Chi Minh City, Vietnam, 2010–2020

ISLA MOCOLI, Guayaquil, Ecuador, 2010–2017

PIERCE BOSTON, Boston, Massachusetts, USA, 2011–2018

606 WEST 57TH STREET, New York, New York, USA, 2011–2018

JLL CENTER, Pittsburgh, Pennsylvania, USA, 2011–2016

THE EMERSON, Los Angeles, California, USA, 2011–2014

CHINA STAR SQUARE, Macau, China, 2011–2019

GDH MIXED-USE, Panyu, China, 2011–2018

TESTIMONIO AND ECOLE INTERNATIONALE MONACO, Monte Carlo, Monaco, 2011–2019

KLCC TOWER, Kuala Lumpur, Malaysia, 2012–2020

HOBHOUSE, London, England, 2012–2019

TRINITY PLACE - PHASE 3 - 33 EIGHTH STREET, San Francisco, California, USA, 2012–2017

CITYPLACE DORAL, Doral, Florida, USA, 2012–2017

ONE MISSION BAY, San Francisco, California, USA, 2012–2018

SWIRE DALIAN WATERFRONT, Dalian, China, 2012–2020

ZHUJIANG PLAZA, Guangzhou, China, 2012–2020

DAYABUMI, Kuala Lumpur, Malaysia, 2012–2021

HAIZHU PLAZA, Guangzhou, China, 2012–2019

SLS BRICKELL HOTEL AND RESIDENCES, Miami, Florida, USA, 2012–2016

PH PREMIERE, Orlando, Florida, USA, 2012–2017

MARINA VILLAGE, West Palm Beach, Florida, USA, 2013–2020

TCTL 11 DEVELOPMENT, Hong Kong, China, 2013–2019

ONE BRICKELL CITY CENTRE, Miami, Florida, USA, 2013–2020

SLS LUX BRICKELL HOTEL AND RESIDENCES, Miami, Florida, USA, 2013–2018

BRICKELL HEIGHTS, Miami, Florida, USA, 2013–2017

SELECTED WORKS

1061 WEST VAN BUREN, Chicago, Illinois, USA, 2013–2019

HYDE MIDTOWN, Miami, Florida, USA, 2013–2018

HALL OF THE SUN, Shanghai, China, 2014–2020

ONE BRICKELL AND PARK HYATT MIAMI, Miami, Florida, USA, 2014–2020

AUBERGE BISCAYNE RESIDENCES AND SPA, Miami, Florida, USA, 2014–2020

4800 YONGE STREET, Toronto, Canada, 2014–2020

SM MEGAMALL TOWER, Manila, Philippines, 2014–2019

THE INFINITY, LUXEMBOURG, 2014–2019

CENTRO SANTA FE, Mexico City, Mexico, 2014–2019

WYNDHAM AVENUE OF THE ARTS, Costa Mesa, California, USA, 2014–2019

ENGLE BUILDING REDEVELOPMENT, Miami, Florida, USA, 2014–2017

TRINITY PLACE - PHASE 4 - 1169 MARKET STREET, San Francisco, California, USA, 2015–2020

SOBRATO SAN JOSE BLOCK 3, San Jose, California, USA, 2015–2019

245 QUEEN STREET EAST, Toronto, Quebec, Canada, 2015–2020

ONE WEST PALM, Palm Beach, Florida, USA, 2015–2020

CUBE WYNWD, Miami, Florida, USA, 2017–2018

40 HUDSON YARDS, New York, New York, USA, 2017–2021

5TH AND HILL, Los Angeles, California, USA, 2017–2020

PORT OF XIAMEN CRUISE SHIP TERMINALS, Xiamen, China, 2017–2021

255 JULIAN STREET, San Jose, California, USA, 2017–2020

PORT OF XIAMEN MIXED-USE DEVELOPMENT, Xiamen, China, 2017–2021

RESIDENTIAL

THE PINK HOUSE, Miami, Florida, USA, 1976–1978

THE BABYLON, Miami, Florida, USA, 1978–1982

THE PALACE, Miami, Florida, USA, 1979–1982

THE ATLANTIS, Miami, Florida, USA, 1980–1982

ENSENADA HOUSES, Coconut Grove, Florida, USA, 1980–1981

THE IMPERIAL, Miami, Florida, USA, 1980–1983

RIVERBAY, Miami, Florida, USA, 1981

MABA HOUSE, Houston, Texas, USA, 1982

TAGGART TOWNHOUSES, Houston, Texas, USA, 1982–1983

HADDON TOWNHOUSES, Houston, Texas, USA, 1982–1983

MILFORD TOWNHOUSES, Houston, Texas, USA, 1982–1984

MANDELL TOWNHOUSES, Houston, Texas, USA, 1982–1984

MULDER HOUSE, Lima, Peru, 1983–1985

STERLING PLAZA, New York, New York, USA, 1983–1985

NANTUCKET TOWNHOUSES, Houston, Texas, USA, 1983–1984

SUMMIT TOWNHOUSES, Denver, Colorado, USA, 1984–1985

NEWTON TOWNHOUSES, Dallas, Texas, USA, 1984

WALNER HOUSE, Glencoe, Illinois, USA, 1985–1987

STEWART HOUSE, Miami, Florida, USA, 1985–1989

KUSHNER HOUSE, Northbrook, Illinois, USA, 1986–1988

CARRAZANA RESIDENCE, Key Biscayne, Florida, USA, 1986

2100 BRICKELL AVENUE APARTMENTS, Miami, Florida, USA, 1987–1992

THE RIVER CLUB, North Bergen, New Jersey, USA, 1987

700 MIAMI AVENUE APARTMENT BUILDING, Miami, Florida, USA, 1988

WILSHIRE VICTORIA RESIDENTIAL TOWER, LOS ANGELES, CALIFORNIA, USA, 1988

LICHT HOUSE, Little Compton, Rhode Island, USA, 1989–1990

DEN HAAG HOUSING FESTIVAL - HOUSING BLOCK KAVEL 28, The Hague, Netherlands, 1989–1994

BEVERLY HILLS RESIDENCE, BEVERLY HILLS, CALIFORNIA, USA, 1989–1990

GROVE POINT IN THE GABLES AFFORDABLE HOUSING, Miami, Florida, USA, 1990–1996

EDISON TERRACE AFFORDABLE HOUSING, Miami, Florida, USA, 1990–1992

SANCHEZ HOUSE, Coral Gables, Florida, USA, 1991–1992

EDIFICIO DE SAN GABRIEL, Lima, Peru, 1991–1995

RINCONAVILA, Caracas, Venezuela, 1992–1998

GRANDE CORNICHE, Miami Beach, Florida, USA, 1993

BONA VISTA GARDENS, Jakarta, Indonesia, 1993–1997

WINSLAND HOUSE II, Singapore, 1994–1998

ORCHARD SCOTTS , Singapore, 1994–2005

RIMINI BEACH, Miami Beach, Florida, USA, 1994–1996

70 GRANGE ROAD LUXURY CONDOMINIUM, Singapore, 1994–1998

CAIRNHILL RISE, Singapore, 1994–1996

80 GRANGE ROAD LUXURY CONDOMINIUM, Singapore, 1994–1997

NICOLAS DE RIVERA RESIDENCE, Lima, Peru, 1995–1998

NEXUS WORLD, Fukuoka, Japan, 1995–2000

PACIFIC PLAZA TOWERS, Manila, Philippines, 1996–2001

MANILA GOLF CREST, Manila, Philippines, 1996–2000

CASTELLO DEL SOLE / MARQUARD RESIDENCE, Miami Beach, Florida, USA, 1996–1997

THE WAVERLY AT SOUTH BEACH, Miami Beach, Florida, USA, 1997–2001

OCEAN PLACE, Miami Beach, Florida, USA, 1997–2003

EDIFICE AT JIAN SU ROAD SUBWAY STATION, Shanghai, China, 1997–2005

EDIFICIO NICOLAS DE RIVERA, Lima, Peru, 1997–2000

HUGHES COVE RESIDENCE, Miami, Florida, USA, 1997–2000

WATER PLACE, Singapore, 1997–2002

HILTON BENTLEY SOUTH BEACH, Miami Beach, Florida, USA, 1997–2003

THE BENTLEY BAY, Miami Beach, Florida, USA, 1997–2004

THE STRAND OCEAN DRIVE, Miami Beach, Florida, USA, 1998–2005

VILLA VENETIA APARTMENTS, Marina del Rey, California, USA, 2000

BRICKELL STATION RESIDENTIAL TOWERS, Miami, Florida, USA, 2000

330 EAST 57TH STREET CONDOMINIUMS, New York, New York, USA, 2000

ONE MIAMI, Miami, Florida, USA, 2000–2005

QUEENS WEST - TOWER 6 - 47-20 CENTER BOULEVARD, Queens, New York, USA, 2001–2007

QUEENS WEST - TOWER 7 - 47-05 CENTER BOULEVARD, Queens, New York, USA, 2001–2008

QUEENS WEST - TOWER 2 - 45-45 CENTER BOULEVARD, Queens, New York, USA, 2001–2013

QUEENS WEST - TOWER 4 - 46-15 CENTER BOULEVARD, Queens, New York, USA, 2001–2012

QUEENS WEST - TOWER 3 - 46-10 CENTER BOULEVARD, Queens, New York, USA, 2001–2015

QUEENS WEST - TOWER 1 - 45-40 CENTER BOULEVARD, Queens, New York, USA, 2001–2012

CENTURY GARDEN, Shanghai, China, 2001

OLYMPIC HEALTH GARDEN, Shanghai, China, 2001

NATIONAL BASKETBALL ASSOCIATION'S PLAYERS ASSOCIATION CONDOMINIUM, New York, New York, USA, 2001

THE VENTURE, Aventura, Florida, USA, 2001–2004

THE PHOENIX AND EXCELSIOR TOWERS, Jersey City, New Jersey, USA, 2001–2005

THE SLADE, West Palm Beach, Florida, USA, 2001–2004

BROADWAY LOFTS, Cincinnati, Ohio, USA, 2002–2005

MANGROVE WEST COAST, Shenzhen, China, 2002–2005

BLUE, Miami, Florida, USA, 2002–2005

SANYO RESIDENTIAL TOWERS, Osaka, Japan, 2003–2005

SHAMA CENTURY PARK, Shanghai, China, 2003–2006

SELECTED WORKS

CENTRE STREET LOFTS, San Pedro, California, USA, 2003–2005

GATEWAY LOFTS AND PARKING GARAGE, Cincinnati, Ohio, USA, 2003–2005

EDIFICIO CIURLIZZA, Lima, Peru, 2004–2005

VELA TOWNHOMES, Edgewater, New Jersey, USA, 2004–2007

PARAMOUNT BAY, Miami, Florida, USA, 2004–2008

THE INFINITY, San Francisco, California, USA, 2004–2009

AXIS, Miami, Florida, USA, 2004–2008

AVALON MISSION BAY, San Francisco, California, USA, 2004–2009

CASA ROMERO, Lima, Peru, 2005–2006

CASA POPPE, Lima, Peru, 2005–2008

ARTECITY AND GOVERNOR HOTEL RENOVATION, Miami Beach, Florida, USA, 2005–2012

CASA PEDRO BRESCIA MOREYRA, Lima, Peru, 2005–2008

ONE ROCKWELL, Manila, Philippines, 2005–2011

SOLARIA AND ARIA, Milan, Italy, 2005–2014

MYBRICKELL, Miami, Florida, USA, 2005–2013

REGALIA, Sunny Isles, Florida, USA, 2006–2015

GC TOWERS, Beirut, Lebanon, 2006–2018

ICON VALLARTA, Puerto Vallarta, Mexico, 2006–2010

ALBA, Singapore, 2006–2015

THE FORFAR, Hong Kong, China, 2007–2010

BEAUFORT, Manila, Philippines, 2007–2015

ICON PANAMA COSTA DEL ESTE, Panama City, Panama, 2007–2008

CASA ALIAGA, Lima, Peru, 2007–2010

EDIFICIO CORONADO, Lima, Peru, 2008–2010

EDIFICIO EL VALLE, Lima, Peru, 2008–2010

EDIFICIO LA JOLLA, Lima, Peru, 2008–2010

EDIFICIO DEL MAR, Lima, Peru, 2008–2010

MARINELLA, Hong Kong, China, 2008–2012

SEYMOUR, Hong Kong, China, 2008–2012

EDIFICIO VICTOR MAURTUA 1, Lima, Peru, 2009–2011

MOUNT PARKER RESIDENCES, Hong Kong, China, 2009–2014

BAY OF MODERN ART (BOMA), Xiamen, China, 2010–2018

OCEANA KEY BISCAYNE, Key Biscayne, Florida, USA, 2010–2014

EDIFICIO VICTOR MAURTUA 2, Lima, Peru, 2010–2011

LUMINA, San Francisco, California, USA, 2010–2017

BEACH HOUSE 8, Miami Beach, Florida, USA, 2010–2017

LINEA, San Francisco, California, USA, 2011–2014

AQUALINA AT WATERFRONT TORONTO, Toronto, Quebec, Canada, 2011–2018

ICON BAY, Miami, Florida, USA, 2011–2015

FENDI CHATEAU RESIDENCES, Surfside, Florida, USA, 2012–2017

AVIVA CORAL GABLES, Coral Gables, Florida, USA, 2012–2015

OLUME, San Francisco, California, USA, 2012–2016

THE ELLIPSE, Jersey City, New Jersey, USA, 2012–2018

HOMANTIN HILLSIDE, Hong Kong, China, 2012–2016

OCEANA BAL HARBOUR, Bal Harbour, Florida, USA, 2012–2017

KAI AT BAY HARBOR, Bay Harbor Islands, Florida, USA, 2012–2017

TERRENO JUNTO RESIDENTIAL LOT 1, Macau, China, 2013–2018

PARAISO BAY, Miami, Florida, USA, 2013–2018

GRAN PARAISO ON THE BAY, Miami, Florida, USA, 2013–2018

ARIA ON THE BAY, Miami, Florida, USA, 2013–2018

AQUAVISTA AT WATERFRONT TORONTO, Toronto, Quebec, Canada, 2013–2018

ONE PARAISO, Miami, Florida, USA, 2013–2018

8800 DORAL APARTMENTS, Doral, Florida, USA, 2013–2017

BASADRE 3, Lima, Peru, 2013–2017

33 TEHAMA, San Francisco, California, USA, 2013–2018

EDIFICIO KLIMT, Lima, Peru, 2014–2017

RITZ-CARLTON RESIDENCES AND SPA, Sunny Isles, Florida, USA, 2014–2019

2100 MARKET STREET, San Francisco, California, USA, 2014–2018

THE HAMPTONS, Cupertino, California, USA, 2014–2020

MALECON DE LA MARINA, Lima, Peru, 2014–2017

PARAISO BAYVIEWS, Miami, Florida, USA, 2014–2018

SABBIA BEACH, Pompano Beach, Florida, USA, 2014–2018

25 MASON STREET, San Francisco, California, USA, 2014–2020

655 FOLSOM STREET, San Francisco, California, USA, 2014–2020

QUITO RESIDENTIAL TOWER, Quito, Ecuador, 2014–2018

ELYSEE, Miami, Florida, USA, 2014–2019

CASA MARIO BRESCIA, Lima, Peru, 2014–2017

THE VILLAGES, Miami, Florida, USA, 2015–2018

SOLEMIA, North Miami, Florida, USA, 2015–2019

MANOR RIVERWALK, Tampa, Florida, USA, 2015–2018

CARLYLE SOUTH, Alexandria, Virginia, USA, 2015–2020

31 PARLIAMENT STREET, Toronto, Quebec, Canada, 2015–2020

VITACON FIANDEIRAS, Sao Paulo, Brazil, 2015–2020

1825 LAS PALMAS AVENUE, Hollywood, California, USA, 2016–2020

UNIVERSITY OF MIAMI STUDENT HOUSING VILLAGE, Coral Gables, Florida, USA, 2016–2019

CASA CUENCO-LINDLEY, Lima , Peru, 2016–2019

3816 DUNN DRIVE, Los Angeles, California, USA, 2017–2020

888 DEVON STREET, Los Angeles, California, USA, 2017–2020

VITACON LOBAO, Sao Paulo, Brazil, 2017–2020

HOSPITALITY

HOTEL LIBERTADOR CUZCO RENOVATION, Cuzco, Peru, 1986–1987

HOTEL LIBERTADOR TRUJILLO RENOVATION, Trujillo, Peru, 1986–1987

HOTEL LIBERTADOR AREQUIPA RENOVATION, Arequipa, Peru, 1986–1987

SAN JOSE CONVENTION HOTEL, San Jose, California, USA, 1987

DISNEYLAND PARIS, VARIOUS PROJECTS, Marne la Vallée, France, 1990–1993

DISNEY'S ALL STAR SPORTS RESORT, Orlando, Florida, USA, 1991–1994

DISNEY'S ALI STAR MUSIC RESORT, ORLANDO, FLORIDA, USA, 1991–1995

PARQUE FUNDIDORA CONVENTION CENTER HOTEL, Monterrey, Mexico, 1992–1998

HYATT REGENCY HOTEL, Lima, Peru, 1994–1998

THE WESTIN NEW YORK AT TIMES SQUARE, New York, New York, USA, 1994–2002

DISNEY'S ALL STAR MOVIES RESORT, Orlando, Florida, USA, 1996–1999

THE STANDARD HOTEL RENOVATION, West Hollywood, California, USA, 1996–1998

HILTON LIMA HOTEL AND OFFICE TOWERS, Lima, Peru, 1996–2004

JW MARRIOTT LIMA HOTEL, Lima, Peru, 1997–2000

DISNEY'S POP CENTURY RESORT, Orlando, Florida, USA, 1998–2003

GOLDEN MOON HOTEL AND CASINO RESORT, Choctaw, Mississippi, USA, 1998–2002

LE MERIDIEN CYBERPORT, Hong Kong, China, 1999–2004

RITZ-CARLTON HOTEL AT PARK PLACE, Irvine, California, USA, 1999–2000

MARINA BAIE DES ANGES RESORT, Nice, France, 2000

THE VICEROY HOTEL RENOVATION, Santa Monica, California, USA, 2000–2002

HILTON AMERICAS - HOUSTON CONVENTION CENTER HOTEL, Houston, Texas, USA, 2000–2003

APOLLO RESORT, Volos, Greece, 2001–2005

DISNEY'S HOLLYWOOD HOTEL, Hong Kong, China, 2001–2005

NOVOTEL CITYGATE HOTEL, Hong Kong, China, 2003–2006

SHERATON PHOENIX CONVENTION CENTER HOTEL, Phoenix, Arizona, USA, 2005–2008

CITY OF DREAMS RESORT AND CASINO, Macau, China, 2005–2009

WESTIN LIMA HOTEL AND CONVENTION CENTER, Lima, Peru, 2006–2011

MANDARIN ORIENTAL HOTEL AND RESIDENCES, Shanghai, China, 2006–2013

SLS SOUTH BEACH, Miami Beach, Florida, USA, 2006–2012

LUXURY COLLECTION TAMBO DEL INKA RESORT & SPA, Urubamba, Peru, 2007–2009

REVEL RESORT AND CASINO, Atlantic City, New Jersey, USA, 2007–2012

FAIRMONT HOTEL AND RAFFLES SUITES AND RESIDENCES, Manila, Philippines, 2007–2012

LUXURY COLLECTION PARACAS RESORT & SPA, Paracas, Peru, 2007–2009

LE MERIDIEN COLUMBUS, THE JOSEPH, Columbus, Ohio, USA, 2010–2015

NAUTILUS HOTEL RENOVATION, Miami Beach, Florida, USA, 2011–2015

JW MARRIOTT NASHVILLE, Nashville, Tennessee, USA, 2014–2018

MR. C BY CIPRIANI, Miami, Florida, USA, 2014–2018

CIPRIANI IBIZA RESORT, Ibiza , Spain, 2014–2016

ALOFT MIRAFLORES HOTEL, Lima, Peru, 2016–2018

ALOFT COSTA VERDE HOTEL, Lima, Peru, 2016–2018

LUXURY COLLECTION NASHVILLE, THE JOSEPH, Nashville, Tennessee, USA, 2016–2020

LAKE NONA TOWN CENTER HOTEL, Orlando, Florida, USA, 2017–2019

LAKE NONA RESORT, Orlando, Florida, USA, 2017–2020

OFFICE

EL PORTAL RECONSTRUCTIVE SURGERY CENTER, Miami Shores, Florida, USA, 1978–1979

OVERSEAS TOWER, Miami, Florida, USA, 1980–1982

CREDITBANK OFFICE TOWER, Miami, Florida, USA, 1982–1986

BANCO DE CREDITO HEADQUARTERS, Lima, Peru, 1982–1988

CREDITBANK HEADQUARTERS, Coral Gables, Florida, USA, 1983–1985

CAPITAL PARK WEST, Houston, Texas, USA, 1983–1983

CAPITAL BANK, SOUTH MIAMI, Florida, USA, 1983–1984

SOUTH FERRY PLAZA CENTER COMPETITION, New York, New York, USA, 1984

BAYOUD OFFICE BUILDING, Dallas, Texas, USA, 1984

COLSON HICKS EIDSON OFFICE INTERIORS, Coral Gables, Florida, USA, 1985–1986

THE CENTER FOR INNOVATIVE TECHNOLOGY, Herndon, Virginia, USA, 1985–1988

TANG INDUSTRIES HEADQUARTERS INTERIORS, Chicago, Illinois, USA, 1987–1989

BMG REGIONAL HEADQUARTERS/BANK OF AMERICA BUILDING, Beverly Hills, California, USA, 1988–1991

COMMERCIAL PLACE, Fort Lauderdale, Florida, USA, 1988–1990

YERBA BUENA GARDENS OFFICE BUILDING COMPETITION, San Francisco, California, USA, 1988

BANQUE DE LUXEMBOURG HEADQUARTERS – I Luxembourg, 1989–1994

ARBED S. A. HEADQUARTERS COMPETITION, Luxembourg, 1989

WEST AND COMPANY ADVERTISING HEADQUARTERS INTERIORS, Tampa, Florida, USA, 1991–1993

BBVA OFFICE BUILDING, Monterrey, Mexico, 1992–1995

ESTEFAN ENTERPRISES OFFICES, Miami Beach, Florida, USA, 1993–1994

BELLO CAMPO OFFICE TOWER, Caracas, Venezuela, 1993

MTV LATINO HEADQUARTERS INTERIORS, Miami Beach, Florida, USA, 1993–1994

HONG KONG BANK, Singapore, 1994–1998

CITY NATIONAL BANK, Miami Beach, Florida, USA, 1994–1997

WISMA BOUNALI RENOVATION, Jakarta, Indonesia, 1995–1996

SHANGHAI INFORMATION TOWN, Shanghai, China, 1995–1999

WIESE HEADQUARTERS, Lima, Peru, 1995–2000

SONY MUSIC INTERNATIONAL REGIONAL HEADQUARTERS RENOVATION, Miami Beach, Florida, USA, 1995

THE NEW TIMES REGIONAL HEADQUARTERS, Miami, Florida, USA, 1995–1996

550 BRICKELL RENOVATION, Miami, Florida, USA, 1995–1998

POST AND TELECOM HEADQUARTERS COMPETITION, Shanghai, China, 1995

JIN HUI PIAZA TOWERS/COMMERCIAL AND INDUSTRIAL BANK OF CHINA, Shanghai, China, 1995

SHANGHAI FINANCE MINISTRY TOWER, Shanghai, China, 1996–2002

EXALTIS TOWER, Paris, France, 1996–2006

TORRE LOS NARDOS RENOVATION, Lima, Peru, 1996–1997

LZM TOWER COMPETITION, Shanghai, China, 1997

TORRE PARQUE MAR OFFICE BUILDING, Lima, Peru, 1997–2000

ATLANTIC CENTER / WILLIAM MORRIS AGENCY BUILDING, Miami Beach, Florida, USA, 1997–2003

CITYPLAZA 2 OFFICE TOWER, Hong Kong, China, 1998

UBS HARBOUR CENTRE, Aventura, Florida, USA, 1998–2004

WARNER MUSIC LATIN AMERICA HEADQUARTERS, Miami Beach, Florida, USA, 1998–2002

OFFICE BUILDING ISSY LES MOLINEAUX, Paris, France, 1998

SURESNES OFFICE BUILDING, Paris, France, 1998–2000

IXL ENTERPRISES HEADQUARTERS INTERIORS, Atlanta, Georgia, USA, 1999–2000

THE LINCOLN / BB&T BANK BUILDING, Miami Beach, Florida, USA, 1999–2003

THE MIAMI HERALD PULITZER PRIZE SHRINE, Miami, Florida, USA, 1999

IXL ENTERPRISES OFFICE INTERIORS, San Diego, California, USA, 2000

IXL ENTERPRISES OFFICE INTERIORS, Los Angeles, California, USA, 2000

IXL ENTERPRISES OFFICE INTERIORS, London, England, 2000

OFFICE BUILDING 4B AT PARK PLACE, Irvine, California, USA, 2000

IXL ENTERPRISES OFFICE INTERIORS, Sao Paulo, Brazil, 2000

CORPORATE POINTE OFFICE DEVELOPMENT, Culver City, California, USA, 2000–2002

THE RELATED GROUP CORPORATE HEADQUARTERS, Miami, Florida, USA, 2000–2005

WOODLAND PARK OFFICE DEVELOPMENT, Herndon, Virginia, USA, 2001

BRIGHT DAIRY GROUP HEADQUARTERS, Shanghai, China, 2001–2002

THE SARASOTA HERALD-TRIBUNE HEADQUARTERS, Sarasota, Florida, USA, 2002–2006

EAST HOPE GROUP HEADQUARTERS, Shanghai, China, 2002–2004

HOMETOWN STATION, Miami, Florida, USA, 2003–2005

LUDI CHANGNING TOWER, Shanghai, China, 2003–2006

TERRANOVA HEADQUARTERS INTERIORS, Miami Beach, Florida, USA, 2004–2005

MICROSOFT EUROPE HEADQUARTERS, Paris, France, 2004–2009

ADARO ENERGY TOWER, Jakarta, Indonesia, 2004–2007

STANDARD CHARTERED BANK TOWER, Jakarta, Indonesia, 2004–2008

LANDMARK EAST, Hong Kong, China, 2004–2008

AIR2 TOUR, Paris, France, 2004–2020

BAO MINERALS TOWER RENOVATION, Shanghai, China, 2005–2006

ARQUITECTONICA STUDIOS, Miami, Florida, USA, 2005–2010

RIMAC PLAZA DEL SOL, Lima, Peru, 2005–2006

ONE E-COM CENTER, Manila, Philippines, 2005–2008

ACCOR HEADQUARTERS AND EQWATER, Paris, France, 2005–2010

CAOHEJING HIGH-TECH PARK, Shanghai, China, 2005–2009

ROCHE PHARMACEUTICALS, Lima, Peru, 2006–2010

AGRICULTURAL BANK OF CHINA AND CHINA CONSTRUCTION BANK, Shanghai, China, 2006–2011

TEMPO SCAN TOWER, Jakarta, Indonesia, 2007–2012

BANCO GNB, Lima, Peru, 2007–2014

BANCO DE CREDITO DATA CENTER, Lima, Peru, 2008–2010

TWO E-COM CENTER, Manila, Philippines, 2008–2013

GREEN TOWERS, Brasilia, Brazil, 2009–2016

BANQUE DE LUXEMBOURG HEADQUARTERS — II, Luxembourg, 2009–2012

W HIGH STREET OFFICE BUILDING, Manila, Philippines, 2009–2011

VASANT E ZONE IT PARK, Mumbai, India 2010

INTURSA HEADQUARTERS, LIMA, PERU, 2010–2011

FIVE E-COM CENTER, Manila, Philippines, 2010–2015

SEA WORLD SALES OFFICE, Tianjin, China, 2010–2011

WHIRLPOOL GLOBAL HEADQUARTERS, Benton Harbor, Michigan, USA, 2010–2017

SHATIN COMMUNICATIONS AND TECHNOLOGY CENTER, Hong Kong , China, 2010–2016

DENIZBANK TORUN TOWER, Istanbul, Turkey, 2011–2014

BBVA TOWER, Buenos Aires, Argentina, 2011–2017

W FIFTH TOWER, Manila, Philippines, 2011–2013

BELCORP HEADQUARTERS, Lima, Peru, 2011–2015

BG GROUP GLOBAL TECHNOLOGY CENTRE, Rio de Janeiro, Brazil, 2011–2016

BANCO DE ORO REGIONAL OFFICES, various locations in the Philippines, 2011–2015

TORRE DEL ARTE, Lima, Peru, 2011–2017

RIMAC HEADQUARTERS, Lima, Peru, 2011–2019

SATRIO SQUARE, Jakarta, Indonesia, 2012–2016

PERSHING OFFICES, Lima, Peru, 2012–2015

TORRE DEL PARQUE 1, Lima, Peru, 2012–2017

TORRE TRAZO, Lima, Peru, 2012–2015

CHITALAND OFFICE TOWER, Jakarta, Indonesia, 2013–2019

FOUR E-COM CENTER, Manila, Philippines, 2013–2021

THREE E-COM CENTER, Manila, Philippines, 2013–2018

ALPHA PLUS TOWER, Manila, Philippines, 2013–2018

MERCY HOSPITAL MEDICAL OFFICE BUILDING, Miami, Florida, USA, 2013–2017

PHILAMLIFE CENTER CEBU, Cebu, Philippines, 2013–2017

BANCO DE LA NACION HEADQUARTERS, Lima, Peru, 2013–2015

COCONUT GROVE BANK INTERIORS, Miami, Florida, USA, 2014–2017

FORUM AVENTURA, Aventura, Florida, USA, 2014–2018

SIX E-COM CENTER, Manila, Philippines, 2015–2021

AK REALTY OFFICE, Sao Paulo, Brazil, 2015–2016

EXQUADRA TOWER, Manila, Philippines, 2016–2020

PATHLINE PARK TECHNOLOGY CAMPUS, Sunnyvale, California, USA, 2016–2020

SOBRATO SAN JOSE BLOCK 8, San Jose, California, USA, 2016–2021

TORRE DEL PARQUE 2, Lima, Peru, 2016–2020

THE RELATED GROUP CORPORATE HEADQUARTERS, Miami, Florida, USA, 2017–2019

RETAIL/ENTERTAINMENT

THE SQUARE AT KEY BISCAYNE, Key Biscayne, Florida, USA, 1979–1982

DECORATIVE ARTS PLAZA SHOWROOM CENTER, Miami, Florida, USA, 1980–1982

THE VAULT FUR SHOWROOM AND STORAGE, Paramus, New Jersey, USA, 1983

MESA EAST RICHMOND SHOPPING CENTER, Houston, Texas, USA, 1984

ZEPHYR SHOWROOM CENTER, Houston, Texas, USA, 1984–1985

THE RIO SHOPPING MALL, Atlanta, Georgia, USA, 1985–1989

MIRACLE CENTER SHOPPING MALL, Coral Gables, Florida, USA, 1985–1988

HONDA CARLAND, Roswell, Georgia, USA, 1985

VAULT FUR SHOWROOM AND STORAGE, Stamford, Connecticut, USA, 1986

MELROSE AVENUE SHOPS, Los Angeles, California, USA, 1986

SAWGRASS MILLS MALL, Sunrise, Florida, USA, 1987–1990

THE WASHINGTONIAN CENTER, Gaithersburg, Maryland, USA, 1987–1990

FLORIDA TURNPIKE PLAZAS, throughout State of Florida, USA, 1988–1989

ITALIAN TILE SHOWROOM INTERIORS, Miami, Florida, USA, 1991–1992

BALLET VALET PARKING GARAGE AND RETAIL SHOPS, Miami Beach, Florida, USA, 1993–1996

CITYPLAZA SHOPPING CENTER RENOVATION, Hong Kong, China, 1995–2005

JOCKEY PLAZA SHOPPING CENTER, Lima, Peru, 1995–1998

BONGO'S CUBAN CAFÉ AT DISNEY SPRINGS, Orlando, Florida, USA, 1996–1997

ESPN GAMEPOINT SKYBOX BAR INTERIORS ON DISNEY MAGIC CRUISE SHIP, Port Canaveral, Florida, USA, 1996–1997

CHINA WORLD TRADE CENTER RENOVATION & EXPANSION, Beijing, China, 1997–1999

NEW WORLD CENTRE RENOVATION, Hong Kong, China, 1999–2001

THE BOATYARD, Marina del Rey, California, USA, 2000–2002

BALLY'S TOTAL FITNESS CENTER, Coral Gables, Florida, USA, 2000–2001

THE PODIUM / SM KEPPEL MALL INTERIOR RENOVATION, Manila, Philippines, 2001–2002

MANHATTAN MALL RENOVATION, New York, New York, USA, 2001–2003

SM MALL OF ASIA, Manila, Philippines, 2001–2007

HONG KOU SHOPPING CENTER, Shanghai, China, 2003–2005

YOUYICHENG / NEW ERA MALL, Shanghai, China, 2003–2005

SM MEGAMALL EDSA, Manila, Philippines, 2003–2012

SPEED MALL, Wuxi, China, 2003–2005

KING GLORY PLAZA, Shenzhen, China, 2003–2004

SM CITY NORTH EDSA MALL, Manila, Philippines, 2004–2006

SM XIAMEN MALL, Xiamen, China, 2004–2008

SINOLINK VI CITY SHOPPING MALL, Shenzhen, China, 2004–2010

DALIAN TIMES SQUARE RETAIL, Dalian, China, 2004–2008

GRAND METROPOLIS MALL, Changzhou, China, 2005–2005

BLEU CAPELETTE, Marseilles, France, 2007–2017

1000 17TH STREET, Miami Beach, Florida, USA, 2007–2014

SM CITY NORTH EDSA MALL SKY GARDEN, Manila, Philippines, 2007–2009

SM CITY CHONGQING MALL, Chongqing, China, 2007–2012

SUNSET HARBOUR GARAGE AND RETAIL SHOPS, Miami Beach, Florida, USA, 2007–2012

SM XIAMEN 1 REFURBISHMENT, Xiamen, China, 2008–2013

THE AURA / SM TAGUIG CITY MALL, Manila, Philippines, 2008–2013

SKYRISE, Miami, Florida, USA, 2008–2020

SM ZIBO, Zibo, China, 2009–2015

TIANJIN TEEMALL, Tianjin, China, 2009–2017

SENADO SQUARE, Macau, China, 2010–2021

LA RAMBLA SAN BORJA, Lima , Peru, 2010–2013

SM SEASIDE CITY, Cebu, Philippines, 2010–2015

SM TIANJIN MALL, Tianjin, China, 2011–2016

KOMODO RESTAURANT, Miami, Florida, USA, 2011–2015

SHUM YIP UPPERHILLS, Shenzhen, China, 2012–2018

MANDARIN ORIENTAL BRICKELL KEY FOOD & BEVERAGE RENOVATION, Miami, Florida, USA, 2012–2013

LA RAMBLA BRASIL, Lima, Peru, 2013–2015

WYNWOOD DINER BUILDING RENOVATION, Miami, Florida, USA, 2013–2015

TCTL 2 A & A WORKS, Hong Kong, China, 2013–2019

SM MALL OF ASIA EXPANSION & RENOVATION, Manila, Philippines, 2013–2020

CAMINO REAL SHOPPING CENTER, Lima, Peru, 2016–2019

CULTURAL/EDUCATIONAL

INTERNATIONAL SWIMMING HALL OF FAME MUSEUM AND EXHIBITION HALL, Fort Lauderdale, Florida, USA, 1987–1991

BIBLIOTHÈQUE NATIONALE DE FRANCE COMPETITION, Paris, France, 1989

FIREFIGHTERS MEMORIAL MUSEUM, Miami, Florida, USA, 1990–1992

SANTA CLARA ELEMENTARY SCHOOL, Miami, Florida, USA, 1990–1996

DIJON PERFORMING ARTS CENTER, Dijon, France, 1991–1998

FOSTER CITY PUBLIC LIBRARY AND COMMUNITY CENTER, Foster City, California, USA, 1992–1997

GALLERY MA ART EXHIBITION, Tokyo, Japan, 1993

ENEIDA M. HARTNER ELEMENTARY SCHOOL, Miami, Florida, USA, 1994–1996

DISCOVERY SCIENCE CENTER, Santa Ana, California, USA, 1995–1999

RANSOM EVERGLADES MIDDLE SCHOOL SCIENCE CLASSROOM BUILDING, Miami, Florida, USA, 1996–1988

MIAMI CITY BALLET, Miami Beach, Florida, USA, 1997–2000

MIAMI CHILDREN'S MUSEUM, Miami, Florida, USA, 1997–2003

LINCOLN CENTER THEATER RENOVATION, New York, New York, USA, 2000–2002

LEARNING EXPERIENCE SCHOOL, Miami, Florida, USA, 2000–2003

SOUTH MIAMI-DADE CULTURAL ARTS CENTER, Cutler Bay, Florida, USA, 2000–2011

THE BRONX MUSEUM OF THE ARTS, New York, New York, USA, 2001–2006

EF INTERNATIONAL LANGUAGE SCHOOL RENOVATION, Miami Beach, Florida, USA, 2001

JOHN W. MACK ELEMENTARY SCHOOL, Los Angeles, California, USA, 2001–2005

HIGH SCHOOL FOR CONSTRUCTION TRADES, ENGINEERING AND ARCHITECTURE, Queens, New York, USA, 2001–2006

CALIFORNIA STATE POLYTECHNIC UNIVERSITY BIOMEDICAL RESEARCH LABORATORY, Pomona, California, USA, 2001–2002

RANCHO SANTIAGO COMMUNITY COLLEGE DIGITAL MEDIA CENTER, Santa Ana, California, USA, 2002–2005

PLYMOUTH CONGREGATIONAL CHURCH CAMPUS MASTER PLAN, Miami, Florida, USA, 2003–2004

EAST LOS ANGELES COLLEGE ARTS CAMPUS, Los Angeles, California, USA, 2003–2011

BELMONT ELEMENTARY SCHOOL # 9, Los Angeles, California, USA, 2003–2006

IRVINE VALLEY COLLEGE PERFORMING ARTS CENTER, Irvine, California, USA, 2003–2007

YOUNG OAK KIM ACADEMY, Los Angeles, California, USA, 2003–2008

UNIVERSITY OF MIAMI DONNA E. SHALALA STUDENT CENTER, Coral Gables, Florida, USA, 2003–2013

RANSOM EVERGLADES MIDDLE SCHOOL BRAMAN FAMILY MEDIA CENTER, Miami, Florida, USA, 2004–2006

NASA COLUMBIA MEMORIAL SPACE LEARNING CENTER, Los Angeles, California, USA, 2005–2008

FLORIDA INTERNATIONAL UNIVERSITY SCHOOL OF INTERNATIONAL AND PUBLIC AFFAIRS, Miami, Florida, USA, 2006–2010

ALONZO AND TRACY MOURNING HIGH SCHOOL, Miami, Florida, USA, 2006–2009

UNIVERSITY OF MIAMI WHITTEN LEARNING CENTER RENOVATION, Coral Gables, Florida, USA, 2011–2013

UNIVERSITY OF MIAMI SCHOOL OF ARCHITECTURE STUDIOS, Coral Gables, Florida, USA, 2012–2018

UNIVERSITY OF MIAMI PEDESTRIAN "FATE BRIDGE", Coral Gables, Florida, USA, 2013–2016

NIHERST SCIENCE CITY, Port of Spain, Trinidad, 2013–2020

CUSHMAN SCHOOL PLAY TO LEARN FACILITY, Miami, Florida, USA, 2014–2019

COCONUT GROVE PLAYHOUSE REDEVELOPMENT, Miami, Florida, USA, 2015–2021

CIVIC

NORTH DADE JUSTICE CENTER, Miami, Florida, USA, 1983–1988

CENTRAL BUS TERMINAL FOR BROWARD COUNTY, Fort Lauderdale, Florida, USA, 1987–1988

UNITED STATES EMBASSY, Lima, Peru, 1988–1995

U.S. PAVILION PROPOSAL FOR 1992 WORLD'S FAIR EXPOSITION, Seville, Spain, 1989

UNITED STATES COAST GUARD HOUSING CAMPUS, Bayamón, Puerto Rico, 1990–1997

DIJON CONVENTION CENTER, Dijon, France, 1991–1997

DIJON CONFERENCE CENTER, Dijon, France, 1991–1999

PHOEBE MORSE CHILDREN'S CENTER, Miami, Florida, USA, 1994–1995

DISNEY CRUISE LINE TERMINAL, Port Canaveral, Florida, USA, 1995–1997

MIAMI INTERNATIONAL AIRPORT TERMINAL EXPANSION AND RENOVATION, Miami, Florida, USA, 1996–1999

WILKIE D. FERGUSON, JR. UNITED STATES COURTHOUSE, Miami, Florida, USA, 1997–2007

AVENTURA GOVERNMENT CENTER, Miami, Florida, USA, 1998–2001

PITTSBURGH CONVENTION CENTER COMPETITION, Pittsburgh, Pennsylvania, USA, 1998–1999

JORGE CHAVEZ INTERNATIONAL AIRPORT TERMINAL EXPANSION, Lima, Peru, 1999–2005

MIAMI INTERNATIONAL AIRPORT TERMINAL EXPANSION AND RENOVATION, Miami, Florida, USA, 2000–2001

BUS STOP SHELTERS, BUS STOP BENCHES, INFORMATION KIOSKS AND STREET SIGNAGE, Miami Beach, Florida, USA, 2000–2002

ALBANY HOUSES COMMUNITY CENTER & GYMNASIUM, New York, New York, USA, 2000–2004

MISSISSIPPI TELECOMMUNICATIONS & CONFERENCE CENTER, Jackson, Mississippi, USA, 2000–2006

JACKSON CONVENTION COMPLEX, Jackson, Mississippi, USA, 2000–2009

UNITED NATIONS PEACEKEEPERS MEMORIAL, New York, New York, USA, 2002–2003

CHANGNING DISTRICT GOVERNMENT CENTER, Shanghai, China, 2003–2005

TOWN OF GATES PUBLIC SAFETY FACILITY, Rochester, New York, USA, 2003–2004

EAST WILMINGTON RECREATION CENTER, Los Angeles, California, USA, 2003–2005

FLORIDA TURNPIKE TOLL PLAZAS, throughout State of Florida, USA, 2005–2007

MANILA CONVENTION CENTER, Manila, Philippines, 2005–2007

FRANKLIN COUNTY COURTHOUSE, Columbus, Ohio, USA, 2006–2011

PORT MIAMI TUNNEL, Miami, Florida, USA, 2012–2014

SM MOA RETAIL AND MUSEUM, Manila, Philippines, 2013–2017

LAS OLAS PARKING GARAGE AND BOULEVARD IMPROVEMENTS, Fort Lauderdale, Florida, USA, 2014–2019

MIAMI BEACH CONVENTION CENTER REDEVELOPMENT, Miami Beach, Florida, USA, 2014–2018

SPORTS

FLORIDA INTERNATIONAL UNIVERSITY FITNESS CENTER RENOVATION, Miami, Florida, USA, 1992–1995

PHILIPS ARENA, Atlanta, Georgia, USA, 1995–1999

AMERICAN AIRLINES ARENA, Miami, Florida, USA, 1996–1999

CORINTHIANS SOCCER STADIUM, Sao Paulo, Brazil, 1999–2002

WUSA SOCCER STADIUMS RENOVATION AND VENUE PLANNING, various US locations, USA, 2000–2001

NEW YORK/NEW JERSEY METROSTARS STADIUM CONCEPTUAL DESIGN, Harrison, New Jersey, USA, 2000–2002

ST. JOHN'S UNIVERSITY BELSON STADIUM, New York, New York, USA, 2000–2002

BALTIMORE VELODROME, Baltimore, Maryland, USA, 2001

AMERICAN BANK CENTER ARENA AND CONVENTION CENTER, Corpus Christi, Texas, USA, 2001–2004

ST JOHN'S UNIVERSITY SOFTBALL FIELD, New York, New York, USA, 2001–2002

ST. JOHN'S UNIVERSITY CAREY MULTIPURPOSE ACTIVITY CENTER, New York, New York, USA, 2001–2003

NORTH CAROLINA STATE UNIVERSITY ATHLETIC FACILITIES RENOVATIONS, Raleigh, North Carolina, USA, 2003–2006

LONG ISLAND UNIVERSITY WELLNESS RECREATION AND ATHLETIC CENTER, Brooklyn, New York, USA, 2003–2006

MANILA ARENA, Manila, Philippines, 2004–2012

RANSOM EVERGLADES MIDDLE SCHOOL GYMNASIUM, Miami, Florida, USA, 2005–2008

MIAMI DOLPHINS HARD ROCK STADIUM REDEVELOPMENT, Miami, Florida, USA, 2009–2019

SEA WORLD TIANJIN ENTERTAINMENT CENTER, Tianjin, China, 2009–2013

BECKHAM STADIUM FEASIBILITY STUDIES, Miami, Florida, USA, 2013–2014

MASTER PLANNING

VINTAGE PARK RESIDENTIAL COMMUNITY, Foster City, California, USA, 1987

VILAMOURA RESORT, Algarve Coast, Portugal, 1990–1991

DIJON URBAN DISTRICT, Dijon, France, 1991–1996

MEERHOVEN DISTRICT, Eindhoven, Netherlands, 1992

NANWAITAN DISTRICT, Shanghai, China, 1993

TAIKOO SHING / ISLAND EAST, Hong Kong, China, 1995–1998

PUERTO RICO WORLD TRADE & CONVENTION CENTER DISTRICT, San Juan, Puerto Rico, 1998–1999

CHOCTAW COMMUNITY, Choctaw, Mississippi, USA, 1999

CHOCTAW RECREATIONAL LAKE DISTRICT, Choctaw, Mississippi, USA, 2000

GEORGIA TECH SAVANNAH TECHNOLOGY CAMPUS, Savannah, Georgia, USA, 2000

QUEENS WEST COMMUNITY, Queens, New York, USA, 2001–2005

SWAINSBORO/EMANUEL COUNTY TECHNOLOGY PARK, Swainsboro, Georgia, USA, 2001

TRINITY PLACE COMMUNITY, San Francisco, California, USA, 2001–2006

AXA BUSINESS PARK, Roissy Gonesse, France, 2002

HUDSON YARDS / WEST MIDTOWN MANHATTAN REDEVELOPMENT, New York, New York, USA, 2002–2003

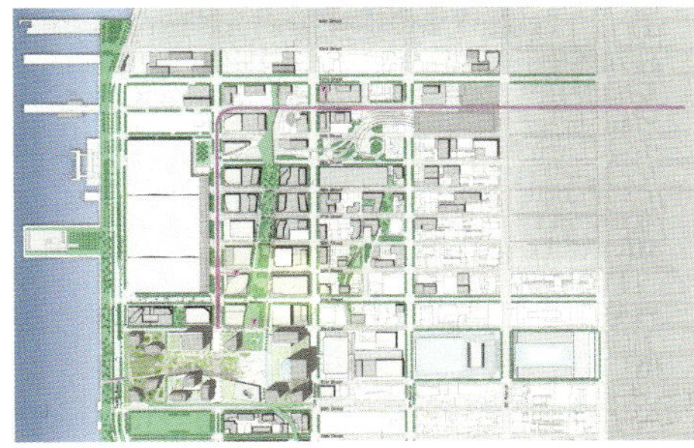

MOROCOPO RIVER DISTRICT, Caracas, Venezuela, 2003

WEST KOWLOON CULTURAL DISTRICT, Hong Kong, China, 2004

QINGDAO WATERFRONT, Qingdao, China, 2004–2005

BAY CITY DISTRICT, Manila, Philippines, 2004–2005

WANCHAI AND CAUSEWAY BAY WATERFRONT DISTRICT, Hong Kong, China, 2005

CONEY ISLAND URBAN REVITALIZATION, Brooklyn, New York, USA, 2006–2007

LULU ISLAND, Abu Dhabi, UAE, 2006–2009

AL MASHTAL, Abu Dhabi, UAE, 2006–2009

SMART CITY MALTA, Ricasoli, Malta, 2007–2015

MONACO SEALAND EXTENSION, Monte Carlo, Monaco, 2007–2008

PARK AVENUE RESIDENTIAL, Shenyang, China, 2008

GAO QI RESIDENTIAL, Shenyang, China, 2008

AL MANHAL DISTRICT, Abu Dhabi, UAE, 2008–2009

AIRPORT ROAD, Abu Dhabi, UAE, 2008–2009

CONCORD CHONGQING DISTRICT, Chongqing, China, 2008–2009

SAN ISIDRO FINANCIAL DISTRICT, Lima, Peru, 2009–2011

LA JOLLA LUXURY BEACH COMMUNITY, Asia, Peru, 2009–2016

MIAMI BEACH CONVENTION DISTRICT, Miami, Florida, USA, 2009–2011

INTERNATIONAL OIL AND GAS UNIVERSITY, Ashgabat, Turkmenistan, 2009–2010

SEA WORLD TIANJIN AQUATIC PARK COMMUNITY, Tianjin, China, 2009–2010

SHANGHAI BAOSHAN INTERNATIONAL RESEARCH AND DEVELOPMENT HEADQUARTERS, Shanghai, China, 2009–2012

SM CEBU SOUTH ROAD PROPERTIES 1, Cebu, Philippines, 2009–2010

SOUTHSIDE COMMERCIAL DISTRICT, Abu Dhabi, UAE, 2009–2010

SM CEBU MIXED-USE DEVELOPMENT, Cebu, Philippines, 2013

SM MALL OF ASIA COMPLEX, Manila, Philippines, 2013–2014

SM PASUDECO, Pampanga, Philippines, 2013

JOCKEY CITY, Lima, Peru, 2014–2015

PORTALIA, Lima, Peru, 2014–2015

SM CEBU SOUTH ROAD PROPERTIES 2, Cebu, Philippines, 2015–2016

ACKNOWLED

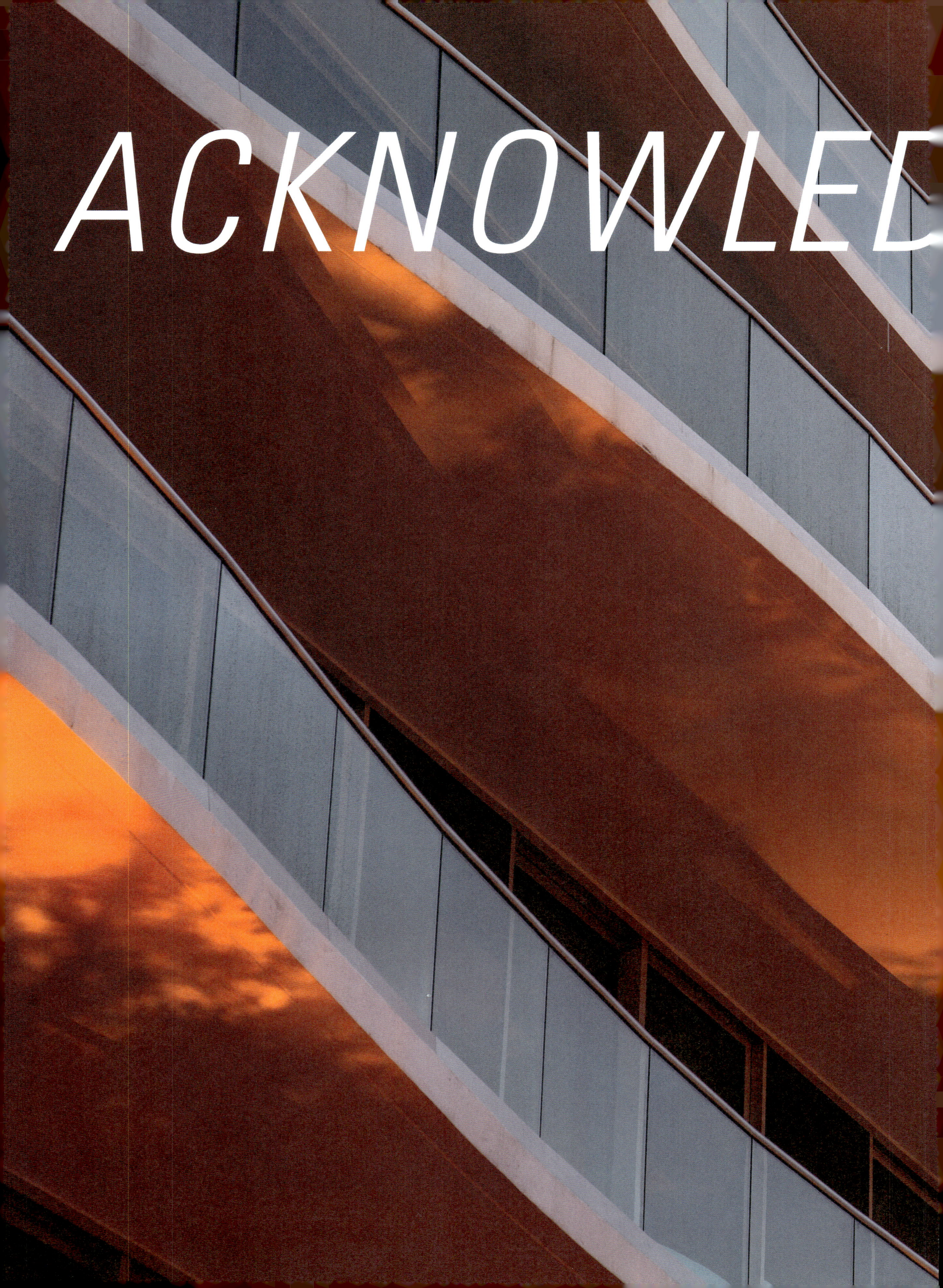

GMENTS

ACKNOWLEDGMENTS

What starts as a sketch ends up, years later, often circuitously, as a realized building — inhabited by people, animating streetscapes and cities, contributing to civic identity and pride. This can only happen with the immense contributions of more people than we can name. There are literally thousands of people who have contributed to what Arquitectonica has achieved over the years.

With a firm as active as Arquitectonica, and with projects as complex as the ones presented in this monograph, collaboration is especially essential. It is a process that is deeply embedded in our firm's founding ethos, and it spreads quickly outwards, encompassing a diverse group of partners:

To our staff through the decades and around the globe who makes our projects a reality by contributing ideas, energy, intelligence and skill;

To our local partners who are integral to the work we do at home and in far-flung locations around the world;

To the specialists and consultants who provide their expertise in every imaginable field;

To the artists who are our collaborators and who contribute their imagination and inspiration;

And to our clients, whose vision, aspirations, resources, and trust make everything we do possible.

Thank you, each and every one of you, for everything you have done and continue to do to make Arquitectonica what it is.

TEAMWORK

Laurinda Spear and Bernardo Fort-Brescia wish to acknowledge the collaboration of the following individuals:

Andrés Duany
Principal, 1977-79

Elizabeth Plater-Zyberk
Principal, 1977-79

Hervin A.R. Romney
Principal, 1977-84

Timothy Reedy
Chief Executive Officer

Jorge Jimenez
Chief Financial Officer

Sherri Gutierrez
Principal / Miami

Alejandro Gonzalez
Principal / Miami

Katia Robreño
Principal / Miami

Samuel Luckino
Principal / New York

Michael O'Boyle
Principal / Los Angeles

Yves Berranger
Director / Paris

Raymond Chu
Director / Shanghai

Peter Brannan
Director / Hong Kong

David Zaballero
Director / Manila

Guillermo Stuart
Director / Lima

Sheila Zynger
Director / São Paulo

Sergio S. Bakas
Senior Vice President

Anna Caruso
Vice President

Michelle Cintron
Vice President

John Ben Hutchens
Vice President

Victor Malerba
Vice President

Jooyeol Oh
Vice President

Thomas Westberg
Vice President

Maria Casuscelli
Senior Associate

Leon H. Cheng
Senior Associate

Charles Crain
Senior Associate

Kenneth Farrell
Senior Associate

Marisa Fort
Senior Associate

Raymond Fort
Senior Associate

Murdo Fraser
Senior Associate

Augusto Garcia
Senior Associate

Scott Kitchen
Senior Associate

Rene Llanes
Senior Associate

Mario Macias
Senior Associate

Jaime Muñoz
Senior Associate

Alejandro Perez
Senior Associate

Ronald Rosell
Senior Associate

Carey Press
Senior Associate

Fidel Zabik
Senior Associate

Liliana Andrade
Associate

Luis Asturias
Associate

Earl E. Brown, Jr.
Associate

Kenlong Castillo
Associate

Karen Chan
Associate

Daniel Garcia
Associate

Rafael Guissarri
Associate

Lourdes Hernandez
Associate

Claire Imatani
Associate

Bewketu Kassa
Associate

Ilon Keilson
Associate

Xin Liu
Associate

Vito Mazzocca
Associate

Isis Mojicar-Hunt
Associate

Amy Newborn
Associate

Ana Ortiz
Associate

Kennieth Richardson
Associate

Felipe Romero
Associate

Daphne Rosas
Associate

Aida Sanchez-Gomez
Associate

Christopher Short
Associate

Elizabeth Suarez
Associate

Heather Tingler-Alonso
Associate

Vera Tse
Associate

Harutyun Voskanyan
Associate

Kirk Weng
Associate

Susan Ibrahim Abed
Aly M. Abouzeid
Leslie Abraham
Andrea Acuña
Myra Acuña
Aurelia P. Adams
Ajibade R. Adebowale
Felipe Agapito
Bea Clare A. Aglibot
Ana Maria Agüero Macher
Anne Caroline Aguinaldo
Alec Aguirre
Natalia Aguirre
Robert P. Aitcheson
Bilal Ajami
Amira Ajlouni
Judith A. Akin
Christopher Akins
Yeison Alarcon
Diego Alata
Gustavo Alberti
José Albertini
Ryan Alderman
Luther Alejandro
Aidin Alejo
Michel Alfonso
Majda Almarzooqi
Meltiades Q. Alog
Heather A. Alonso
Randall Alonso
Benjamin Alopari
Adam Alter
Natalie Alter
Mario Alvarez
Peter Alvarez
Rey Baltazar Alviar
Bryan Anthony Alzati
Andrea Amaral
Thomas S. Ames
Asli Amir
Marion Ancheta
Paula Anderson
Miguel Andrade Jr.
Stephen B. Andrews
Gerard Ang
Vantar Angardi
Shanton K. Antolin
Carlos Antón
Giorgio G. Antoniazzi
Claudia Aparicio
Natalye Appel
Alexander Aptekar
Jesus M. Aquino
Beatriz Arauz-Fernandez
Claudia L. Aravena
Camila Arboleda
Paolo A. Arce
Michael S. Arellanes II
Manuel Arias
Stephanie J. Armentrout
Carlos E. Arredondo
Eddie H. Ashki
Amir Asli
Juan Carlos Attanasio
Alfredo Austria
Carlos Avila
Amir Azadeh
Samira Azgua
Andrea Azzinnari
Raffaella Maria Bacigalupo
Chandler Bailey
Katarina A. Bakas
Jaime Balaguera
Melissa Balcazar
David Balian
Francis Ballescas
Roger Balling
Eduardo Balta
Carlos Baluyot Jr.
Joe Banerjee
Luis Felipe Barahona
Omar Barcena
Andrea M. Barei
Paul Barke
Chris Barker
Matthew Barker
Scott W. Barnholt
Claudia Baroni
Enrique Barrantes
Damian J. Barton
Aaron D. Baseman
Yara Bashoor
Beatrice Bastidas
Nicholas Batelli
Julie Bateman
Anny Batista
Felecia Batson
Olivier Baudry
Stuart Baur
Kareem S. Bayram
Elizabeth Becerra
Jonathan Becerra
Raquel Becerra
Neal Beckstedt
Rachel Begalke
John B. Begeman
Giselle C. Behnan
Heidi Behr
Jonathan C. Bell
Marc Philip Bell
Leah J. Bellian
Brigitte Beltran
Tai Benes
Ronald Benson
Jose Berdecia-Colon
Andrew C. Berger
Vanessa Bermudez
Yolanda Bernardo
Stuart Berriman
Ruth Alina Berrios
Victor Berrios
Madeline Bertot
Benay A. Betts
Florencia C. Biaggi
Mark Bichel
Jodie Bielun
Rodrigo Bilbao
Thomas Bittner
Raymond Biscocho
Peter Blackburn
Christopher Blanch
Lorna Roxana Blanco
Margarita Blanco
Verity M. Blevins
Alisa Block-Sommer
Eric Blumberg
Jeffrey L. Blydenburgh
Joseph C. Bodwin
Beatris Bogomilova
Mariana Boldu Dallmann
José Bon
Louis Bond
Daniel J. Bonham
Antonio Bonifacio
Veronique Bonnard
Elizabeth S. Bonsato
Mercy Borges
Reinaldo Borges
Xavier Borja
Dieter Borrell
Craig R. Bosket
Stephanie Z. Bou-Ghannam

Myriam Boutin
Peter Brand
Pedro Bravo
Natasha Brewer
Dan Brezniceanu
Jenifer Briley
Alexander Briseno
Andrew P. Bristow
Peter C. Britton
Melanie S. Brooks
Jennifer Broutin
Edward Brown
Elissa A. Brown
Jason R. Brown
Shawn Hubertus Bruins
Guillermo Brunzini
Olyvia Buana
Steven Bugay
Roman Bugryn
Ben Burns
Santiago Bustamante
Ruslanas Byckovas
Lourdes Cabanas
Christian Cabrera
Jose Angelo Cacal
Francisco N. Caceres
Maria Caicedo
Gabriela Caicedo-Hillis
Patricia L. Calasich
Jeremy M. Calleros-Gauger
Romina Caluste
Juan Calvo
Laura Camejo
Ansley Campbell
Alfredo Campos
Elizabeth L. Canon
Sergio Canton
John D. Cantu
Alex Cao
Eric Cao
Alexandra Cardenas
Katherine Carley
Juan Carlos
Alina A. Carmona
Phillip Cartagena
Natalia Castaneda
Levy Castañeda
Luis Castellon
Daniel A. Castillo
Johnstein Castillo
Daniel M. Castro
Felicitas Castro
Jorge Castro
David Castro-Blanco
Elaine M. Catane
Andrew Catterick
Olga Cech
Bruce Celenski
Jedmy Centeno
Damion Cera
Amauri Chacon
Candy Chan
Catherine M. Chan
Joshua Chan
Christopher Chan
Ho Fu Chan
Ho Wa Chan
Arron Chan
Kwan Chan
Wicky Chan
Joyce Chan
Yuen Yeung Cecilia Chan
Yiu Bun Chan
Abigail A. Chang
Chuan-Chih Chang
Jerome Chang
Monica Chavarri
Jovany A. Chediak
Bob Chen
Daren Chen
Linda Chen
Somy Chen
Pitt Chen
Yuchuan Chen
Zhenyu Chen
Alvin Cheng
Irene Cheng
Lawrence Cheng
Felix K. Cheong
Doris Cheung
Lai Ming Cheung
Chieu Chih Chiang
Leslie M. Chimelis
Lukas Ching
Abbey Chiu
Bernard Chiu
Min Kyung Cho
Ye Sul Cho
Geena Choi
Raul Choque
Gabriela M. Chorobik
Jacqueline Chow
Raymond Chow
Christopher Choy
Angela Chu
Taesik Chu
Wesly Chu
Juanluis Chueca
Eric Chui
Alexander Chun
Taesik Chun
Jaewoo Chung
Steven C. Chung
Cher Chung
Enrique Chuy
Gigi C. Chuy
Gustavo Chuy
Dennis Cimatu
Gerald M. Cipriano
Angelica Loraine Ciscar-Castillo
Donna Claus
Lorenzo Cobiella
Maria G. Cobos
Thomas Coco
Christopher Coe
Tracey Coffman
Susana P. Colarte
Carlos R. Colon
Danny Colon
Hector L. Colon
Jose A. Colon-Berdecia
Matthew R. Compeau
Marc Compton
Cinthia Condor
John L. Conley
Whitney K. Conley
John L. Conley AIA
Patrick Connolly
Kirk H. Conover
Aline Constantinides
Miklos Conti
Raquel M. Contreras
Tonia B. Coomler Long
Ashley L. Cooper
L. Ashley Cooper
Karen Corrales
Anne Seton Cotter
Rodney D. Covington
Douglas H. Cox
Ronald Cox
Chad R. Cramer
Eve Creighton
Guy Crims
Eric Crotty
William E. Crotty
Alvin Cruz
Javier J. Cuardros
Jorge Cuba
Lourdes Cubanas
Judy Cui
Julia Cullen
Christopher Cummock
Delphine Cunin
Donald Cupit
John Andrew Curtis
Ana E. da Silva
Alexander L. Dale
Gustavo Dallmann
Mariana Boldu Dallmann
José Abraham Dalman
Joan Dalupang
Patrick Daniels
Maria Daroy
Isabel Daser
Courtney D. Davies
Jorge Davila
Philip Davis
David Michael Dax
José Daza
Alexander A. de Armas
Kimberly Elie de Armas
Alejandra De Diego Llopis
Maria de Fatima Montoya
Noel De Guzman
Angel De Jesus
Foster De Jesus
Antonino Dela Cruz
Carolina De La Horra
Rigoberto de la Paz
Jorge De la Torriente
Luis De Lance
Karem De Leon
Mac Einstein De Leon
Natalie H. de los Hoyos
Ramon De Mier
Nicholas de Rochefort
Tom Decker
Nurys Decreouy
Chanel Dehond
Meredith P. Deinema
Michael DeJong
Jose M. Del Risco
Tania Del Socorro Nuno
Luis Delance
Karem DeLeon
Adalberto A. Delgado
Dan Delgado
Diego Delgado
Mervin Delgado
Monica D. Delmonte
Christopher Delusky
Ramon DeMier
Margina A. Demmer
William M. Denkinger
Deborah Desilets
George Despues
Frederick Deza
Joel Di Giacomo
Ownery Rose Diala
Carmen L. Diaz
Julio Diaz
Loribeth Diaz
Maribel Diaz
O. Francisco Diaz
Laura M. Diaz De Leon
Reynolds Diaz Jr.
Ryan Diaz-Bringas
Alvin Diego
Juan Camilo Diez
Douglas Diggle
David Digiacomo
Bernard Joseph Dimacali
Wendell Dimaculangan
Timur Erin Dincer
Tri Do
Nan J. Doelling
Christopher J. Doherty
Catherine E. Dolan
Cathy Dong
Mary Dong
David W.N. Donnelly
Alvaro S. Donoso
Danielle Dorfman
Eduardo Dorta
R. Conner Dowling
Eric Dufour
Antoine Durand
Isil Duzgun
Magdalena Dzialo Balian
Maria Eboli
Mateo Echegaray
Daviela Eckols
Marie Edouard
Eddie Edwards
Paul T. Edwards
Steven L. Egwele
Suzanne Ekaitis
Fedaa Eldosougi
Maria Beatriz Elias
Benson Ellis
Mohamed Elnagar
Martín Endo
Leonardo Enea Spilimbergo
Tony Engelberg
Rafell Enriquez
Ryan Enz
Adriana R. Epelhoim
Barry Erlanda
Peter E. Erni
Rodrigo Escardo
Francisco M. Escobar
Carlos H. Escuti
David Espana
Julio Cesar España
Lourdes Sanchez Espinell
Monserrat Espino
Christine Espinosa
Frank Espinosa
Olga Espinosa
Theodore Evangelakis
Renelyn B. Evora
Milton Ewell
Gregory Ewest
Ruben Fabregat
Basil Fakhri-Papazian
Mahasti Fakourbayat
Sandra Fandre
Faris Faraj
Jane Fare
Ana V. Faria-Delfino
Maurice Farinas
Diana Farmer
Rodrigo Faro
Killian Farrelly
Margaret Fatovic
Robert J. Fatovic
Keren Feilgut-Reshef
Tiziana Felice
Renzo Felices
David Fenster
Gigi Fernandez
José A. Fernandez
Juan F. Fernandez
María Gracia Fernández
Martin Fernandez
Ricardo Fernandez
Alejandro Fernandez de Mesa
Johann Fiallo
Michael Figueredo
Jeremy S. Finnell
Tania C. Fiorani
Paul S. Fischman
William Fitzpatrick
Kharina Fiuza
Washington Fiuza

TEAMWORK

Frederick Fleshman
Anne Marie Fletcher
Damaris Flores
Luis Alberto Flores
Audrey M. Flynn
Wendy Folk
Anisleidy Fombona
Adrian Fong
Ernesto Mock Fong
Violet Fong
Alexander Fort
Gabriel Fort
Harold Fort
Nicholas Fort
Lorenzo Forteleoni
Nicolo Forteleoni
William Foti
Raymond Fowler
Aleksandra B. Fradin
Susana M. Franco
Melissa K. Franzak
Anthony H. Freedman
Tricia Freedman
Charles Freyre II
Melissa Frye
Toshio Fudimoto
Andres Fuentes
Michel Fuller
Higino Fungo Jr.
Lolit Borja-Fungo
Robin Fyfe
Ranses A. Galindo
Robert Gallagher
Ronnie Gallego
Ashley V. Galvankar
Gilberto Gamez
María del Pilar Gárate
Alexander D. Garcia
George Garcia
Henry Garcia
Jorge García
Karen Garcia
Maria Garcia
Noah D. Garcia
Jennifer M. Gareau
Rodrigo Garrido
Le Roy Garriques
Paul Gasiorkiewicz
Lourdes H. Gavilanes
Jose A. Gaviria
Antonio Gelia
Lara Genovese
Patrick Giannini
Laura B. Gilmore
Alex Ginard
Robert Given
John Glagola
Robert S. Glennie
Marjorie Goldman
Adan Henry Gom
Bethany R. Gomes
Allen Gomez
David Gomez

Gerald Peter Gomez
Richard L. Gonser
Alvin Gonzales
Archibald Gonzales
Annette Gonzalez
Barbara Gonzalez
Barbara M. Gonzalez
Edgar Gonzalez
Elisa M. Gonzalez
Emmanuel Gonzalez
Enrique R. Gonzalez
Felix Gonzalez
Jacqueline Gonzalez
Juan Gonzales
Miguel E. Gonzalez
Roberto Gonzalez
Veronica Gonzalez
Hiram E. Gonzalez-Chuy
Willis Gortner II
Maria Gradin Pernas
Mary Graham
Lauren Gratenstein
Nathaniel Greenberg
Kasey M. Greenough
Keith D. Greer
Jovita Gregorio
Olivia Gridelli
Arturo Griego
Michael Griffiths
Monica I. Grigorescu
Eva Grimard
Michael Grimshaw
Alvaro E. Grisales
Andy Gruber
Nicole L. Gualdarrama
Li Ting Guan
Ana Guaracao
Leonel Guedes
Nathalie Guedes
Mario E. Guerra
Juan Carlos Guerrero
John Guffey
Idil Gumruk
Emily Guo
Vera Guo
Daphne Gurri
John E. Gustin
Candi Gutierrez
Dario Gutierrez
Monica X. Gutierrez
Marianela Guzman
Dina Ha
Tae Kyung Ha
Judith Haase
Rasha Habiby
Alexander Hache
Herman Hagelsteen
Erik Hagen
Andrew Haidar
Anthony Haines
Michael Halland
Shahrixan Amir Hamzah
Michelle Patrice Hanna

Helen Hansen
Franz Hanzlicek
Michael Harris
Geron Lee Harrison
Frances Haugen
David Hay
Jonathan Haynal
Christopher Hazlett
Katherin E. Healy
Aaron Michael Heinrich
Erik Hemingway
Giovana Henao
Lidia Heres
George Hernandez
Kevin M. Hernandez
Nidia Hernandez
Novel Hernandez
Raul Hernandez
Rodrigo Hernandez
Violeta Hernandez
Yessenia M. Hernandez
Michael Heron
Ricardo Herran
David O. Herrera
Melissa Herrera
Oscar Herrera
Yvette Herrera
Luis H. Herrero
Robert Herrick
Ava Dawn Hetzer
Jamison Heyliger
Rod Hidalgo
Caridad Hidalgo-Gato
Luis Higa
Alexander Higbee
Kevin Craig Higham
Samantha Hill
Maria Luisa Poller Hipol
Dina Ho
Jayson Y. Ho
Angela Ho
Ester Ho
Jane Hobbs
Alejandro Hoch
Philip M. Hoffer
Michel Holland
Brad Hollenbeck
Bill Holt Jr.
Tomsgin Hong
Arthur Horton
John E. Houston
Krikor S. Hovaguimian
Terry Howells
Luis G. Hoyos
Jason Hsun
Owen Hu
Coco Huang
Jenny T. Huang
Lilian Huang
Brian R. Hubbard
Leslie G. Huber
Eduardo Huergo
Jorge Huertas

Heather L. Hughes
Kin Ho Andy Hui
Michael J. Hunton
Gilberto Hurtado
Erik Hutson
Felipe E. Igualt
Amral Imran
Ismail Imran
Natalie S. Imran
Venbiye Duygun Inal
Yehuda Inbar
Ryan Inman
Cindy I-Jung Ionita
Cindy I. Ionita
Joyce Ip
Daniel Irizarry
Yoko Isaji
Seitairo Ishida
Ericson Isip
Nathaniel C. Jakus
Tamara Z. Jamil
Tabatha Janna
Omar G. Jarrett
James G. Jenkins
John Jenkins
Reginald Jennings
Jie Ping Ji
Anthony Jimenez
Day J. Jimenez
Suquito Joa
Paulina E. Johansson
Robert A. Johnson
Liselott Johnsson
Eric A. Jones
Justin Jones
Andy Jordan
Jennifer Jordan-Lock
Caroline J. Jordi
Ericka M. Joseph
Flamina Jouve
Igor L. Jozsa
Han Koon Juan
Alfredo Julien
Alfonso Jurado
Alexa S. Kalandiak
Nikhil Kamat
Megan S. Kamayatsu
Angélica Castro Kamimoto
Isamu Kanda
Stephanie Kander
Allen Kanter
Marta Emilia Karamuz
Thea Karlavaris
Simon Kates
Apoorv Kaushik
Elias Kawass
Shabbir Kazmi
Tara Keens-Douglas
Chloe Keidaish
Meredith Kenny
Scott A. Kepford
Sarah Khalid
Saeed Khalili

Andre N. Khoury
Christopher Kiefer
Peter Kiernan
Ihnil Kim
Ihnil Tony Kim
Jae Wook Kim
Nathan Kim
Qu H. Kim
Shaina Kim
Andrew King
Jonathan Kinsley
Scott Kirk
Satsuki Kitagawa
Carolina Klingelfus
Glen Knight
Youngah Ko
Kendra Koblenzer
Jean-Pierre Kocher
David Kocieniewski
George Koehler
Peter C. Kohn
Matthew C. Kopp
Bradford Korder
Viviane Fort Korder
Yoshikado Koyama
David Kraft
Natalie L. Krakovsky
Irene Kulis
Jarod W. Kurzner
Jennifer Kutnow
Catherine Kwancharoen
Ana Maria La Rosa
Antonio La Rosa
Renato S. Lacson
Christopher J. Laedlein
Melbelena Lagos
Gaston Laguna
Anthony Lai
William Lai
Robert Laird
Tsz Wai Eveline Lam
Miranda Lam
Wittawat Lamson
Alejandro Landes
Barry Langer
Robert Langford
Henry Lares
Chad Larson
Crisanto Lasola
Claudine Lau
Layla Lau
Queenly Lau
Susan Lau
Kit Lau
Francisco Laurier
Chun Kau Kenneth Law
Cynthia Lazarte
Edmond Le Blanc
Jose Lecca
Yuri L. Lechtholz
S.V. Jeanne Ledesma
Chris Lee
Chung Hyun Lee

Clement Lee
Dorothy Lee
David D. Lee
Dean S. Lee
Dohyung Lee
Jessica Lee
Cathy Lee
Kenneth Lee
Lisa R. Lee
Quenifer Lee
Wan Lung Vincent Lee
Sandy Leff
Gabriel V. Legaspi
Grit Leipert
Scott K. Lelieur
Jacob A. Lenard
Carla Leon
Isabelle Leprince
Karoline Leuenberger
Jenny Leung
Tak Yi Leung
Gary Leus
Larry Levis
Daniel Levy
Bertram Lewars
Dean Lewis
Edward Leyva
Ada Li
Lynn Li
Sau Yan Grace Li
Shan Li
Xintian Li
Colin Lienhard
Rebecca A. Liggins
Jawn Lim
Jawn Tze-Hin Lim
Jonathan Y.E. Lim
Mi Sun Lim
Lillian Lin
Joan Lin
Andrew J. Linn
Michael Liss
Andrew Liu
Ao Liu
Lingfei Liu
Mela Liu
Ronda Liu
Victor Lizardo
Rolando Llanes
Eduardo Llano
Robert H. Lloyd
Joseph Lo
Wan Lok Lo
Joséph Lo Hoi Wai
Jennifer C. Lock
Jesse Lockwood
Karl Loescher
Mark Joseph Lojo
Jelena Loncar
Tonia Long
Carmen Loo
Benjamin Lopez
Carlos A. Lopez
Christopher Lopez
Danny G. Lopez
Dina C. Lopez
Manuel Lopez
Oscar Lopez
Veronica Lorenzo-Luaces
Jean-Jacques Lorraine
Victoria L. Losada
Giorgio Lostao
Tommy Lou
Noaman Louagh
John Loughran
Mae Keng Louie
Arthur Lowe
Jennifer Lowe
Michelle K. Lozano
Rosalynn Lu
Eduardo Luaces
Talia Luaces
Nicholas Lucarelli
Armand Luceres
Carol L. Luis
Lydia Lun
Wan Lung
Yi Luo
Andres Luque
Elena Ma
Mylene Macauyag
Mark Maccagno
Joseph MacDonald
Julie Mackenzie
Rossana Macher
Madison I. Macheske
Emily Maemura
David F. Magee
Michel Magloire
Moises X. Magro
Gloria H. Mah
Nashin K. Mahtani
Raymond C. Majewski
Nicolas Majluf
Claire Malone Matson
Afagh A. Mamaghani Zadeh
Nays Mandilego
Fernando E. Mane
Noreena Manio
Monika Manios
Alberto Manrique
Rene Mansito
Douglas Mar
Sandra Marcheco
Romyr Mariano
Ana Marin
Marco G. Marini de Freitas
Alvaro Echevarria Marmolejo
Janet Marquetti
Marcus Martin
Todd Martin
Carla Martinez
German Martinez
Herman Martinez
Hernan Martinez
Louis Martinez
Natalia Martinez
John Maruszczak
Audrey Marvez
Gustavo A. Masis
Zion I. Mass
José Matute
Anca Matyiku
Edmond MacLeod Maurice
April May
Gerhard W. Mayer
Michael McBride
Michael D. McBride
Matthew McCallum
Michael McCann
Michael McCaw
Mick McConnell
Raymond McConnell
Valeria McCue
Christopher McCullough
Eden McDowell
Cristina A. McKelligott
Olin McKenzie
Margaret McMahon
Peggy McMahon
Kathy McMurphy
John McQuown
Naga Medapti
Damaris Medina
Mario Medina
Jose Mejia
Gabe Mejia
Mark Melchi
Marcia Mello
Julio Mendez
Kennet A. Mendez
Glenn Mendoza
Jay-R Mendoza
Maria S. Mendoza
Endri Meneri
Saul Meneses
Diya M. Menezes
Henry G. Mera
Faith Mercado
Mirtha I. Mercado
Lindsay M. Mercer
Frederic G. Merle
James D. Merriman
Melissa S. Meyer
Jonathan Meyers
Bi-Ying Miao
Thomas Miel
Carlos Mieles
Raul G. Mieres
Ronald Migoya
Francisco Miguez Jr.
Ruben Mijares
Adam Mikulicz
Anna Giselle Milanis
Christopher L. Miles
Timothy B. Miller
Elaine Mills
Cara Mimun
Anna B. Miorelli
Ana Maria Miyares
Ziyad Mneimneh
Robert Moehring
Robert M. Moehring
Ali Mohebali
Philip Mohr
Marcelo Moino
Maria Molina
Adrian Monarrez
Juan Montalvan Jr.
Erik Montalvo
Armando Montero
Rodrigo Diaz Montero
Jeffrey Montes
Armando E. Montilla
Arturo Montoya
Cassandra Mooney
Princess Moquette
Lucia Mora
Frank J. Moradiellos
Aimee Morales
Johanna Catalina Morales
Vanessa Valerio Morales
Stephanie Morales Casariego
Mickey Moran
Tatiana Moreira
Antonio Moreno
Solange Moreno
Richard Moreta
Anne Marie Morley
Cinda Morris
Derona Moss
Robert Mothershed
Rafael Muci
Michael Muench
Inaki Muguruza
Paul F. Mulder-Fort
Richard Mullis
Luisa Munoz
Neil S. Muntzel
Luisa Murai
George Murillo
Ryan Myburgh
Eduardo F. Nabua
Hijiri Nagasawa
Andrea L. Nagy
Rosa M. Napoles
Drew Napolitano
Carlos Navarrete
Lauren D. Nayman
Tal Nealy
Florent Nedelec
Allen Neff
Kelly Neill
Sara K. Nejad
James A. Neville
Barrett L. Newell
Andrew Isaac Ng
Angie Ng
Dennis Ng
Patricia Ng
Sherene Ng
Shengyan Mary Ng
Stanley Ng
Yat Lun Ng
Joyce Ngo
Christina Nguyen
Joseph Nibo
Georgiana E. Nicoara
Youkun Nie
Eric Niemy
Laticia Nobell
Michael Nogoy
Consuelo Noguer
Margaret K. Nolan
Peter Norgaard
Jesus Novoa
Andres F. Nunez
Martin J. Nunez
Margarita Nuvhe
McKenzie J. O'Neill
Olman Oberti
Jessica Obregon
Sergio S. Ochoa
Vaughn Ochsner
Bennett Oh
Maria Paz Olavide
Olga Olbinsky
Marina Oliveira
Jessica Oliveri
Alexis Olle
Stephen N. Olson
Carolyn Ong
Raymond C. Ong
Anna Oppel
Chad Oppenheim
Matthew Paul Oravec
Alberto Orellano
Mikhail K. Orosz
Maria Elena Ortega
Veronika Ortega
German E. Ortiz
Joy Ortiz
Ana Ortiz-Ramos
Schinichi Ozawa
Erwin Pacamarra
Cynthia D. Pacheco
Ashley Pacheco
Carol Pad
Pallavi Padgilwar
Lisa Padilla
Luis Padron
Emily Padua
Grace Pae
Pablo Pajares
Steve Palmier
Miguel Panetta
Joe Pang
Katherine Pangilinan
Basil Papazian
Florencio V. Paraon
Gonzalo Pardo
Manon Pare
Rafael Pareja
Allegra Parisi
Hansol Park

TEAMWORK

Jonathan Parke
Renato Patricio
Thelma Joy Patmore
Linda Patton
Geoffrey J. Pauwels
Juan Pablo Pava
Ventzislav P. Pavloz
Manuel Paz
Louis Pedraza
Ulises N. Peinado
Brian G. Pelcak
Magaly Pena
Joel Peña
Olga Barbara Penalver
Nino Pender
Meila Penn
Jacqueline Peralta
Cesar Perea
Marie C. Perea
Marny A. Pereda
Esther Perez
Ileana Perez
Jesus Perez
Jorge Luis Perez
Patricia Perez
Rossana Perez
Luis E. Perez Montero
Alex J. Perez-Daple
Richard Perlmutter
Ignacio Permuy
Jorge Alberto Pernas
Hannah K. Perrino
Caitlin M. Perry
Andrew E. Persoff
Gabriel S. Peschiera
Gonzalo Peschiera
Kriss Peterson
Steven Peterson
Cristian Petschen
Peter Pham
Jennifer T.A. Phan
Steven Phillip
Roberta Phillips
Nick Picciurro
Joel Piecowye
Carl Pierce
Grace Pierce
Graydon Pierce
Joel L. Piercowye
Marie Pierre
Laurent Pierre-Philippe
Gianpaolo Pietri
Andrea Pietrucci
J. Brian Pignanelli
Alfred Pili
Mari-Carmen Pina
Michele Pina
Justin Pinchback
Andres S. Pinero
Carli Pino
Kathy Pino
Michelle Piotrowski
Elizabeth Piotrowski
Hornbuckle
Ratima Pisalyaput
Robert Piscioneri
Orlando J. Pizarro
Campion Platt
Mindy L. Ploss
Magda Polec
Maria Luisa Poller Hipol
Natalie Pollet
Rodrigo A. Poma
Damian Ponton
Adrian G. Portal
Alexis M. Porten
Alex Portilla
Raphael Portuondo
Bradley Potts
Ramiro Poyaoan
Merve Poyraz
Jennifer Press
Prithula Prosun
Michael Proteau
Natale Prudente
Michelle Prutschi
Daniel Pryor
Anna Pujdak
Joseph Punzalan
Alexander Purdue
Bret Quagliara
Cesar Querales
Lizette Quimper
Michael J. Quinones-Lebron
Monica Quirch
Alicia A. Rabadan
Nemanja Radusinovic
David Ramer
Aiko Ramirez
Carolina Ramirez
Oscar E. Ramirez
Royde Ramirez
Yesenia Ramirez
Alice Ramos
Carola Ramos
Claudio Ramos
José Luis Ramos
Olivia Ramos
Rudy Ramos
Rufino Ramos
Sandro Rastelli
Janice Rauzin
Georgia R. Read
Nigel Reading
Carolina Reategui
Stefanos Rebori
Suchi Reddy
Kevin J. Regalado
Roberto Regazzoni
José Rego
Ramon Rego
Ronald B. Regulacion
Natalia Reina
Sarah Reitelman
Christopher Reiter
Patricio R. Renato
Carla V. Rengifo
Cristino Resente
Elise Reyes
Maybelle Reyes
Valeria Reyes Bijos
Christian Reynolds
Brandon Richard
Joaquin Riera
Anthony Rimore
Michael J. Ritus
Hernan M. Rivera
Mariana Rivera
Chris Roberts
Brian Robertson
Karla M. Robertson
Damian Robledo
Damien Robledo
Roberto Roca
Alexander Rodak
Alain L. Rodriguez
Anashiely Rodriguez
César Rodriguez
Christina M. Rodriguez
Daniel Rodriguez
Fernando Rodriguez
Juan Carlos Rodriguez
Marie Rodriguez
Monica M. Rodriguez
Sue Rodriguez
Victor H. Rodriguez
Victor L. Rodriguez
Sue Rodriquez
Lester Rojas
Suhey V. Rojas
Patrick G. Roldos
Yajaira Roman
Nancy Romero
Robin Romero
Luis Rondon
Sara C. Rondon
Juanita Rosa
Camilo Rosales
Julio Rosales
Mercedes Rosales
Cesar O. Rosario
Michael Rosen
Debra Rosenbaum
Juliana Ross
Theodore Ross
Michelle Rouffer
Jaime Rouillon
Ethan Royal
Nicole J. Rubin
Alana B. Rudolph
Cécile Rudolf
Joan Ruffe
Ronald Rufin
Plutarco Ruiz
Jonathan Rukma
Erika A. Rullman
Mario Rumiano
Ronald Rupay
Quinn R. Russell
Jennifer Ryan
Pavlina Ryvola
Alex Sabatier
Hira Sabuhi
John Sacco
Joseph Saha
Scott Saikley
Helene Saint Laurent
Jorge Salcedo
Seth O. Salcedo
Emilia Salde
Jorge Salgado
Paul S. San Gemino
Antonio Sanchez
Arnaldo Sanchez
Arnold Sanchez
Arnulfo Sanchez
Jocelyn Sanchez
Ramon Sanchez
Renota R. Sanchez
Lourdes Sanchez Espinell
Derek Sanders
Ruya I. Saner
Luzviminda T. Sanez
David Sang
Anisha Sankar
Jessica Santaniello
Shelley M. Santo
Arlene Santos-So
Carlos Sardina
Giorgio Saumat
Anne Scheffels
Neal Schefil
Karen Scheinberg
Gregory Schenker
Paula Schiavini Cadier
Peter Schlecht
Caelin H. H. Schneider
Gabriele Schneider
Neal Schofel
Benjamin T. Schulte
Ben W. Schumacher
Norman Schwartz
Jorge Sciupac
Ryan Sears
Nikola Seferovic
Lauren A. Segall
Lizbeth Segovia
Nada Sellami
Kelsey A. Sellenraad
Jonathan Seltzer
Marta Sensidoni
Won J. Seol
Guylene Sermeno
Alma Serna
Dalila L. Serrao
Laura Sewell
Ronetta A. Seymour
Jeff Shaddock
Ashraf A. Shahin
John Sharon
Stephanie Shaw
Paul Sheehan
Xiao Yang Shen
Larisa Sherbakova
Russell Sherman
Carter Shi
Tadao Shimizu
Sohrab Shokraee
Charlene Shum
Evan Siegel
Massimo Silipo
Daniel Silverman
Victoria P. Sim
Kaitlin Simmons
Lance Simon
Ailsa Simone
Temple W. Simpson
Jessica Sin
Jessica Siu
Catherine Siu
Julie Siu
Raphael Sixto
Roberto Sixto
Jennifer Slavik
Richard Smart
Daziano L. Smith
Gregory Smith
Karl Smith
Kyle J. Smith
Mitch Smith
Shane Smith
Tracy Smith
Martin John Smyth
Dominick Snell
Mikaile Solomon
Claudio Solorzano
Leticia S. Soo Hoo
Tina Soo Hoo
Kant Soong
Frank Soriano
Guillermo Sosa
Fernanda A. Sotelo
Eduardo M. Soto
Isabel Diane Soto
Jerome Soustra
Maria Spada
Alison L. Spear
Caylin Spear
Leslie C. Spear
Michael Spitzer
Gustavo A. Spokoiny
Cynthia Spray
B. Louis St. Clair
Alastair Standing
Rebecca Stanier
Tina Stanisci
Don Starr
Michael Steffens
Paul Stevens
Karl Stewart
Leif Stigson
Gabriel Stock
Kevin Storm
Mary Strowbridge
Katherine Stull

Edwin L. Suarez
Mario Suarez
Frederick Suatengco
Ramkumar Subramanian
Ha R. Suh
Saskia Suite-Hardt
Hisham Suliman
Sri Sumantri
Paulette Summers
Angela Sun
Psyche Sung
Cory J. Surovek
Trevor Sze
Christopher M. Sweeney
Brent Swingle
Johanny Takayama
Richard Talbet
Maria Paula Taluban
Julius Tamba
Crisencio Tan
Fannie Tan
Miguel L. Tan
Patricia Tan
Suzanne Tanascaux
Dennis Tang
Sandy Tang
Simone Tang
Sue Anne S. Tang
Lawrence Tao
Felomena Tapawan
Jason Tapia
Maneu Tataryn
Stephanie R. Tatem
Jordan Tatlonghari
Shawn Tavares
Kan Wee Wagen Teh
Alvaro Tejada
Felipe Tejeda
Ana Tejidor
Bettsy Tello
Alexis Teltser
Victoria Teofilo
Dana Terp
Pablo Terrazas
Alma Theresa Dizon
Lisa M. Thompson
Robert Thompson
Diana Tigani
Rolando Tillit
Roxana Tillit
Manuel Timana
Steven J. Timana
Etai Timna
Samuel Tizon
Tammy To
Michael Todd
Daylis Toledo
Robert Tolmach Jr.
Carl Tominski
Jennifer H. Tomooka
Chi Fun David Tong
Paul Topogna
Jose Joel V. Toribio
Rafael Torrens
Martin G. Torrentes
Tania Torrentes
Arleen Torres
Fausto R. Torres
Mark Josef Torres
Carlos Prio Touzet
Jason R. Trahan
Raphael T. Tran
Virginia Tran
Lilyana Traub
David Trautman
Ruben Travieso
Timothy Tremaine
Carol Trent-Dufresne
Jean-Marc Tribie
Carl Trominski
Vilmar Gordo Troncoso
Armando Trujillo
Charles Tsang
Clinton Tsoi
Caleb Tsui
Kate Tsui
Ariel T. Tuazon
Drew Tucker
Shreejaya Tuladhar
Tania Tzamtzis
Alfred Tze
Rudolf Uhlemann
Adam C. Umber
Kenneth Ung
Lloyd Ungson
Benny J. Urena
Darlene S. Urgola
Rosa Uriarte
Ariel Valdes
Osvaldo Valdes
Teresita Valdes
Jessica L. Valdivia
Erwin Valeña
Nora Valencia
Benjamin Valera Jr.
Fabio Vallebona
Cristhian D. Vallejo
Rosemarie Van Der Linde
Denise M. Van Vriesland
Ingrid Van Wormer
Luis Vanselow
Michael Vascellaro
Ronald Velarde
Roberto Velasco
Andrea J. Velez
Maria S. Velez
Maria Gabriela Velutini
Octavio Venegas
William Verdaguer
Isabelle Verwaay
Francisco Viacava
Andrea Viana
Antonia Vick
Daniel Villa
Ariel Villanueva
Mylene Villanueva
Roberto Villazon
Carlos Eduardo Pereira Villela
Raymond Viloria
Gustavo Vivas
Mark Volpendesta
Kyle Vreeland
Jerry Wagner
Matt Waitkus
Marek Walczak
Seth L. Waldman
Pierre Walgenwitz
Jason C. Walker
Jordan M. Walker
Whitnie Walker
Jennifer Walton
Martin Wander
Bei Wang
Joe Wang
Mark Wang
Nina Wang
Derek Warr
Allison F. Watkins
John Watkins
Vincent F. Weaver
Julio Weber-Valls
Renee A. Webley
Matthew C. Weeks
Bruce Weinstein
James Wells
Zhi Wen Hu
Ching-Wen Yang
Charlene West
Gerald West
Yann Weymouth
Joséph White
Shawn F. Whitehorn
Lisa Whitney
Michael Wilbur
Dennis Wilhelm
Robert R. Williams
Allen Wilson
Bruce Allan Wilson
Emmanuel D. Wilson
Kristin Wingart
Allen Wipon
Malcolm Wiseheart III
Dennis Witnauer
Jacob B. Woloshin
Benjamin Wong
Binh Wong
Darci Wong
Debbie Wong
Francis Wong
Elise Wong
Jeremy Wong
Maury Wong
Matthew Wong
Selina Wong
Rex Wong
Anson Wong
David Woo
Janice Woo
Kelly Woodward
Roberto Woodworth
J. Michael Woollen
Michael Woollen
Christy Wright
Corina Wright
Benson Wright
Steve L. Wright
Kenny Wu
Mandy Wu
Walter Wu
Rowland Wu
Yun Yun Wu
Yvonne Wu
Claire Yang
Xuwen Xing
Alec Xu
Rebecca Xu
Chloe Xu
Juan M. Yactayo
Itaru Yanagawa
Fariba Yazdani
Charles F. Ye
Felema Yemaneberhan
Ging Yeung
Po Wah Yeung
Tommy Yeung
Tsz Ling P. Yeung
Christine Ying
Pei Ching Ying
Petrina Yiu
Claire Young
Carl Young III
Victor Yue
Amy Yuen
Kei Dawson Yukon
Dan Zabowski
Ana Zacharias
Silvio O. Zafra
Maryam Zamani
Federico Zapata
Jorge M. Zardoya
Christine F. Zavesky
Lillian Zayas-Bazan
Andrew Zdzienicki
Dario Zeco
Cathy Zhang
Hai Zhang
Ray Zhang
Rui Zhang
Yihui Zhang
Ice Zheng
May Zheng
You Hui Zhou
Zhi Gang Zhou
Teresa M. Zix
Corinne Zuñiga

COLLABORATIONS

ARCHITECTS

360 ARCHITECTURE
Hard Rock/Miami Dolphins Stadium

AA CONSULTANTS
Terreno Junto Residential, Macau

AEDAS
W Square Refurbishment, Hong Kong

AGC DESIGN
Novotel Citygate Hotel, Hong Kong
Disney Hollywood Hotel, Hong Kong
New World Center, Hong Kong
Grand Hyatt at City of Dreams, Macau

AGENCE D'ARCHITECTE BRIDOT WILLERVAL
Exaltis / Mazars Headquarters
EOS / Microsoft Headquarter

AIDEA
Philamlife Center, Cebu

ALAOUI OMAR + EL KASRI YASMINE
Anfa Club

ALEXANDRE GIRALDI
Testimonio II

ARQ WF
Santander Tower, Sao Paulo
WT JK Complex, Sao Paulo
WT JK Bloco B, Sao Paulo
Green Towers, Brasilia
GTC BG, Rio de Janeiro
V House, Sao Paulo
The City Business District, Rio de Janeiro

ARTHUR C S KWOK ARCHITECTS
Landmark East, Hong Kong

ATHIE WOHNRATH
Tek Nacoes Unidas, Sao Paulo

AZAP (AZ ARCHITECTURAL PLANNERS INC.)
BDO Regional Offices

BATES SMART
City of Dreams, Macau

BAUM ARCHITECTS
International Finance Center, Seoul

BEA INTERNATIONAL (BRUNO ELIAS ARCHITECTS)
Disney Cruise Terminal at Port Canaveral

BEIJING INSTITUTE OF ARCHITECTURAL DESIGN
Beijing 5th Square, Beijing

BELLON & TAYLOR
Miami International Airport Terminals D-E-F-G-H Expansions and Renovations
The Royal Palm Resort

BEN LEONG CHONG IN ARQUITECTO
Nam Van Lake, Macau
Senado Square, Macau
China Star Square, Macau

BEYOND HOSPITALITY
Brickell City Centre EAST Hotel - Hospitality

BIURO PROJEKTOWE KAZIMIERSKI I RYBA
CBD ONE

BLT ARCHITECTS
Revel Resort & Casino

BRISAC GONZALEZ
Hobhouse

BUREAU D'ARCHITECTURE CAVALLINI
Immeuble de Bureaux et de Logements rue Sainte Zither- Rue Dicks

CAPARRA ENTELMAN
Luxury Collection Paracas Resort & Spa, Paracas, Peru
Luxury Collection Tambo del Inka Resort & Spa, Urubamba, Peru
Westin Lima

CAPOL
Upperhills, Shenzhen

CAPUTO PARTNERSHIP
Aria and Solaria residential Towers

CARBONDALE
JK Iguatemi Mall - Interior design

CARUNUNGAN & PARTNERS CO.
Four E-Com Center, Manila
Five E-Com Center, Manila

CBT ARCHITECTS
Pierce Boston

CENDES ARCHITECTURAL DESIGN CONSULTANTS (CHENGDU)
SM Zibo, Zibo

CHHADA SIEMBIEDA & ASSOCIATES LTD
Mandarin Oriental Hotel and Residences, Shanghai

CHINA NORTHEAST BUILDING XIAMEN DESIGN INSTITUTE
SM Xiamen 1 Refurbishment, Xiamen
SM Xiamen Mall, Xiamen

CHRISTIAN BAUER & ASSOCIÉS ARCHITECTES S.A.
Banque Du Luxembourg extension

CIGLER MARANI
Luxembourg Plaza

CLODAGH DESIGN INTERNATIONAL
Brickell City Centre EAST Hotel - Interior Lobbies/Event Spaces/Rooms/Suites

COOPER ROBERTSON & PARTNERS
Hudson Yards master planning

DALE & ASSOCIATES
Jackson Convention Center Complex

DENNIS LAU & NG CHUN MAN
Festival Walk, Hong Kong
Mount Parker Residences, Hong Kong

DESIGN GLOBAL INTERNATIONAL (DGI)
Chitaland Office Tower, Jakarta

DGLA
Pôle de Commerce et de Loisirs Bleu Capelette

EAST CHINA ARCHITECTURAL DESIGN & RESEARCH INSTITUTE CO., LTD
Agricultural Bank of China and China Construction Bank Headquarters, Shanghai
Mandarin Oriental Hotel and Residences, Shanghai

EHAF CONSULTING ENGINEER
Sharm El Sheikh Resort, Sharm El Sheikh, Egypt

EL-CHEIKH & PARTNERS
Al Madinatayn Makkah Complex (Mecca)

ELNESS SWENSON GRAHAM ARCHITECTS
Le Meridien Columbus
The Joseph Luxury Collection Nashville

EPSTEIN
Whirlpool Corporate Headquarters
1061 West Van Buren

ESTEBAN Y. TAN AND ASSOCIATES
The W Fifth Tower, Manila
W Office Building, Manila
SM Mall of Asia Expansion, Manila

FELIX S. LIM & ASSOCIATES
One E-Com Center, Manila
Two E-Com Center, Manila
Three E-Com Center, Manila
SM Keppel Center & BDO Tower, Manila

FENTRESS ARCHITECTS
Miami Beach Convention Center

FRIEDMUTTER GROUP
The Cosmopolitan Resort & Casino

GDP ARCHITECTS
KLCC Lot 91 Mixed-Use, Kuala Lumpur

GENSLER
Hilton Americas Houston Convention Center Hotel

GETTYS
City of Dreams, Macau

GIGNAC & ASSOCIATES
American Bank Center Arena and Convention Center

GLOVER SMITH BODE
Bongo's restaurant (Disney Springs)

GRAHACIPTA HADIPRANA
Tempo Scan Office Tower, Jakarta

GUANGZHOU DESIGN INSTITUTE
Poly Dongrui Plaza, Foshan
TaiKoo Hui, Guangzhou

GUANGZHOU URBAN PLANNING & RESEARCH CENTER DEPARTMENT OF DISTRICT PLANNING
Haizhu Plaza, Guangzhou

HEINLEIN SCHROCK STEARNS
American Airlines Arena

HELLER MANUS ARCHITECTS
Infinity
Lumina

HKS
Westin Times Square
Disney's All-Star Resorts
Disney's Pop Century Resort
Miranova Residential & Office Towers
Gallery Place

HLW INTERNATIONAL
Ellipse

HOK
Philips Arena
Wilkie D. Ferguson Jr. Federal Courthouse

INTERIOR ARCHITECTS (IA)
Whirlpool Corporate Headquarters

ISMAEL LEYVA
MiMa and Yotel

THE JERDE PARTNERSHIP
Cyberport Retail Mall, Hong Kong
City of Dreams, Macau

JORGE L. HERNANDEZ ARCHITECT
Coconut Grove Playhouse

JOSE SIAO LING & ASSOCIATES
SM Mall of Asia Arena, Manila
SMX Convention and Exhibition Center, Manila
SM Cebu Arena & SMX, Cebu
Exquadra Tower, Manila
Ecoprime Tower, Manila

KELL MUNOZ ARCHITECTS
Grand Hyatt San Antonio Convention Hotel

KLEIHEUS + KLEIHEUS
Wertheim Mixed Used Development

LEIGH & ORANGE
City Of Dreams, Macau

LPA ARCHITECTS
Peery Park Office Campus, Sunnyvale

LUPTON RAUSCH ARCHITECTS
The Offices at The Joseph

LWK & PARTNERS
China Star Square, Macau
Citygate TCTL 11 Development, Hong Kong
Homantin Hillside, Hong Kong
Nam Van Lake, Macau
TaiKoo Hui, Guangzhou

M3 ARCHITECTES
IMPE / Infinity

MAP ARCHITECTURE & PLANNING
City of Dreams, Macau

MILTON PATE & ASSOCIATES
The Rio, Atlanta

MVE + PARTNERS
Hamptons Residential Community

NATIONAL ENGINEERING BUREAU ARCHITECTURAL & ENGINEERING CONSULTANTS
The Gate Shams, Abu Dhabi

NRY ARCHITECTS
Dayabumi, Kuala Lumpur

OMA (REM KOOLHAAS)
Park Grove

OMAR YEUNG ARCHITECTS & ASSOCIATES
City Of Dreams, Macau

ONG & ONG ARCHITECTS
Orchard Scotts, Singapore

ORA ITO

ORBI ARQ

PANDEGA DESAIN WEHARIMA
Satrio Office Tower, Jakarta

PAUL CAMILLERI & ASSOCIATES
Smartcity Malta

PIMENTEL RODRIGUEZ SIMBULAN & PARTNERS
Fairmont Hotel and Raffles Suites
and Residences, Manila
The Podium, Manila
One Rockwell Residential, Manila

R. VILLAROSA ARCHITECTS PARTNER & ASSOCIATES
BeauFort, Manila

RECIO + CASAS ARCHITECTS
Pacific Plaza Towers, Manila

ROBERT CARAG ONG & ASSOCIATES
SM Mall of Asia, Manila

ROSSER INTERNATIONAL
Philips Arena

RSP ARCHITECTS
Sheraton Phoenix Convention Hotel
Vision Crest, Singapore
Winsland House and Lanson Place, Singapore

RICHARDSON SADEKI
Brickell City Centre Reach and Rise
residential condominiums

SASAKI ASSOCIATES
Puerto Rico convention district master planning

THE SCHIFF GROUP
Aventura Government Center

SEKAWAN DESIGNINC ARSITEK
Standard Chartered Bank Tower, Jakarta

SERGIO ECHEVERRIA, CHILE
Westin Lima

SERGIO GATTASS ARQUITETOS ASSOCIADOS

SHANGHAI INSTITUTE OF ARCHITECTURAL DESIGN & RESEARCH CO.
Youyicheng, Shanghai

SHENZHEN CHINA MERCHANTS ARCHITECTS & ENGINEERS
King Glory Mall, Shenzhen

SLCE ARCHITECTS
Queens West towers
606 West 57th Street
Avalon Bowery I
Avalon Bowery II
Avalon Christie place
Phipps place (separate affordable housing)

SMALLWOOD REYNOLDS STEWART & STEWART
JW Marriot Nashville Convention Hotel

SOSH ARCHITECTS
Revel Resort & Casino

SOUTH CHINA UNIVERSITY OF TECHNOLOGY
Wanbo Mixed-Use, Panyu
Zhujiang Plaza, Guangzhou
Buxin Mixed-Use, Shenzhen

STUDIO ARTHUR CASAS
JK Iguatemi Mall - Interior furnishings

STUDIO COLLECTIVE
Brickell City Centre EAST Hotel -
Interior Restaurant/Night Club/Bar/Lounge

STV ARCHITECTS
New York High School for Construction Trades,
Engineering and Architecture

TAA ARCHITECTS
66-70 Grange Road, Singapore
80 Grange Road, Singapore
Alba, Singapore

THE ARCHITECTS HALL / THE HALL GROUP
South Miami-Dade Cultural Arts Center

THOMSON ARCHITECTS

THORN GRAFTON / ALLEGUEZ AND ASSOCIATES
The Royal Palm Resort

TIANJIN ARCHITECTURAL DESIGN INSTITUTE (TADI)
Sea World Water Park, Tianjin
Sea World Sales Office, Tianjin
SM Tianjin, Tianjin
Tianjin Teemall, Tianjin

TONY CHI ASSOCIATES
TaiKoo Hui, Guangzhou
Westin Lima

TVS DESIGN
American Bank Center Arena and
Convention Center

VIETNAM NATIONAL CONSTRUCTION CONSULTANT COMPANY (VNCC)
The Spirit of Saigon, Ho Chi Minh City

W.V. COSCOLLUELA & ASSOCIATES
SM Aura Premier, Manila
SM Seaside City, Cebu
SM City North Elevated Park, Manila
SM Megamall Expansion, Manila
SM Megamall Tower, Manila
SM North EDSA Expansion &
Refurbishment, Manila

WARD/HALL ASSOCIATES
The Center for Innovative Technology

WCWP INTERNATIONAL
Forfar, Hong Kong
Seymour, Hong Kong
Shatin Communications & Technology Centre,
Hong Kong

COLLABORATIONS

ARTISTS

WILLIAM DORSKY & ASSOCIATES
The Palace

WILMOTTE ET ASSOCIES ARCHITECTES
Banque de Luxembourg Headquarters

WILSON ASSOCIATES
The Spirit of Saigon, Ho Chi Minh City
Sharm El Sheikh Resort, Sharm El Sheikh

WIRATMAN & ASSOCIATES
Menara Karya, Jakarta

WONG TUNG & PARTNERS
Cityplaza Renovation, Hong Kong
Cyberport, Hong Kong
Marinella, Hong Kong

XIAMEN HORDOR ARCHITECTURE & ENGINEERING DESIGN GROUP CO.
Bay of Modern Art, Xiamen

CARLOS ALVES
West & Company Offices in Tampa, Florida, USA
mosaic ceramic tile floors

DARA BIRNBAUM
The Rio Shopping Mall, Atlanta, Georgia, USA
"Garden and Frogs", collaboration with Martha Schwartz
"Video wall"

POLO BOURIEAU
Landmark East, 102 How Ming Street, Hong Kong, China
"Man Walking East"

Taikoo Hui, Guangzhou, China
"BAGODA!"

FABIÁN BURGOS
Brickell Heights, Miami, FL
applied mural on podium wall
SLS Lux Brickell Hotel and Residences, Miami, FL
applied mural on podium wall

ROBERT CHAMBERS
South Miami-Dade Cultural Arts Center, Cutler Bay (Miami), Florida, USA
"Light Field"
"Orbital 1" and "Orbital 2"

Sarasota Herald-Tribune Headquarters, Sarasota, Florida, USA
"Elipsota"

APRIL GREIMAN
Wilshire Vermont Mixed-Use Development, Los Angeles, California, USA
"Hand Holding A Bowl of Rice"

RALPH HELMICK AND STUART SCHECHTER
American Airlines Arena, Miami, Florida, USA
"Double Vision"

CHRISTOPHER JANNEY
American Airlines Arena, Miami, Florida, USA
"Turn Up the Heat"
Revel Casino-Hotel, Atlantic City, New Jersey, USA
"Sonic Fireflies"
Miracle Center Shopping Mall, Coral Gables, Florida, USA
acoustical kinetic sculpture

L'OBSERVATOIRE INTERNATIONAL
Dijon Performing Arts Center
American Airlines Arena
Philips Arena
Cyberport Technology Campus

MAYA LIN
Wilkie D. Ferguson, Jr. United States Courthouse, Miami, Florida, USA
"Flutter" environmental sculpture

MARKUS LINNENBRINK
SLS Brickell Hotel and Residences, Miami, Florida, USA
monumental city facade (painted mural on podium wall)

KATJA LOHER
SLS Brickell Hotel and Residences, Miami, Florida, USA
video installations

CHRISTIAN MOELLER
Centre Street Lofts, San Pedro, California, USA
"A Robot named Mojo"

TOM PATTI
Marquis, Miami, Florida, USA
architectural glass and metal wall sculpture

BERNARDÍ ROIG
SLS Brickell Hotel and Residences, Miami, Florida, USA
mysterious sculpture

RAY SMITH
SLS Brickell Hotel and Residences, Miami, Florida, USA
canvases in the residential lobby

FRANK STELLA
American Airlines Arena, Miami, Florida, USA
musical bandshell sculpture

ELYN ZIMMERMANN
North Dade Justice Center, Miami, Florida, USA
landscaped environmental sculpture

IMAGE CREDITS

© **PETER AARON/OTTO**
UNITED STATES EMBASSY LIMA
p. 25

© **BANQUE DE LUXEMBOURG**
BANQUE DE LUXEMBOURG
p. 86 (top)

© **PAVEL BENDOV PHOTOGRAPHY**
ELLIPSE
p. 348

© **JOERN BLOHM**
THE INFINITY
p. 234 (bottom)

© **AMY K. BOYD**
MOUNT PARKER
pp. title page, 305, 310 (bottom), 311(bottom)

© **RICHARD BRYANT/ARCAID**
BANQUE DE LUXEMBOURG
p. 88

AMERICAN AIRELINES ARENA
pp. 121, 124, 125, 126

© **KWAN CHAN FOR ARQUITECTONICA**
LANDMARK EAST
p. 216

© **DICK & AARON CHOW/PACE PUBLICATION**
CYBERPORT
p. 157 (bottom)

© **ENRIQUE CHUY FOR ARQUITECTONICA**
SAN ISIDRO FINANCIAL DISTRICT
pp. 302, 305

© **ROGAN COLES**
LANDMARK EAST
pp. 218 (bottom), 219

AGRICULTUTAL BANK OF CHINA AND CONSTRUCTION BANK OF CHINA 270
All photos

© **ALEXANDRE FAGUNDES DE FAGUNDES/ DREAMSTIME**
BANCO REAL SANTANDER / JK IGUATEMI
p. 280

© **TARIQ DEJANI**
SUN AND SKY TOWERS
p. 253

© **DANIEL DUCCI**
BANCO REAL SANTANDER / JK IGUATEMI 280
All photos except p. 284 (bottom)

© **PAUL DYER**
TRINITY PLACE
pp. 30, 191 (top)

© **JULIO ESPANA FOR ARQUITECTONICA**
STUDENT CENTER AND FATE BRIDGE UNIVERSITY OF MIAMI, CORAL GABLES
p. 211

© **RÔMULO FALDINI**
BANCO REAL SANTANDER / JK IGUATEMI
p. 284 (bottom)

© **BRAD FEINKOPF** 2015
FRANKLIN COUNTY COURTHOUSE 264
All photos

© **FRANK FISCHBECK**
FESTIVAL WALK
pp. 9, 107

© **PATRICIA FISHER**
NORTH DADE JUSTICE CENTER
p. 23

THE RIO SHOPPING CENTER
p. 23

SAWGRASS MILLS MALL
p. 24

© **DAN FORER**
AVENTURA GOVERNMENT CENTER
p. 153 (top)

© **YUKIO FUTAGAWA/GA PHOTOGRAPHERS**
PINK HOUSE
pp. 7, 42, 45, 46, 47

BEVERLY HILLS RESIDENCE
p. 83 (top)

© **DANIEL GIANNONI**
BANCO DE CREDITO
p. 65 (top)

© **FERNANDO GUERRA**
BANQUE DE LUXEMBOURG 86
pp. title page, 8, All photos except 86, and 88

ARIA AND SOLARIA 254
All photos except p. 257

© **KEN HAYDEN**
REGALIA
pp. table of contents, 276, 277

© **ROBIN HILL**
ATLANTIS
p. 16

IMPERIAL
p. 16, 19

ESTEFAN ENTERPRISES OFFICES
p. 22

ARQUITECTONICA STUDIOS
p. 33

RIMINI BEACH
p. 34

BABYLON
p. 51

MIAMI CHILDREN'S MUSEUM
p. 138

WILKIE D. FERGISON, JR. UNITED STATES COURTHOUSE
pp. 143, 144 (bottom), 148 (bottom)

SOUTH MIAMI DADE CULTURAL ARTS CENTER
pp. 158, 162

SARASOTA-HERALD TRIBUNE 192
All photos except pp. 192, 197 (bottom)

500 BRICKELL
pp. front end sheet, 34, 221, 222

ICON BRICKELL 244
All photos except pp. 245

SCHOOL OF INTERNATIONAL FINANCE FLORIDA INTERNATIONAL UNIVERSITY, MIAMI
pp. 38, 258, 262, 263 (top)

ICON BAY 320
All photos except pp. 320 and 321

PORT MIAMI TUNNEL 331
p. 33

FENDI CHATEAU
pp. 343, 344, 346

© **HI-SHOTS**
CYBERPORT
pp. 154, 155 (top)

© **TIM HURSLEY**
PALACE 52
All photos execpt pp. 52 (top), 54 (bottom)

BANCO DE CREDITO
pp. table of contents, 24, 62, 65 (bottom), 66, 69

MULDER HOUSE 70
All photos except p. 72

© **AMAL IMRAN**
LANDMARK EAST
pp. 217, 218 (top)

© **MIKE KELLEY**
BEVERLY HILLS RESIDENCE 78
p. 27, all photos except pp. 81, 83 (top)

AMERICAN AIRLINES ARENA
p. 122

WILKIE D. FERGISON, JR. UNITED STATES COURTHOUSE
pp. back cover, 140, 144-148 (top), 149

AVENTURA GOVERNMENT CENTER 151
All photo except p. 152 (top)

SOUTH MIAMI DADE CULTURAL ARTS CENTER
pp. 161, 163

TRINITY PLACE 189
All photos except p. 191 (top)

PERFORMING ARTS CENTER IRVINE VALLEY COMMUNITY COLLEGE, IRVINE, CALIFORNIA
pp. 200, 201

ARTS CAMPUS 202
EAST LOS ANGELES COLLEGE, LOS ANGELES
All photos except p. 204 (top)

STUDENT CENTER AND FATE BRIDGE UNIVERSITY OF MIAMI, CORAL GABLES
pp. 208, 211, 212, 213

500 BRICKELL
pp. 220, 223

AVALON MISSION BAY
p. 230

INFINITY 232
All photos except p. 234 (bottom)

ICON BRICKELL
p. 245

SCHOOL OF INTERNATIONAL FINANCE FLORIDA INTERNATIONAL UNIVERSITY, MIAMI
p. 263 (bottom)

REGALIA
pp. 274, 278, 279

BRICKELL CITY CENTRE 286
Back end sheet, all photos except p. 292 (bottom)

BEACH HOUSE 8 312
All photos

LINEA 316
All photos

ICON BAY
pp. 34, 40, 320, 321,

FENDI CHATEAU
pp. 34, 342, 345

© DODDY KOROMPIS
ADARO ENERGY TOWER
p. 215 (top)

© ROBERT LAUTMAN
PINK HOUSE
pp. 44, 47 (bottom)

© CATHY LEE FOR ARQUITECTONICA
TAIKOO HUI
pp. table of contents, 187

MOUNT PARKER
pp. 310 (top), 311 (top)

© KITMIN LEE
FESTIVAL WALK
pp. 106, 108 (top)

INTERNATIONAL FINANCE CENTER
p. 241, 242

© JONATHAN LEIJONHUFVUD
TAIKOO HUI 182
p. 39, all photos except p. 187

© PAUL MAURER PHOTOGRAPHY
PERFORMING ARTS AND CONVENTION
CENTER DIJON 98
pp. table of contents, 28, All photos except p. 104

EXALTIS 132
All photos

MICROSOFT EUROPE HEADQUARTERS 226
p. 29, All photos

ACCOR AND EQ WATER 248
All photos

© NORMAN MCGRATH
BABLYLON
pp. 15, 50

ATLANTIS 56
All photos except p. 56

WESTIN TIMES SQUARE
pp. 31, 117, 118, 119

BRONX MUSEUM OF THE ARTS 169
pp. 401, 31, all photos

HIGH SCHOOL FOR CONSTRUCTION
TRADES, ENGINEERING AND ARCHITECTURE,
NEW YORK 175
All photos

QUEENS WEST
pp. 180 (left)

SARASOTA-HERALD TRIBUNE
pp. 192, 197 (bottom)

© ERIC MORRIL
PERFORMING ARTS AND CONVENTION
CENTER DIJON
p. 104

© ANDRE NAZARETH
BG GROUP GLOBAL TECHNOLOGY CENTRE 336
Cover, all photos

© NEW YORK FOCUS
SCHOOL OF INTERNATIONAL FINANCE
FLORIDA INTERNATIONAL UNIVERSITY, MIAMI
p. 261

© ERIC NIEMY FOR ARQUITECTONICA
CYBERPORT
pp. 155, 156, 157 (top)

© JOSE ORIHUELA
SAN ISIDRO FINANCIAL CENTER
pp. 302, 304

© RICHARD PAYNE
HADDON & TAGGART TOWNHOUSES
p. 22

AMERICAN BANK CENTER 165
All photos

© STEVE PROEHL
ARTS CAMPUS
EAST LOS ANGELES COLLEGE, LOS ANGELES
pp. 36, 204,

© JANICE RETTALIATA
PHILIPS ARENA 128
All photos

© SILVIA ROS
ESSAY
pp. 13, 14, 18, 20, 21, 23, 26

BABLYLON
pp. 15, 48, 49

PALACE
pp. 17, 52 (top)

ATLANTIS
p. 56 (top)

BANCO DE CREDITO
p. 52

MULDER HOUSE
p. 72

BEVERLY HILLS HOUSE
p. 81

STUDENT CENTER AND FATE BRIDGE
UNIVERSITY OF MIAMI, CORAL GABLES
pp. 212 (bottom), 213 (bottom)

© CARLOS ROSSO/RELATED PROPERTIES
SLS BRICKELL
p. 35

© SIMONE SIMONE / SIMONESIMONE.IT
AIRA AND SOLARIA
p. 257 (Left)

© SCOTT B. SMITH
AMERICAN AIRLINES ARENA
p. 127

MIAMI CHILDREN'S MUSEUM
pp. 136, 137

© SOROUH
SUN AND SKY TOWERS
p. 252

© TIM STREET-PORTER
WALNER HOUSE
p. 27

PINK HOUSE
p. 46

© RAY SUGIHARTO
ADARO ENERGY TOWER
p. 215

© NAMGOOG SUN
INTERNATIONAL FINANCE CENTER
pp. 238, 240, 243

© DAVID SUNDBERG/ESTO
QUEENS WEST
pp. 178, 179, 180 (right), 181

ELLIPSE 348
All photos except p. 348

© RALPH THOMAS
FESTIVAL WALK
p. 106 (bottom)

© PAUL TURANG
PERFORMING ARTS CENTER
IRVINE VALLEY COMMUNITY COLLEGE,
IRVINE, CALIFORNIA
p. 198

© DAVID WAKELY PHOTOGRAPHY
AVALON MISSION BAY
p. 231

© PAUL WARCHOL
BANCO DE CREDITO
pp. 64, 67, 68

© MICHAEL WEBER/SWIRE PROPERTIES
BRICKELL CITY CENTRE
p. 278 (bottom)

© MARIO WIBOWO
ORCHARD SCOTTS 110
All photos except p. 113

© WIREDNEWYORK.COM
WESTIN TIMES SQUARE
p. 114

© ALEJANDRO WIRTH
BBVA 326
All photos

© JOSE A. ZABALLERO
SM ARENA AND CONVENTION CENTER 236
All photos

© JI ZHENG QI
MANGROVE WEST COAST
p. 32

All renderings provided by Arquitectonica.

Every effort has been made to contact the holders of copyrighted material. Omissions will be corrected in future editions if the publisher is notified in writing.

IMAGE CREDITS

SELECTED WORKS

Pp. 370-371 (top to bottom, left to right)

CANYON RANCH LIVING @**WEST AVENUE REALTY**

MIRANOVA CONDOMINIUM AND OFFICE TOWERS @ **???**

LONGMONT HOTEL AND OFFICE TOWER @ **ZHANG SI-YE**

WILSHIRE VERMONT STATION @ **PAUL TURANG**

ZENDAI FORUM @ **ACD SYSTEMS DIGITAL IMAGING**

MARINA BLUE @ **ROBIN HILL**

COSMOPOLITAN RESORT AND CASINO @ **RICK FOWLER**

MARQUIS AND ME MIAMI @ **ROBIN HILL**

MIMA AND HOTEL @ **NORMAN MCGRATH**

GRAND HYATT SAN ANTONIO CONVENTION CENTER HOTEL AND ALTEZA CONDOMINIUMS @ **ACD SYSTEMS DIGITAL IMAGING**

THE GATE AND ARC TOWERS AND BOUTIK MALL @ **LESTER ALI**

BANCO DE ORO TOWER @ **PATHFINDER**

JLL CENTER @ **CONNIE ZHOU FOR ARQUITECTONICA**

SLS BRICKELL HOTEL AND RESIDENCES @ **CARLOS ROSSO FOR RELATED**

BRICKELL HEIGHTS @ **AZEEZ BAKARE**

Pp. 372-373 (top to bottom, left to right)

THE IMPERIAL @ **YUKIO FUTAGAWA**

HADDON TOWNHOUSES @ **???**

MANDELL TOWNHOUSES @ **RICHARD PAYNE**

WALNER HOUSE @ **TIM HURSLEY**

NEXUS WORLD @ **???**

PACIFIC PLAZA TOWERS @ **JOHN K. CHUA**

THE WAVERLY AT SOUTH BEACH @ **SCOTT B. SMITH**

MANGROVE WEST COAST @ **JI ZHENG QI**

BLUE MIAMI @ **PAUL MORRIS**

SHAMA CENTURY PARK @ **ZHANG SI YE**

Pp. 374-375 (top to bottom, left to right)

PARAMOUNT BAY @ **JULIO ESPANA FOR ARQUITECTONICA**

AXIS @ **???**

ICON VALLARTA @ **???**

ALBA @ **ONG & ONG**

LUMINA @ **MIKE KELLEY**

OLUME @ **MONOGRAM APARTMENT COLLECTION**

OCEANA BAL HARBOUR @ **MIKE KELLEY**

DISNEY'S ALL STAR SPORTS RESORT @ **DAN FORMER**

JW MARRIOTT LIMA HOTEL @ **??? (PERMISSIONS?)**

GOLDEN MOON HOTEL AND CASINO RESORT @**MARTIN ALLRED FOR ALLRED & ASSOCIATES**

Pp. 376-377 (top to bottom, left to right)

LE MERIDIEN CYBERPORT @ **GRAHAM UDEN FOR LE MERIDIEN CYBERPORT**

HILTON AMERICAS - HOUSTON CONVENTION CENTER HOTEL @ **???**

NOVOTEL CITYGATE HOTEL @ **NEWFOUNDWORLD**

CITY OF DREAMS RESORT AN CASINO @ **COURTESY OF CITY OF DREAMS**

LUXURY COLLECTION TAMBO DEL INKA RESORT AND SPA @ **COURTESY OF LUXURY COLLECTION**

REVEL RESORT AND CASINO @ **MICHAEL KINERK**

LUXURY COLLECTION PARACAS RESORT & SPA @ **COURTESY OF LUXURY COLLECTION**

LE MERIDIEN COLUMBUS, THE JOSEPH @ **BRAD FEINKNOPF**

OVERSEAS TOWER @ **???**

THE CENTER FOR INNOVATIVE TECHNOLOGY @ **TIM HURSLEY**

BMG REGIONAL HEADQUARTERS/BANK OF AMERICA BUILDING @ **TIM HURSLEY**

ESTEFAN ENTERPRISES OFFICES @ **ROBIN HILL**

WISE HEADQUARTERS @ **ENRIQUE CHUY FOR ARQUITECTONICA**

ATLANTIC CENTER / WILLIAM MORRIS AGENCY BUILDING @ **DAN FORER**

Pp. 378-379 (top to bottom, left to right)

EAST HOPE GROUP HEADQUARTERS @ **ARQUITECTONICA STAFF**

AIR2 TOUR @ **YANN ROSSIGNOL**

ARQUITECTONICA STUDIOS @ **JULIO ESPANA**

RIMAC PLAZA DEL SOL @ **ENRIQUE CHUY FOR ARQUITECTONICA**

TEMPO SCAN TOWER @ **ACD SYSTEMS DIGITAL IMAGING**

TWO E-COM CENTER @ **JOSE A. ZABALLERO**

GREEN TOWERS @ **???**

WHIRLPOOL GLOBAL HEADQUARTERS @ **STEINKAMP PHOTOGRAPHY**

SHERATON COMMUNICATIONS AND TECHNOLOGY CENTER @ **CATHY LEE FOR ARQUITECTONICA**

BANCO DE LA NACIÓN HEADQUARTERS @ **???**

SAWGRASS MILLS MALL @ **PATRICIA FISHER**

THE WASHINGTONIAN CENTER @ **TIM HURSLEY**

BALLET VALET PARKING GARAGE AND RETAIL SHOPS @ **DAN FORER**

JOCKEY PLAZA SHOPPING MALL @ **???**

SM MALL OF ASIA @ **???**

SM CITY NORTH EDSA MALL @ **PATHFINDER**

Pp. 380-381 (top to bottom, left to right)

INTERNATIONAL SWIMMING HALL OF FAME MUSEUM AND EXHIBITION HALL @ **???**

FOSTER CITY PUBLIC LIBRARY AND COMMUNITY CENTER @ **COLIN MCCREA**

DISCOVERY SCIENCE CENTER @ **COURTESY OF DISCOVERY SCIENCE CENTER**

MIAMI CITY BALLET @ **DAN FORER**

JOHN W. MAC ELEMENTARY SCHOOL @ **PAUL TURANG**

YOUNG OAK KIM ACADEMY @ **ACD SYSTEMS DIGITAL IMAGING**

ALONZO AND TRACY MOURNING HIGH SCHOOL @ **ROBIN HILL**

NORTH DADE JUSTICE CENTER @ **PATRICIA FISHER**

UNITED STATES EMBASSY @ **PETER ARRON/ OTTO**

DIJON CONVENTION CENTER @ **PAUL MAURER**

DIJON CONFERENCE CENTER @ **PAUL MAURER** (???)

Pp. 382-383 (top to bottom, left to right)

DISNEY CRUISE LINE TERMINAL @ **BOB BRAUN/SEVEN**

JORGE CHAVEZ INTERNATIONAL AIRPORT TERMINAL EXPANSION @ **PERMISSION?**

MISSISSIPPI TELECOMMUNICATIONS & CONFERENCE CENTER @ **JIMMY WINSTEAD**

JACKSON CONVENTION COMPLEX @ **SHANNON SHERIDAN**

UNITED NATIONS PEACEKEEPERS MEMORIAL @ **GERMAN ORTIZ FOR ARQUITECTONICA**

MANILA CONVENTION CENTER @ **PATHFINDER**

PORT MIAMI TUNNEL @ **ROBIN HILL**

AMERICAN AIRLINES ARENA @ **SCOTT B. SMITH**

SEA WORLD TIANJIN ENTERTAINMENT CENTER @ **COURTESY TIANSHAN GROUP**

DIJON URBAN DISTRICT @ **???**

MEERHOVEN DISTRICT @ **???**

SMART CITY MALTA @ **??? PERMISSION?**

First published in the United States of America in 2018 by
Rizzoli International Publications, Inc.
300 Park Avenue South, New York, NY 10010

ISBN 978-0-8478-5999-3

Library of Congress Control Number: 2017958395

Front cover: BG Group Global Technology Centre, Andre Nazareth
Back cover: Wilkie D. Ferguson, Jr. United States Federal Courthouse, Mike Kelley
Inside front cover: 500 Brickell, Robin Hill
Inside back cover: Brickell City Centre, Mike Kelley

Design and type composition by Group C Inc / New Haven

Printed and bound in Italy

2018 2019 2020 2021 / 10 9 8 7 6 5 4 3 2 1

www.arquitectonica.com